The Politics and Economics of Britain's Foreign Aid

The Pergau dam in Malaysia was the most controversial project in the history of British aid. Because of its high cost, it was a poor candidate for aid funding. It was provided in part to honour a highly irregular promise of civil aid in connection with a major arms deal. After two parliamentary inquiries and intense media coverage, in a landmark judgement the aid for Pergau was declared unlawful.

Tim Lankester offers a detailed case study of this major aid project and of government decision-making in Britain and Malaysia. Exposing the roles played by key politicians and other stakeholders on both sides, he analyses the background to the aid/arms linkage, and the reasons why the British and Malaysian governments were so committed to the project, before exploring the response of Britain's Parliament, and its media and NGOs, and the resultant legal case. The main causes of the Pergau debacle are carefully drawn out, from conflicting policy agendas within the British government to the power of the business lobby and the inability of Parliament to provide any serious challenge. Finally, Lankester asks whether, given what was known at the time and what we know now, he and his colleagues in Britain's aid ministry were correct in their objections to the project.

Pergau is still talked about as a prime example of how not to do aid. Tim Lankester, a key figure in the affair, is perfectly placed to provide the definitive account. At a time when aid budgets are under particular scrutiny, it provides a cautionary tale.

Tim Lankester worked at the World Bank and the British Treasury before serving as Private Secretary (Economic Affairs) to Prime Minister James Callaghan and then to Margaret Thatcher. He was later Britain's Executive Director on the boards of the IMF and World Bank, and Permanent Secretary of the Overseas Development Administration. After leaving the civil service, he was Director of the School of Oriental and African Studies and President of Corpus Christi College, Oxford. He was knighted in 1994.

'This book is a very readable and fair-minded insider's account of how government occasionally goes badly wrong. It shows how brave and strong-minded civil servants sometimes have to be to preserve integrity and decency in government.'

Lord Patten, Chancellor of Oxford University; former EU Commissioner for External Relations; former Minister for Overseas Development, UK.

'This book is an excellent example of something too little practised – a rigorous post-event evaluation. Tim Lankester showed great courage in speaking truth unto power, albeit unsucceessfully, and he has also confronted the reasons for ODA's failure to stop a poor project. Despite that, the Pergau Dam affair has generated many lessons and changed UK aid policy for the better.

The evaluation shows that the Pergau Dam was not the disaster many predicted (unlike the groundnuts project it actually works effectively). But nor was it the best option at the time, and as a way of generating British jobs it was very poor value for money. The real scandal was the improper confusion of defence and development objectives which the government then tried to cover up. The good news is that, as result of this affair, we will no longer waste development money on middle income countries as a backdoor industrial subsidy.'

Lord Turnbull, former Cabinet Secretary, UK.

'This is an unusual book. Very few senior civil servants, in the UK or elsewhere, are either willing or able to write a scholarly analysis of a controversial policy issue with which they were closely involved. Tim Lankester has done just that in his book on the Pergau dam. The result is a fascinating study of the political pressures which drive decisions about aid projects. In the Pergau case, aid officials tried to use rational economic analysis to bolster their case against the project, but ran up against powerful vested interests in both the UK and Malaysia. The book discusses the reasons for the resulting controversy and examines the lessons for British aid policy. It deserves to be read not just by those with a direct interest in the formulation and implementation of aid projects, but by all those interested in international development issues.'

Professor Anne Booth, School of Oriental and African Studies, UK.

'A fascinating account of one of the shabbier episodes of the late Thatcher premiership.... a case study in bad government which should be read by anyone seriously interested in the inner workings of Whitehall and Westminster.'

Simon Jenkins, political journalist and author, UK.

'Tim Lankester has written a brilliant insider's account of a pivotal event in UK development policy. Read it for its gripping narrative of this low water mark in British aid, in which civil servants and cost benefit analysis are the unlikely heroes. But read it also to understand how after foolishness can come wisdom. Following Pergau, politicians of all parties decided – and enshrined in the International Development Act – that poverty reduction, and not commercial interest, would be the sole objective of British aid policy, in turn enabling the UK to become a world-leader in international development. Tim Lankester, a central and courageous actor in the Pergau drama, writes with flair and great skill.'

Andrew Steer, President, World Resources Institute, USA; former Director General, Department for International Development, UK.

'Tim Lankester has provided a superb account of the most important turning point in UK aid policy. It is comprehensive, objective and authoritative, as only an insider's reconstruction can be. "The Pergau Dam Affair" is a gripping narrative not just of aid management, but of the way that political disasters happen and the people and institutions that manage to extract beneficial change from folly. I cannot praise it too highly.'

Professor John Toye, Oxford University, UK.

The Politics and Economics of Britain's Foreign Aid

The Pergau Dam Affair

Tim Lankester

Taylor & Francis Group

LONDON AND NEW YORK

First edition published 2013
by Routledge
2 Park Square, Milton Park, Abingdon, Oxon, OX14 4RN

Simultaneously published in the USA and Canada
by Routledge
711 Third Avenue, New York, NY 10017

Routledge is an imprint of the Taylor & Francis Group, an informa business

First issued in paperback 2013

British Library Cataloguing in Publication Data
A catalogue record for this book is available from the British Library

Library of Congress Cataloging in Publication Data
Lankester, Tim.
The politics and economics of Britain's foreign aid : the Pergau Dam affair /
Tim Lankester. -- 1st ed.
p. cm.
Includes bibliographical references and index.
1. Economic assistance, British--Malaysia--Case studies. 2. Economic
development projects--Political aspects--Malaysia--Case studies.
3. Hydroelectric power plants--Malaysia--Kelantan--Case studies. 4. Great
Britain--Foreign economic relations--Malaysia. 5. Malaysia--Foreign
economic relations--Great Britain. I. Title.
HC445.5.Z9E4453 2013
338.91'410595--dc23
2012011259

ISBN: 978-0-415-52952-5 (hbk)
ISBN: 978-0-203-10958-8 (ebk)
ISBN: 978-0-415-72302-2 (pbk)

Typeset in Times New Roman
by Taylor & Francis Books

For Alex, Livy and Laura
and for my many former colleagues at ODA and the
World Bank who strove to secure from limited aid budgets
the maximum benefits for developing countries and
their peoples.

Contents

Tables

Preface

The controversy over the funding of the Pergau hydroelectric project in Malaysia in 1991 was a key episode in the history of British overseas aid. It had a lasting impact on subsequent aid policies. Along with the major arms deal with which it came to be associated, it was also a significant, if ephemeral, cause célèbre in British politics.

In 1991 I was the civil servant with overall responsibility for managing the aid programme and for the effective use of the monies voted for aid by Parliament. Over the years, various myths grew up – some close to the mark, others mistaken – as to how it all came about, who was responsible and whether in fact the funding of the project was quite so bad after all. For unlike some aid projects, the Pergau power station – after some initial teething problems – did at least work as it was intended. Sporadic references to various aspects of the story, particularly on the legal side, appeared in articles and books. But nowhere was there a rounded account covering all the issues.

I had my own personal recollections and there was already a considerable amount of published material available from the two parliamentary inquiries that took place in 1994 and from the legal challenge that followed later that year. I had originally intended to write an extended article drawing on just these. But then in 2010 the Department for International Development generously gave me access to their files and I was able to dig deeper.

The result is this book, which attempts to tell the story in detail and to provide a critical analysis covering all the main aspects. It is as much a story about politics and public administration as it is about aid policy and aid management. It is a story of systemic failure – the unresolved clash of conflicting policy agendas and the botched attempt to run them in parallel.

I have told the story from an aid and development policy perspective because that was my official perspective at the time. This inevitably colours my analysis and conclusions. At the same time, I have tried to stand back and describe objectively why and how, in the then Foreign Secretary Douglas Hurd's words, it turned out to be a "fairish nightmare" – a nightmare for which most of the principals involved, including myself, bear some responsibility.

In reconstructing the course of events and the arguments around them, on the British side I have relied as far as possible on primary documents. Where written evidence is thin, personal recollection – my own and that of others – plays a bigger part. This applies particularly to Chapter 4 where I comment on the attitudes of the key politicians and government departments that played a part. From the various civil service positions I held in the 1980s and early 1990s, I knew all five of the cabinet ministers who were principally involved – and Margaret Thatcher especially well from having served as her private secretary for economic affairs in the period 1979 to 1981. With the exception of the Ministry of Defence, I had also worked in, or worked closely with, all the departments that feature in this account.

On the Malaysian side of the story, I have had to rely mainly on secondary sources. Barry Wain's superb *Malaysian Maverick: Mahathir Mohamad in Turbulent Times* was a key source for my understanding of Dr Mahathir and Malaysia under his leadership.

It is not possible to understand what happened without an appreciation of the overall context – the record of British aid over the preceding years, official aid policy and the political, bureaucratic and commercial tensions surrounding it in the late 1980s, and the political background in Britain and Malaysia. This is why the first few chapters are devoted to these. Readers who are thoroughly familiar with the background may wish to move rapidly to Chapter 6 where the story begins in earnest.

Many former ODA colleagues have helped me with their recollections and by commenting on early drafts: Bob Ainscow, Andy Bearpark, Suma Chakrabarti, Robert Graham-Harrison, Barrie Ireton, Dick Jones, Mark Lowcock, Richard Manning, Michael McCulloch, Alan Whitworth and Myles Wickstead. So too have John Caines and John Vereker, my predecessor and successor respectively as Permanent Secretary. Chris Patten and Lynda Chalker, successive aid ministers over the period of the Pergau saga, shared with me their own recollections. Barrie Ireton showed me the draft of his history of British aid. Others who provided helpful comments included Chris Beauman, Damon Bristow, Robert Cassen, David Colvin, Rosalind English, Elizabeth Fisher, David Hart, Ben Jackson, Harriet Lamb, Anna Marmodoro, Din Merican, Michael Pattison, Adam Raphael, John Toye, Andrew Turnbull and Barry Wain. Malcolm Keay and Malcom Smart were especially helpful on the tricky issues of discount rates and the valuation of carbon emissions. Anand Menon wisely warned me off from trying too hard to invoke political theory to explain the decision-making process. Noreha Hashim kindly allowed me to quote from her unpublished PhD thesis on politics and accountability in relation to the Pergau decisions. Laurence Cockcroft advised me on issues relating to corruption. Most of all, I want to thank Stephen Powell for our many discussions on energy economics; and my wife, Patricia, for all her advice and encouragement. To all of the above I am extremely grateful, though any errors of fact or judgement are of course my responsibility.

I thank the senior management of Tenaga Nasional Berhad who briefed me on the project when I visited Kuala Lumpur in 2009; and likewise my generous hosts, Ahmad Zam Zam Bin W Abd Wahab and Abdul Aziz Derahman, when I visited the project site in 2011. Khanam Virjee, Helena Hurd and Siobhán Greaney at Routledge also provided me with great support.

Abbreviations

ATP	Aid and Trade Provision
BHC	British High Commission
BTU	British Thermal Unit
C and AG	Comptroller and Auditor General
CCGT	Combined cycle gas turbine
CO_2	Carbon dioxide
DAP	Democratic Action Party
DECC	Department of Energy and Climate Change
DESO	Defence Export Services Organization
DFID	Department for International Development
DTI	Department of Trade and Industry
ECGD	Export Credits Guarantee Department
FAC	House of Commons Foreign Affairs Committee
FCO	Foreign and Commonwealth Office
GNP	Gross national product
HC	House of Commons
LNG	Liquefied natural gas
MAC	Marginal abatement cost
MIC	Malaysian Indian Congress
MOD	Ministry of Defence
MOU	Memorandum of understanding
NAO	National Audit Office
NGO	Non-governmental organization
NPV	Net present value
ODA	Overseas Development Administration
OECD	Organization for Economic Cooperation and Development
OCGT	Open cycle gas turbine
PAC	Public Accounts Committee
PAS	Parti Islam SeMalaysia (Islamic Party of Malaysia)
PS	Private Secretary
SCC	Social cost of carbon
SMEC	Snowy Mountain Engineering Corporation
SOC	Social opportunity cost
STP	Social time preference
TNB	Tenaga Nasional Berhad
UMNO	United Malays National Organization

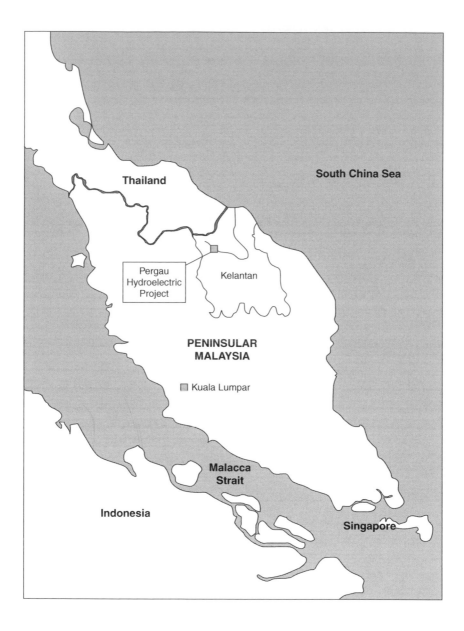

1   Introduction

The Pergau River in the northern Malaysian state of Kelantan is not one of Asia's major waterways. Rising near the Thai border, it is no more than a sub-tributary of the Kelantan River, itself a mere 250 km in length before it flows out into the South China Sea.

Until 1993, only a handful of Britons had ever heard of the Pergau. Outside Kelantan state, not many Malaysians would have heard of it either. That all changed in 1993 when details started emerging about a dam and hydro-power station that were being built on the Pergau, thanks to a massive grant from the British government. The decision to provide the grant quickly became known in Britain as the Pergau Dam Affair.

The grant in question amounted to £234 million and was provided by Britain's Overseas Development Administration (ODA), as the government department responsible for foreign aid was then called.[1] It had been formally approved in February 1991 after more than two years of argument between government departments in London, and two years of lobbying by the British companies bidding for the project and by the Malaysian government. The Pergau grant, once agreed, was not only the largest ever made under the British aid programme for a single project; it also turned out to be the most controversial.

At the time, British aid had a good reputation with the international development community. As a proportion of Gross National Product (GNP), British aid did not rank high: in 1990 the percentage was just 0.27 (compared with the UN target of 0.7 per cent), which put Britain at fourteenth out of 20 donor countries. But in terms of quality, it was judged by the Organization for Economic Cooperation and Development (OECD) as one of the best. British aid was focused mainly on the poorest countries, and ODA was highly rated for its knowledge and technical expertise, and for its systems of project identification, appraisal, monitoring and evaluation. As with other bilateral donors, much of its aid was tied to the purchase of goods and services in Britain – which made it less cost effective than it would have been, had it been fully untied; and by no means all of its projects and programmes succeeded in meeting their objectives. Nonetheless, by the standards of aid generally,

ODA was regarded as an effective and prudent provider of development assistance.

This perception was seriously dented by the Pergau affair. No project in the history of British overseas aid, with the possible exception of the ill-fated Tanganyika groundnut scheme of the late 1940s, provoked such public controversy, not to say outrage, or caused such difficulty for the government of day. (The Tanganyika scheme had as its principal aim the supply of edible oils to Britain at a time of severe post-Second World War shortages. The development of Tanganyika was a secondary consideration, and in that sense it had something in common with the aid for Pergau.)

The purpose of British aid, as stated in repeated policy documents and in the enabling legislation, was to promote the economic and social development of recipient countries and improve the welfare of their peoples. By long established policy and practice, and in accordance with standard Treasury guidelines relating to all government expenditure, this meant supporting projects and programmes that made sense economically. It was well understood that aid could and should serve other goals besides development, such as fostering trade and protecting and promoting political relations with recipient countries; but development and improving welfare had to be the main purpose.

Unlike the Tanganyika scheme, which achieved only a fraction of its planned production levels, the Pergau project was completed and achieved its goal of producing electricity for the Malaysian power system. There was some cost overrun and delay in getting it completed, but by the standards of many infrastructure projects, these were relatively modest. The completed scheme produces 520 million kWh of electricity a year to meet peaking demand as designed. It has not resulted in any serious environmental damage, nor did it require any significant movement of population.

The controversy arose for other reasons. The decision to finance the project was taken in the face of a strongly negative appraisal by economists at the ODA and against the advice of the ODA minister and Accounting officer. According to the economic analysis, which was shared by Malaysia's own power planners, Pergau was not needed until well into the 2000s; and if it was to be built in the early 1990s, it would involve a cost penalty of around £100 million. I was Permanent Secretary of ODA at the time and responsible therefore for the overall management of the aid programme and accountable to parliament, through parliament's Public Accounts Committee, for the efficiency and effectiveness of aid spending. The economic case against the project was so overwhelming that I took the unusual step of advising ministers that, if they were to overrule official advice and approve the financing, as Accounting Officer I would require a formal direction before authorising the expenditure. The issuing of such a direction was rare: there had only been a handful of cases in recent years. It placed on record that the decision had been taken against the advice of the civil service and that ministers alone had to take responsibility for it.

The decision to back the project was taken primarily to boost Britain's trade and political relations with Malaysia. Most controversially of all, there was an indirect linkage to an agreement between Britain and Malaysia on the sale of defence equipment to the tune of £1 billion. This linkage was contained in a secret Defence Protocol entered into by the two governments in March 1988. Although many of Britain's aid recipients were purchasers of weapons from Britain, such purchases had previously – in accordance with international agreement – been kept formally separate from aid. The entanglement between arms sales and aid in the case of Malaysia, though described by British ministers as only temporary, caused immense trouble for the government.

The controversy was further compounded when London's *Sunday Times* mounted a sharp attack on the Malaysian government and the Malaysian Prime Minister in particular for sanctioning or being party to bribery. Allegations of bribery in relation to the project were not new: several MPs had sought answers to these allegations during the negotiations that preceded the approval of the grant. The *Sunday Times* coverage, however, touched a raw nerve in Kuala Lumpur with the result that for seven months all new public sector contracts with British companies were banned.

Finally, to cap it all, the decision to fund Pergau through the aid budget was challenged in the British courts and found to be unlawful. This was on the grounds that, if the project was considered economically unsound by the experts, the government could not claim it was assisting in the development of Malaysia. Previously, government lawyers and most other legal experts had taken the view that aid was within the law provided ministers believed it was assisting the development of the country in question. The court ruling therefore came as a considerable surprise. Its effect was to require the continued funding of the project to be found from outside the aid budget, and it was seen – more widely – as further advancing the role of the courts in relation to government decision making in general. The ruling was a final damning conclusion to the Pergau saga.

For over a year, from the autumn of 1993 when the National Audit Office (NAO) published a critical report about the project until after the adverse court decision in late 1994, the Pergau decision and the factors that led up to it were subject to intense media coverage and extensive examination and debate in Parliament. Although the government tried hard to defend its actions, media coverage generally and the findings of two parliamentary select committees were highly critical. The controversy became a serious political embarrassment for the government. And in the short run, British–Malaysia relations – far from being improved – were severely damaged.

The government faced a barrage of criticism that essentially took two forms: that the aid programme had been wrongly, and it turned out unlawfully, used; and more broadly, that the government had shown itself to be grossly incompetent. It was the latter that was the more damaging since it resonated not just with those who positively supported British overseas aid but with the majority who were either neutral or hostile towards aid. The principal companies that were involved in the project also did not get off lightly for some of their actions.

The Pergau controversy not only raised questions about the competence of government, it also raised issues about the purpose of British aid. Should it be used only or primarily for the purpose of development and poverty alleviation; or should it be used, and if so to what extent, to promote Britain's commercial and political interests?

There were two views. There were many in parliament, in the NGO community, amongst academics and in the media who believed that the basic purpose of British aid – to support development and provide humanitarian relief – had been unduly downgraded during the Thatcher years, and that the shift to a more commercially oriented aid agenda was not in accord with officially declared policy. On the other side were those, particularly in industry and on the right of the Conservative Party, who argued that, since other governments supported exporters through their aid programmes, the British government must do the same; and for similar reasons, the aid programme should be used to support Britain's political and wider foreign policy objectives.

Pergau marked a watershed. The misuse of aid to finance Pergau and the political and legal troubles that followed had a lasting effect on all who were concerned with British aid policy. The lessons from Pergau, alongside international moves to reduce the tying of aid, and then the election of a Labour government in 1997 with a mandate to increase the aid budget and strengthen aid effectiveness – these all brought about changes in British aid policy that gave greater weight to development and poverty alleviation and in due course all but eliminated the commercial influence in aid decisions.

This is a story about commercial interests being improperly entangled with development assistance – certainly to the detriment of Britain's overall public interest and arguably to the detriment of the public interest in Malaysia too. It is a story, to borrow Daniel Moynihan's description of the 1960s War on Poverty in America, of "maximum feasible misunderstanding". It is a story of bad governance in Britain at a time when its ministers and officials were preaching the virtues of good governance to their partners in aid-receiving countries. And it provides an object lesson for the management of overseas aid and perhaps for public administration more generally.

From the start of the Pergau story in 1988 until the start of the parliamentary committee investigations in 1994, I was officially involved: first, as deputy head of the Treasury's Overseas Group with responsibility – amongst other things – for overseeing ODA's budget; and then from July 1989 until January 1994 as Permanent Secretary of ODA. I have already referred to the advice I gave to ministers against funding Pergau. My last act as Permanent Secretary was to appear in January 1994 before the Public Accounts Committee to answer questions on the National Audit Office's report. I was not personally involved in the detailed assessments and discussions that went on within ODA and between government departments; but I received regular reports on them and I was ultimately responsible for the ODA's position at official (i.e. non-political) level.

In the textbooks about British government, civil servants are supposed to be purely the servants of ministers, without views of their own on the aims and application of policy: their role, rather, is to advise in a dispassionate way on the pros and cons of different policy options and their implementation. If they do have views of their own on policy, they are expected to subordinate them to those of the government of the day.

My experience of working for 22 years in the British civil service was that the vast majority of civil servants did their best to comply with this ideal. In the case of my own role as Permanent Secretary of ODA, it was not too difficult. My personal views on aid and development were very much in line with the government's stated policies as articulated in ODA policy statements and in legislation. What I soon discovered was that there were powerful forces in other parts of the government that did not fully support the official policy line. The divergence of actual policy from officially stated policy is at the heart of the Pergau affair.

Although I had come to my post at ODA from the Treasury, my interest in aid and development went back many years. It started when I was an 18-year-old volunteer teacher in Belize in 1961. There, for the first time, I was exposed to serious poverty and economic backwardness, which the British colonial government seemed unable to do very much about. (Belize, then known as British Honduras, was a Crown Colony until it became independent in 1981.) Towards the end of my year in Belize I attended an inspiring lecture by the West Indian economist Arthur Lewis. Lewis was one of the leading development economists of his day. He had been an adviser to Kwame Nkrumah at Ghana's independence and he had written an influential book on the economics of development.[2]

I remember Lewis giving an optimistic account – which I later discovered was the gist of his "dual sector" model – of how under-employed surplus labour in agriculture could move into industrial employment, and how – with increased investment made possible by higher domestic savings and by foreign aid – backward countries could take-off. I was enthralled by Lewis' message and immediately wrote to my prospective university, Cambridge, that I would like to study economics instead of law.

Far from finding economics a "dismal science", I became fascinated and impressed – in retrospect, overly impressed – by its apparent power to explain, predict and improve economic and social conditions in rich and poor countries alike. At Cambridge I had the good fortune to attend lectures by some of the "big name" economists who had been colleagues or disciples of John Maynard Keynes, such as Richard Kahn, Joan Robinson, James Meade and Nicholas Kaldor, as well as lectures on development by the future Nobel laureate Amartya Sen. I continued my studies at Yale – macroeconomics with the great James Tobin, international finance with Robert Triffin, and economic development with an excellent group of younger scholars, including Gerry Helleiner, Werner Baer and Carlos Diaz-Alejandro. I then spent seven years as an economist with the World Bank working on Africa and India, including a spell in the Bank's New Delhi office; and later, for two and a half years I was Britain's representative on the World Bank's board of directors.

In common with many economists trained in the 1960s, I started out believing in the merits of state planning and public intervention; but gradually I came to realise that in many developing countries the "statist" approach had to a large extent failed and that there should be a much greater emphasis on markets and the private sector. By the time I became Permanent Secretary of ODA in 1989 I favoured a mixed economy approach – reliance wherever possible on well-functioning markets, combined with public interventions to offset and correct market failure and undertake activities such as education and health provision where markets typically were unable to deliver.

I believed that wealthier countries had a moral duty to help people in poorer countries achieve a decent standard of life, and that it was in their political and economic interests to do so. As a child of the British colonial state – at times benevolent but more often arrogant and exploitative – I felt that Britain had a particular obligation to our former colonies. I was a believer in aid as an instrument for assisting development and poverty alleviation, in the need for aid volumes to be increased, and in the importance of ensuring that aid resources were used to optimum effect.

I accepted that, as a political reality, British aid policy could not be constructed on a purely technocratic basis and that it had to take into account commercial and wider foreign policy objectives as well. This was clearly a complicating factor. However, I had no difficulty with aid being used to support wider policy objectives provided this was not at the expense of the key objective of maximising aid's development and poverty alleviating impact. With care and imagination, I felt these multiple objectives could be reconciled. Maximising the development impact of Britain's aid was to my mind all the more important in view of its relatively small size.

I have spelt out my own views on aid and development in some detail, and how I had come to them, so that the reader can better understand my attitude to the Pergau project and to the linking of aid to defence sales. The fact that these views in nearly every respect chimed with officially stated policies made me all the more determined to ensure that ministers were given the "correct" advice, even though it might mean rowing against powerful voices inside and outside the government, which, without admitting it, sought to use British aid in ways that contradicted these policies.

It may be objected that, if ministers decide to pursue a policy that is different from their declared policy, they have every right to do so. This of course is true constitutionally. It cannot be for officials to prevent them from doing so – even though parliament and the public may object. What officials have to do is to advise on the consequences of departing from declared policy. This is exactly what ODA attempted to do with Pergau.

Finally, in view of the intense spotlight in this book on the issues surrounding the funding of Pergau, it is worth emphasising that these were amongst a host of other – and for most of the participants much more important – policy issues that British ministers and officials had to address at the time. This is the nature of modern government, and one of the features of good policy-making is to decide how much time and priority to give to particular issues. For the senior ministers involved, such as Mrs Thatcher, Douglas Hurd and John Major, Pergau will have ranked very low amongst all the other issues they were dealing with. In retrospect, Hurd for one certainly regretted that he had not given it more attention.

Certainly, there were mistakes that should and could have been avoided. But many of the difficulties arose simply from the fact that the principal "players" were operating on the basis of different policy agendas. In the end, as the following chapters will explain, it was the dominance of political and commercial considerations over the development objective that led to the decision to fund Pergau a decade or more before it was needed.

2   British overseas aid

By the time the Pergau project became a candidate for ODA financing in late 1988, Britain's overseas aid programme in its modern, post-colonial form had been in existence for nearly a quarter of a century. Under the aegis of the Colonial Office and the Treasury, there had been programmes of technical assistance and budget support in the 1940s and 1950s for Britain's colonies, and through its membership of the World Bank and various UN agencies the UK also provided assistance indirectly to what were then called "under-developed countries". But it was a disjointed effort, lacking strategic direction and political and professional leadership.

Aid in the 1960s and 1970s

The election of the Labour government in 1964 saw the start of a fully fledged, modern aid programme when for the first time a separate government department for aid with its own cabinet minister was established.

The political climate was propitious. There was cross-party support for the idea that we owed it to our former colonies to help them on their feet and assist their development. In the case of the Conservatives, this was partly the logical extension of the de-colonisation process that had reached its apogee under their government in the late 1950s and early 1960s, and of the desire to build a prosperous Commonwealth of independent nations with Britain at its head and the influence and prestige that would go with this. In the late 1950s, the Conservatives had hoped that, once independence came, the former colonies would be able to access the international capital markets for funding their development programmes. But by the early 1960s, it was obvious that this was not to be.[1]

In the case of Labour, the idea of overseas assistance appealed to the sizeable portion of the party that saw themselves as internationalist and socialist – made the more attractive by the fact that the majority of newly independent countries opted for socialism both in their rhetoric and in their policies. Many people across the political divide accepted the idea – implicit in the 1948 UN Universal Declaration of Human Rights to which Britain was party – that the poorest in the world had a moral right to a better standard of life and that governments in the richer world had a moral duty to help them achieve it.[2]

The intellectual climate was also favourable. At around this time development economics as a sub-discipline of economics was taking off. Numerous studies were being published on the problems and prospects for individual countries, and there was a mounting literature on what were likely to be the key ingredients of successful economic "take-off". Amongst the latter was the need to increase domestic savings and investment, and since it would take time to increase savings, the latter would need to be supplemented by foreign savings, most likely in concessional form since the poorer countries would have difficulty in attracting private inflows. And if domestic savings could be increased, aid might still be necessary on account of foreign exchange shortages arising from the difficulties that the poorer countries were likely to have in increasing their export earnings – either because of weak commodity prices or because of the difficulty of developing manufacturing exports.[3]

Allied to this analysis of savings and foreign exchange gaps was the belief amongst most academic economists that markets in the poorer countries were inherently inefficient and incapable on their own in bringing about faster growth; and that government intervention would therefore have to play a key role. This intervention could take a number of forms: public investment in and ownership of key industries, import protection and export subsidies, price controls, controls over private credit allocations and the allocation of foreign exchange. National planning – to determine the balance between investment and consumption and the industries to be encouraged and how this was to be done – was considered a requisite for accelerated development

In establishing the new ministry, the Labour government bought into these ideas. The latter also found a ready reception amongst political leaders in the poorer countries and were widely adopted. Leaders such as Nehru in India and Soekarno in Indonesia, who had no particular interest in economics, were impressed by what socialist planning had achieved in the Soviet Union. They were also attracted by socialist planning precisely because it was an alternative to the capitalist model of their former colonial masters. Yet with varying degrees of enthusiasm, they accepted that aid was a necessary complement to their own countries' efforts.

Only a minority of development economists questioned this approach. Peter Bauer at LSE, whose work was later championed by the Conservative Right and became influential with Margaret Thatcher, was the most prominent amongst them. He argued that government intervention was likely to add to existing market inefficiencies; it would provide enhanced opportunities for corruption; it would postpone necessary policy reform; and it would create an unfavourable climate for private investors, savers and entrepreneurs. He and others like him also argued that, if governments adopted market-oriented policies, then private capital inflows would reduce or eliminate the need for aid. In encouraging or making possible the continuation of anti-market policies, aid was as likely to harm a country's development prospects as enhance them.[4]

If the political and mainstream intellectual context was positive for the new ministry, the economic backdrop was less so. Although economic growth in the 1950s and early 1960s had been respectable, with the incoming Labour government there were promises and heightened expectations of higher public spending that were difficult to fulfil. Moreover, Britain was facing a serious balance of payments problem, which in 1967 led to the devaluation of sterling – seen at the time as a political humiliation on a par with Britain's inglorious exit from the European Exchange Rate Mechanism in 1992.

The new ministry started off with a generous budget. Aid spending in its first full calendar year, 1965, amounted to an extraordinary 0.60 per cent of GNP. With its generous budget and the opportunity to help put into practice some of the new interventionist ideas on development, the ministry was seen as an exciting place to work. Its first minister with a seat in the cabinet was a rising Labour star, Barbara Castle, and several distinguished economists, like Dudley Seers and Paul Streeten, were early joiners.

From the outset, there was a determination to spend the aid budget wisely. The guiding principle, which followed precisely from the wording in the enabling legislation, was to spend it in ways that would best promote development and improve welfare in aid-receiving countries. Over time, the concept of "development soundness" came into the aid vocabulary – and it would play an important part in the controversy over Pergau. In operational terms, and in keeping with internationally recognised best practice, this meant undertaking cost–benefit studies on proposed projects to determine whether the project in question was likely to achieve a satisfactory economic return; or where the benefits were hard to quantify, as often was the case with projects in the social sectors, the object was to achieve the project's aims at minimum cost. The minimising of cost was also the approach to be used when considering an incremental investment within a grid system such as electricity generation and distribution – again, another foretaste of the Pergau controversy.

The ministry quickly established itself as one of the leading "players" amongst the official aid-giving community. It has been claimed that there were more economists working at the ministry in the late 1960s than in the whole of the rest of Whitehall. Apart from its economic expertise, it was able to recruit many other able professionals in agriculture, education, engineering, health and other fields, who had experience working in the former colonies. The ministry established a reputation for technical competence and effective spending. The focus was on the poorest Commonwealth countries of which there were plenty in Asia and Africa particularly.

But because of Britain's increasing economic difficulties, the aid budget fell back. By the late 1960s and early 1970s the ratio of aid to GNP had fallen to around 0.4 per cent, well below that of France, Germany and several other European countries, though above that of the US. In 1971, nonetheless, the Conservative government adopted the UN aid to GNP target of 0.7 per cent but without naming a date when it would be reached.

After Labour returned to power in 1974, the volume of aid improved and the ratio to GNP reached 0.51 per cent in 1979 (a figure not to be reached again until 2006); and there was a more clearly defined strategy, with greater emphasis on the poor (ODA 1975).

However, after the optimism of the early years, by the late 1970s significant doubts and stresses were creeping into Britain's aid effort. It was not just a matter of constrained budgets and being unable to match the aid efforts of our European partners: there were other factors too. One was the fact that many of Britain's main aid recipients were performing poorly in economic terms. The largest in terms of size and aid received from Britain was India. Its economic record for the past decade and more had been mediocre, and that of some of the largest recipients in Africa – such as Tanzania, Zambia and Ghana – had been dreadful. They all had in common the interventionist, statist policies that academic economists and much of the aid community had previously extolled. These policies clearly weren't working, yet they were being supported by aid from Britain and from other countries.

A wide-ranging and careful study a few years later led by Robert Cassen entitled *Does Aid Work?* concluded that the majority of aid interventions had a positive impact (Cassen and Associates 1986). At the same time, whilst particular projects in isolation might be considered a success, the overall impact of aid on economic performance had to be in doubt.

Another issue to come to the fore was whether British industry was benefiting sufficiently from British aid. Because of the country's perennial balance of payments problem, it was an article of faith from the beginning that the bilateral portion of our aid – i.e. aid given directly to other countries rather than routed through multilateral organizations like the World Bank and the UN – had to be tied to the purchase of British goods and services unless, exceptionally, it was being used to fund local costs. Because of mounting inflation, loss of competitiveness and industrial strife, the British economy in the 1970s suffered its worst decade since the 1930s. Against this backdrop, there was pressure for the aid programme to do more for British industry and British jobs. Yet this was made the more difficult by the fact that a rising proportion of our aid was going through the European Economic Community, the World Bank and other international agencies where tying to British goods and services was impossible.

Other countries were using their aid budgets more aggressively than we were to promote their exports. They did this through the mechanism of "mixed credits" whereby a grant was combined with an export credit on commercial terms supported by government guarantee. Alternatively, they would provide a "soft loan" whereby a grant was used to provide an interest subsidy in connection with an export credit, i.e. to soften its terms.

Responding to the pressure for aid to do more for British industry and jobs, the then aid minister, Judith Hart, decided in 1977 to establish within the aid budget the Aid and Trade Provision (ATP) to fund mixed credits. Hart was a left-winger within James Callaghan's Labour government. She probably thought the creation of ATP would bolster political support for an expanding aid programme both from the trade unions and from industry without compromising the integrity of the overall aid programme. It turned out to be a serious miscalculation.

The ATP budget was initially set at 5 per cent of the total bilateral aid budget; it rose to nearly 10 per cent in the 1980s. The ATP scheme is described in some detail below because it was this scheme, rather than the regular bilateral country programme, which was used to fund the Pergau project.

The aid programme in the 1980s

With the Conservative election victory of 1979, the aid budget suffered substantial cuts. From 0.51 per cent of GNP in 1979, Britain's aid volume fell to 0.27 per cent in 1990. The cuts were partly driven, along with other spending reductions, by the desire to cut the budget deficit and pay for reduced taxes. The aid budget was also a comparatively easy target. The centre-left of the Conservative Party was still broadly in favour of aid, even though there was concern that aid did not seem to be having the beneficial impact originally hoped for. On the right of the party, however, there was widespread scepticism emanating not just from the practical experience with aid in the 1970s but also from the writings of Peter Bauer and other pro-market economists. The view of the Conservative Right was that if for political reasons there had to be an aid budget, it should be used for humanitarian purposes and, otherwise, much more vigorously to promote Britain's commercial and political interests.

Following an inter-departmental review of aid policy, the ODA minister, Neil Marten, on 20 February 1980 made a statement in the House of Commons that signalled clearly that in future – whilst development would remain the basic objective of aid – political, industrial and commercial considerations would be given greater weight.[5] In reality, these considerations were already being given very considerable weight. According to a 1984 study, the allocation of Britain's aid amongst developing countries in the period 1978–80 was determined to the tune of 90 per cent by "donor interest", and only 10 per cent by "recipient need".[6] If that was already the case in regard to the allocation of aid according to recipient country, Marten's statement could only mean even greater emphasis on non-developmental considerations in terms of both country allocation and in the way that aid was to be used.

Because of a continuing rise in ODA contributions to multilateral organisations, the bilateral budget found itself especially squeezed. With a declining bilateral aid budget, the department would have liked to have concentrated its aid on fewer countries with a view to greater efficiency and impact. But ODA was also once again a wing of the FCO, and its minister no longer in the cabinet. Consequently, the FCO had greater influence over aid policy, and it was resistant to withdrawing aid from any of the more than 50 Commonwealth and other countries that British aid had been supporting.

It was also taken as a given that the remaining nine Overseas Territories had a first call on the aid budget. Whether it made sense to spend several thousand pounds a year on each of the 3,000 inhabitants of tiny St Helena in the mid-Atlantic, rather than pay for them to move to Britain – which most of them would have been delighted to do – was a question that no one wished to debate.

The continued tying of much of ODA's bilateral aid to procurement in Britain was increasingly seen as reducing its effectiveness. By the 1980s, a greater proportion of British aid was tied in this way than that of most of the other main donors. ODA attempted to select projects in respect of which British goods and services would be internationally competitive, but there was no denying that tied aid made it less cost effective. The dangers were especially acute with ATP projects.

Tying of aid in general and the expansion of the ATP, plus the increasing subordination of ODA's decision making to commercial and political pressures, made ODA a less effective aid donor, not to say a less inspiring place in which to work, compared with its first two decades of existence. For those at the helm of ODA, it was a constant struggle to accommodate the commercial pressures whilst not losing sight of aid's development purpose.

Some bad decisions were imposed on ODA. Famously, India received a £65 million grant under the regular bilateral programme to enable it to purchase helicopters from the ailing helicopter manufacturer, Westlands – for machines that turned out to be useless in Indian conditions and were eventually cannibalised for their spare parts for the Indian military.

The ATP budget was also used to prop up the ailing engineering company, Northern Engineering Industries, for the building of a power station in India's Bihar state. There were numerous problems of implementation, serious environmental issues that were not adequately tackled, and a cost overrun that proved disastrous for the company (NAO 1990, pp. 12–16).

In spite of these political inroads, British aid continued to have a relatively good reputation at large. The two ministers who headed the department throughout much of the 1980s, Tim Raison and Chris Patten, were determined to ensure maximum aid effectiveness within the political and policy constraints they faced. Under their leadership, the programme by and large continued to be run to a good standard in terms of process and professional input; and a higher proportion of British aid, compared with that of most of the larger donors, was focused on the poorest countries. ODA received high marks for quality from its peers in the regular OECD reviews of OECD members' programmes.

The balance of the regular (non-ATP) programme in the 1980s shifted away from capital projects in favour of technical assistance and programme aid – in effect, budget support. The extra technical assistance was partly a response to the growing recognition amongst academics and development professionals that poorly functioning institutions – legal systems, parliaments, the media, the police, government ministries – were one of the main blockages to economic take-off. To this was added the need to support the transformation of institutions in the countries of the former Soviet Bloc after 1989. ODA and the FCO established several Know How Funds for technical assistance to these countries.

One aspect of better governance was the need in many countries to tackle corruption. ODA had a twofold interest in this. First, because we believed that corruption – both grand corruption and petty corruption – undermined countries' development efforts and harmed the poor. Second, we were concerned to ensure that no British aid money was used directly or indirectly for the making of corrupt payments – particularly through inflated contract prices allowing excessive agents' fees to be paid, which in turn could too easily be used to line the pockets of local politicians and officials.

The shift to programme aid was a response to what was increasingly seen as the other main blockage – the absence of sound economic policies. Bad policies and incurring of excessive debt in many of the poorest countries required a new approach. Capital projects were too often failing not because they were technically defective but because of a hostile domestic policy environment. The donors, led by the World Bank and the IMF, took the view that the highest priority now was to use aid to underpin – and through conditionality, enforce – economic reform. ODA was in the vanguard amongst bilateral donors in embracing this approach, especially in Africa where policy regimes seemed particularly detrimental and where the donors had the muscle to insist on change.

The package of policies promoted by the World Bank and IMF was dubbed the "Washington Consensus", later in the 1990s to be modified to the "Post-Washington Consensus" when the emphasis became more on a mixed economy approach. Whatever their shortcomings, and whether or not donor conditionality had much effect, policies in most developing countries did change for the better and with improved results. In the 1990s African economies achieved higher growth, albeit not enough to have much impact on the percentage of people in severe poverty. Both China and India liberalised and their economies took off, though in neither case was aid instrumental in bringing this about. Ever since the mid-1960s, the World Bank and other donors had been urging India to liberalise its economy; but it was the financial crisis of 1991 and the success of other liberalising countries, including China, which finally persuaded the Indian government to start ditching its previous statist policies.

When Pergau came over the horizon for financing in late 1988, British aid thus revealed a rather mixed picture. Amongst the bilateral donors, it remained one of the best in terms of professional competence and poverty focus. But against this, there was the slippage against the 0.7 per cent UN aid target while other donors were increasing their aid; there was the continuing tying of aid to British goods and service while other donors were beginning to untie; and there was the increasing emphasis on political and commercial advantage. There was also a sense, albeit partly a symptom of a reduced confidence amongst aid donors generally, that ODA had a diminished profile within Whitehall and externally, and it was less able to hold its own than in earlier years and withstand outside pressures. This was to be become all too evident as the Pergau story unfolded.

The focus on Pergau in this book might give the impression that the project wholly dominated the work of ODA during the late 1980s onwards. The reality is different. The Pergau issue concerned only a narrow range of officials, and for relatively small amounts of their time. While Pergau was on ODA's agenda for several years, there was a huge amount of other work going on. ODA had programmes in over 50 countries, and was engaged directly in many aspects of development: maternal and child health, agriculture, education, climate change, nutrition, water and power supply, transportation, public administration, economic reform, humanitarian relief – and much else. With around 50 per cent of its budget being channelled through the EU, the World Bank, the UN agencies and other multilateral channels, ODA was also heavily engaged with these organizations.

Aid and trade provision

The ATP scheme, established by the Labour minister Judith Hart in 1977, was designed to enable British capital goods exporters and contractors to seek out orders on a negotiated contract basis with the assurance that, if successful, their clients would be able to obtain a "mixed credit" to cover its financing – i.e. a commercial credit mixed with a grant. The commercial credit was to be obtained from a private bank with the credit guaranteed by the government's Export Credits Guarantee Department (ECGD). The grant portion was to come from the ATP line in the aid budget. Later in the 1980s, aid in support of "soft loans" was added to the scheme: that is to say, the exporter would take out a commercial credit to cover the whole financing and ODA would provide an interest subsidy on the credit so as to soften its terms.

To provide some discipline and reduce the scope for competitive subsidisation, under OECD rules there had to be a minimum "grant element". This was 25 per cent in the 1970s and it was raised to 35 per cent in the late 1980s. This meant that for a mixed credit the grant had to be at least 25 per cent (or later, 35 per cent) of the mixed credit (i.e. the credit plus grant); and with a soft loan, the present discounted value of the interest subsidy also had to be 25 per cent (later, 35 per cent) of the value of the loan.[7]

The projects to be financed had to serve a development purpose so as to comply with legislation (the Overseas Aid Act 1966 and its successor, the Overseas Development and Cooperation Act 1980). Accordingly, they were to be appraised against the ODA's standard development and cost-effectiveness criteria. But unlike projects under the normal bilateral (i.e. non-ATP) programme, which were generated through discussion between ODA and the recipient government, ATP projects were to be proposed in the first instance by British firms; then vetted for their commercial and industrial value by the Department of Trade and Industry (DTI); and finally – if the DTI regarded the project as worth supporting – sent on to ODA for appraisal and approval.

Thus, the ODA got involved much later in the process than with the regular aid programme – by which time a head of steam had often built up behind the project with ODA finding itself on the back foot. This was all too evident when it came to Pergau.

There was also a difference between ATP projects and those under the regular programme in terms of substance. Whereas under the regular aid programme whatever benefits came to British industry were merely a consequence of the particular aid project, with ATP the aim was actively to promote British exports alongside the supposed aim of sound development.

This was easier said than done. Because ATP projects were generated in the first instance by British companies whose primary aim was profit rather than development for the country concerned, they were less likely to conform to the ODA's normal development criteria. The proposed project might not be a priority for the recipient country; and even if it was, given that an ATP proposal normally involved a negotiated contract rather than a competitive tender, there was a greater risk that the negotiated price would make the project uneconomic. There was also the greater danger that, even if the project was deemed economic, the contract price might be padded to produce an excessive profit margin. ODA did not want to find itself funding excess profits nor did it wish to fund excessive agents' fees. It therefore instituted "value for money" checks on the price makeup of individual contracts. These provided ODA with some protection but were never entirely satisfactory as the companies were far better informed on the detail and were capable of covering up excess costings.

ODA was inevitably less in control of the process than with the regular aid programme. Because they weren't party to the negotiations between client and exporter, they didn't have control of the timetable and were often under great pressure to take a decision very quickly. Consequently, they were rarely if ever able to conduct the in-depth analysis that was normal for regular aid-funded projects. Furthermore, exporters were often reluctant to have ODA's economists dig too deeply for fear of putting off the client.

ODA officials did their best – albeit with varying degrees of diligence or success depending on the political and commercial pressures – to ensure that the projects funded under the ATP scheme made sense from an economic point of view for the recipient country. John Vereker, who was Principal Finance Officer at ODA in the mid-1980s with lead responsibility for ATP, did all he could to maintain rigorous standards in the appraisal of ATP proposals. Like others in the department, in the face of pressures from exporters and the scepticism and outright opposition to aid in some quarters of the Conservative Party, he felt it was vital to prevent ODA's development mission from slipping away. But it was an uphill struggle and ATP projects were never subject to the same degree of professional scrutiny as projects in the regular programme. The handling of ATP was described by one senior participant as continuous guerrilla warfare between ODA and DTI, with DTI usually the winner.

The export lobby often complained that ODA was slow and unduly negative in its appraisal of ATP proposals. If there was any bias in practice, and despite the complaints of the export lobby, it was that ODA operated the ATP scheme in ways that if anything down-played the developmental purpose of aid in the interests of the exporters. ODA's lighter touch was reflected in the fact that ATP project proposals, unlike proposals under the regular programme, were not subject to review by its Project Evaluation Committee.

In the 1980s, the provision for ATP was increased and soft loans added as an alternative to mixed credits. With soft loans, because the expenditure on an interest subsidy was spread out over a much longer period than the expenditure on a grant for a mixed credit, for a given ATP budget it was possible for ODA to fund a much larger number of projects in terms of overall value – even though this was going to store up a heavy burden of expenditure in later years.

The value of ATP projects supported accordingly expanded enormously. For the whole period 1978/79 to 1991/92, ODA committed £1,370 million in ATP funds for projects valued at £3,730 million in total. They were concentrated inevitably on those countries that were able to access export credits for large projects. The top four recipients in terms of ATP funds committed between 1978/79 and 1991/92 were in order of ranking: Malaysia, Indonesia, China and India. As of November 1990, ODA had made 37 offers of ATP support to Malaysia; 18 of these were eventually converted into aid agreements.[8] Globally, the power sector was much the largest to benefit from ATP funding – with power projects accounting for 43 per cent in terms of total value.[9]

British exporters, or rather the half dozen companies led by the General Electric Company (GEC) and Balfour Beatty who dominated the ATP business, were generally enthusiastic about the scheme, though they would have liked it to be larger in size and they would have preferred it be run by DTI without ODA involvement. They argued that without such a scheme they would effectively be unable to compete in many middle-income countries. British banks liked it because the export credits they provided were guaranteed by ECGD. They liked it better still when ATP supported a soft loan rather than a mixed credit since this meant a larger credit and the interest rate largely paid to them by the British government directly. Accordingly, they had little or no interest in vetting the project for its viability. They were likely therefore to add uncritical support to their exporter clients when the latter lobbied for ATP funding.

DTI officials liked ATP because – superficially at least – it assisted British exports and the relevant capital goods industries that it was their task to promote. ODA officials on the other hand were generally lukewarm. ODA's economists were concerned that projects were being approved without adequate time or information for a proper appraisal, and some were being approved where the economic case was at best marginal.

Their scepticism was reinforced by ex post evaluations of ATP projects on which the economic returns for the recipient country were in many cases shown to be unsatisfactory. Evaluators also found it hard to find genuine economic benefits for the British economy. Without the support of ATP, orders in many cases would have gone elsewhere; but the same could be said for any industrial subsidy. ATP could only really be justified in economic terms if there were unaided follow-on orders or if there were discernible supply-side benefits (such as the development of new technologies), and there was little evidence of either of these effects (Toye & McQuaide 1986, Donaldson & Currie 1991).

Many ODA staff, particularly the economists, felt that ATP undermined the department's integrity as a serious development institution – the more so, as routinely happened, when they were discreetly advised to temper their misgivings about particular ATP proposals.

Others, including successive aid ministers, felt that the existence of ATP was a political necessity; and because it was a discrete, ring-fenced programme, its existence actually protected the rest of the aid programme from undue political or commercial interference. Moreover, at 5–10 per cent of the bilateral aid budget, it was still only a relatively small part of the overall programme. On this view, ATP was a "loss leader", which enabled the rest of the aid programme to be run on thoroughly professional lines.

Academic economists tended to be highly critical of ATP. The co-author of one of the studies just referred to, Professor John Toye, then Director of the Institute of Development Studies at Sussex and later Professor of Development Studies at Oxford, was shocked by the poor quality of some of the projects he was asked to examine. In one project, involving the supply of buses to Zambia, the buses had been built for European roads and fell apart after three months on Zambia's dirt roads. His view was that ATP had built into it two fatal flaws – client capture of the DTI and the joint ability of firms and the DTI to jeopardise ODA's attempts to undertake a serious assessment of development soundness. In a submission to the House of Commons Foreign Affairs Committee in 1986, he gave warning of this (FAC 1987, pp. 195–206). His warnings were more than borne out by Pergau.

In an article in 1991, Dr Oliver Morrissey of Nottingham University wrote:

> ATP is bereft of economic justification; the benefits it confers on some firms are more than offset by the costs imposed on other firms ... and on the taxpayers. It has not increased the net economic welfare of the UK and is unlikely to have been of much net economic benefit to recipient Less Developed Countries. Mixed credits are a "beggar-thy-neighbour" form of competition between industrialised countries which clearly only benefit a small group of firms.
>
> (Morrissey 1991, p. 127)

In short, no one was particularly happy with the ATP scheme. Exporters and the DTI felt the operation of the scheme was too restrictive; many in ODA, with the backing of academic economists (and also by the development NGOs) felt it was too lax. To address both sets of concerns, the House of Commons Foreign Affairs Committee in 1987 proposed the transfer of responsibility for ATP to the DTI. The government felt obliged to reject this as it would have meant removing ATP from the aid budget, thus reducing further the UK's published aid figures.

In December 1991, OECD member countries agreed (in the so-called Helsinki Agreement) a tightening up of the rules so as to restrict tied aid credits to poorer countries and to exclude projects that normally should be commercially viable. ODA's Principal Finance Officer at that time, Barrie Ireton, played a leading role in the negotiations; as we shall see later, he was a key player in the Pergau story also. The new rules came into effect in 1995: had they been in effect in 1991, the Pergau project would have been excluded from ATP funding.

The aid programme after Pergau

Since 1994, there have been many developments in British aid, mostly for the better. The debacle over Pergau played a part in bringing these about. Looking back at it in 2011, one senior official at DFID described it as "totemic": after Pergau, British aid would never be the same again.

Even though ODA had opposed the project, the immediate effect was a decline in ODA's reputation. Its image as a highly professional organisation that could be trusted to spend money wisely was undoubtedly damaged. The Treasury, always looking for opportunities to reduce public spending, tapped into this negative mood about ODA by reducing the aid budget – which had been edging up in the early 1990s – for the years 1995/96 and 1996/97.

At the same time, the failures over Pergau helped to create a new political consensus over how aid should be used. The Labour Party had been highly critical of the Conservatives' handling of Pergau; but the experience caused a serious rethink on the part of Labour as to how, if elected to power, they would manage the aid programme. After the breakup of the Soviet Union, there was a move amongst all the major donors in the direction of poverty alleviation and development: strategic reasons for giving aid became less important. In any event, the Labour Party concluded that development and poverty alleviation must be the overriding focus. The party also drew the lesson from ODA's failure to hold its own over Pergau that the aid programme should once again be managed by a department fully separate from the FCO, with its own minister in the cabinet.

In slower time, the Conservative Party also shifted its position on aid. The party was deeply scarred by Pergau and made no serious attempt to challenge Labour's policies on aid when Labour came to power in 1997; and as it prepared for government towards the end of the Blair/Brown years, there was little to choose between Conservative policies on aid and those of Labour in terms of both how they would use the aid budget and how much they would spend.

After Labour was elected in 1997, with the dynamic Clare Short as its minister with a seat in cabinet, the department (now renamed the Department for International Development) quickly regained its confidence and positive image. It produced an excellent White Paper (DFID 1997), and the aid budget started to expand at a rapid pace. By 2010 British aid in real terms was roughly two and a half times what it was in the early 1990s. The stronger focus on development and poverty alleviation was enshrined in new legislation.

The International Development Act 2002 established poverty reduction as the over-arching purpose of British aid. The Act requires that all aid – with the exception of aid to the Overseas Territories and for relieving the effects of disasters, and contributions to multilateral development banks – has to meet the tests of sustainable development or improving welfare *and* poverty reduction.[10] The legislation did not prohibit ministers from taking into account political or even commercial considerations in deciding how to spend the aid budget; but in the light of the court ruling on Pergau, no government was likely in the foreseeable future to allow such considerations to override the basic purpose of sound development and poverty alleviation.

With its rising budget and greater poverty focus, DFID was able to play a leading role in getting international agreement in 2000 on the Millennium Development Goals with their aim of halving extreme poverty by 2015 and improving other measures of well-being. DFID has also been a driver in efforts to achieve these goals, though sadly it is virtually certain that for a variety of reasons – including disappointing aid flows from other donors – few of the goals will be fully met.

The new minister abolished ATP as one of her first acts in 1997. The experience of Pergau, and the broader critique of the scheme, certainly influenced her; and so too did the fact that several of the main beneficiary companies had been donors to the Conservative Party. The tying of British aid to purchases of British goods and services was abolished altogether in 2000. As a result, British aid has become more effective and it is no longer subject to the pressures and conflicts that caused so much trouble over Pergau. DFID has also worked hard to secure improved aid effectiveness amongst other donors – which came to partial fruition in 2005 with the Paris Declaration on Aid Effectiveness.

Over the past 15 years, the growing budget and improved efficiency and effectiveness have placed DFID right at the forefront amongst donors. If ODA's reputation prior to Pergau was already quite impressive, it was greatly enhanced in the Labour years 1997–2010. Writing in 1999, the distinguished American aid administrator and academic, Carol Lancaster, had already written that the "British aid programme is among those with the strongest capacity" (Lancaster 1999, p. 143); and with reference to aid to Africa, that it is "by reputation among the more effective" (ibid, p.137). A review of projects and programmes undertaken by ODA/DFID and completed in the late 1990s reported that 75 per cent of them achieved their objectives (Flint *et al.* 2002).

In 2007, DFID was subject to review by an external team under the government's so-called Capability Review Programme and was judged amongst the best of all Whitehall departments in terms of efficiency and effectiveness.

Throughout its history ODA/DFID – perhaps more than most ministries in Whitehall – has been interested in and influenced by new ideas emanating from the academic community. An important influence on recent policy making has been the Oxford economist, Paul Collier. In his book *The Bottom Billion*, Collier argued that the poor economic performance of many of the world's poorest countries (he was referring mainly to Africa) had been due not only to bad policies, but also to bad governance (weak institutions and lack of accountability), civil conflicts, unsatisfactory neighbours in the case of land-locked countries and – for those with valuable natural resources – misuse of natural resource revenues. Such factors were the reason why growth models, which assumed that additional resources would accelerate economic growth, had proved mistaken, and why aid in many countries had failed to improve per capita incomes. Unless aid donors helped to address these issues, the impact of aid would continue to disappoint (Collier 2007).

Charles Kenny, a Senior Fellow at the Centre for Global Development in Washington, in a more recent book has argued a rather more nuanced and optimistic line. Whilst economic growth in many of the poorest countries had been very disappointing from the 1960s to the 1990s, there had been significant improvement over this period in quality of life indicators such as health, education and rights; and at a micro level, aid has made a positive contribution to these improvements (Kenny 2011).

The incoming Conservative–Liberal Democrat government in 2010, unlike the previous Conservative governments, retained DFID as a separate department with its own cabinet minister. The new government also affirmed that, in contrast to the major cuts in most other departments' spending programmes aimed at reducing the fiscal deficit, Labour's plan to reach the 0.7 per cent UN target in 2013 would remain in place. This will mean that Britain's aid will increase from £8.4 billion in 2010 to £12.0 billion in 2013 (DFID 2010).

In March 2011, DFID published its plan for spending this large increase. Its main features are a concentration on fewer countries (country programmes are to be reduced to 27 in number) with one-third of the bilateral programme spent in fragile and conflict-affected states, and a strong emphasis on aid effectiveness and results. An Independent Commission on Aid Impact has been established to provide regular reports to Parliament and the public (DFID 2011).

Project and programme evaluation has a long and creditable history at ODA/DFID – more so than in most other Whitehall departments. The government's declared focus on this area can be seen partly as a means of shoring up political support for an expanding programme at a time of economic difficulty at home.

The emphasis on fragile and conflict-affected states carries risks. The idea is admirable – that development and poverty alleviation are essential to prevent conflicts breaking out in the first place, or to prevent a recurrence after relative stability has been restored. It is in line with Paul Collier's recommendation that aid donors need to concentrate their aid on these countries since they are the ones that are most in need of assistance. Actually identifying and implementing effective projects and programmes for support is typically very difficult in such countries, and until relatively recently aid professionals have taken the view that it is hard to spend substantial aid funds effectively in these places. However, DFID, the World Bank and other donors in recent years have shown that in carefully chosen locations and with carefully chosen partners – often NGOs rather than government – it is possible. The World Bank's World

REGENT'S UNIVERSITY LONDON

Development Report in 2011 was entirely devoted to this issue and offered practical suggestions as to what can be achieved.[11] As Collier argued, it means taking greater risks with aid funds, but how this squares with the commitment to demonstrate aid effectiveness in each and every aid intervention remains to be seen. On the other hand, it seems unlikely in the foreseeable future that risks will be taken with the British aid budget of the kind that were taken in the period 1988 to 1991 – with the aid/arms linkage and the funding of Pergau; and of all the aid donors DFID is as well positioned as any to achieve good results.

3 The Pergau hydroelectric scheme

Malaysia is one of the smaller states of Southeast Asia. With just under 30 million people, it is far outstripped in terms of population by Thailand, Vietnam, Burma, Philippines and Indonesia. However, in terms of per capita income it is well above each of these countries, and third only to tiny Singapore and Brunei. Geographically, it is split between peninsular Malaysia to the west and, 600 miles across the South China Sea, its two eastern states of Sabah and Sarawak.

The country has been fortunate in its natural endowments. In colonial times, rubber, palm oil and tin were the mainstays of the economy. More recently, petroleum and natural gas discoveries have given the economy a massive boost. From the 1970s Malaysia also developed a sizeable manufacturing base and became an important exporter of manufactured products, especially electronic goods. This came about through a mix of market-oriented and interventionist government policies known as the New Economic Policy (NEP) and patterned on those of Japan and other East Asian "success stories". The NEP was the brainchild of Malaysia's second Prime Minister, Tun Abdul Razak bin Hussein (1970–76). But it was under the direction of Dr Mohamad Mahathir, Prime Minister from 1981 to 2003, that the NEP was implemented – and given a strong pro-Malay bias. From the 1970s until the late 1990s Malaysia enjoyed rapid growth: for the 25 years to 1997, per capita incomes grew by an average of 5 per cent a year. A concomitant of this was a very rapid rise in demand for electricity and the need to expand generating capacity.

Malaysia was badly hit by the Asian financial crisis of 1997–98, with its economy contracting in 1998 by almost 8 per cent. But it recovered quite rapidly, and without the support of the IMF. Over the past decade, growth has slowed somewhat, partly due to increased competition from China, and Malaysia was inevitably affected by the global financial crisis of 2007–08.

Taking the last five decades overall, Malaysia's economic record has been remarkable. Not only did the country achieve rapid growth, but absolute poverty was virtually eliminated; virtually all classes benefited, and in contrast to other rapidly growing economies, there was little or no increase in inequality.[1] This was largely due to the Bumiputera ("sons of the soil") policy under which the majority indigenous Malay community were given preference over the more privileged Chinese (and other communities) in jobs, in education and in the ownership of property. Malays benefited from the rapid expansion of the public sector in the 1980s and then from the switch to mass privatisation in the 1990s when many Malay individuals and companies received preferential allocations of shares.

Although there were some negative side effects, such as the emigration of skilled labour and undue capture of the benefits by politically well-connected Malays, taken overall the policy was extremely successful. Professor Hal Hill of the Australian National University, one of the leading experts on the Southeast Asian economies, has described Malaysia's affirmative action programme as the most successful in the developing world. It achieved its redistributive objective without undermining growth and without causing undue political tensions. More broadly, Hill attributes Malaysia's outstanding economic success to "its openness to the global economy, prudent macroeconomic management, its excellent physical infrastructure, and its above average institutional quality" (Hill 2005, p. 17). Malaysia avoided what Paul Collier calls the "resource curse" – the curse of having plentiful revenues from natural resources and misusing them (Collier 2007). There were some bad examples of wasted expenditure on large industrial projects such as the Perwaja steel and Proton car projects.[2] But on the whole, Malaysia spent its natural resource endowment well.

Peninsular Malaya became independent from Britain in 1957. In 1963, Malaya combined with Singapore, Sabah and Sarawak to form the Malaysian federation. In 1965 Malaysia and Singapore agreed a peaceful separation. Without Singapore, the federation consisted of an elected central government and 13 states with elected governments in which the hereditary rulers retained residual powers.

In the early years, competitive party politics existed at state and federal level; but increasingly after 1970, a single party representing the Malay community, the United Malays National Organization (UMNO), came to dominate. Under Dr Mahathir's leadership, the party was able to drive through its political and economic policies, achieving the economic success story outlined above.

But the success came at a price. Dr Mahathir and his party's domination, and the Bumiputera policy, increasingly came to be seen to be associated with cronyism, money politics and lack of accountability.[3] Malaysia's ranking in Transparency International's Corruption Perception Index has become steadily worse in recent years. Many examples of financial malfeasance are described by opposition MP Tony Pua in his book *The Tiger that Lost its Roar* (Pua 2011). The problem was admitted by Malaysia's prime minister, Najib Razak, in 2010 when he said: "We can no longer tolerate practices that support the behaviour of rent-seeking and patronage which have long tarnished the altruistic aims of the New Economic Policy".[4] In the 2008 national elections, the UMNO-dominated Barshad Nasional (National Front) lost the two-thirds majority it had enjoyed in parliament since the 1970s, and five states were lost to opposition parties. Allegations of cronyism, corruption and inefficiency in government were major issues in the election campaign.

Pergau: basic data	
Generating capacity	600 MW
Annual electricity output	520 million kWh
Contract price – current prices	RM 1,824 million (£415 million)
– 1990 prices	RM 1,420 million (£323 million)
Final cost	RM 1,880 million (£427 million)
Soft loan	£306 million
ODA interest subsidy	£234 million (NPV £133 million)

Britain's relations with Malaysia over the past 50 years have been mixed – often positive in reflection of historical ties, but at times rocky as Malaysia sought to assert itself against its former colonial ruler. By the 1970s, diversification of the Malaysian economy and a weakened British economy led to Britain being overtaken by Japan, Germany and the US, and later by China, as Malaysia's principal trading partners outside Southeast Asia. Under Dr Mahathir's nationalistic leadership, there was a weakening of political ties, and in 1981 – in retaliation for sharply higher university tuition fees for foreign students and other alleged slights – Malaysia brought in a "Buy British Last" policy that continued for two years until Mrs Thatcher persuaded Dr Mahathir to bring it to an end.

Thereafter, strenuous efforts were made by British companies, and by Mrs Thatcher and her ministers on their behalf, to take advantage of Malaysia's booming economy and ambitions for a modernised defence force. As a relatively well-off developing country, and without the incentive of particularly close political ties, Malaysia had not been a significant recipient of British aid. However, once the Aid and Trade Provision had been established in 1977, because of its appetite for foreign-financed capital projects, Malaysia became an obvious target and eventually the largest recipient of ATP funding.

This, in brief, is the Malaysia in which the idea of British aid for the Pergau hydroelectric scheme was conceived in the late 1980s. After all the controversy surrounding its financing, it was completed in 1997. It is owned and operated by the national power utility, Tenaga Berhad Nasional (TNB).[5] Its official name is Sultan Ismail Petra Power Station – after a former sultan of Kelantan state.

The power station is located on the Pergau River close to Malaysia's border with Thailand. The river is shallow and quite narrow and winds through heavily forested mountains. Though there has been some logging in the area, the area remains largely forested.

The dam and reservoir are not large by the standards of the great dams on the Indus, the Three Gorges Dam in China or the Bakun Dam in Malaysia's eastern territory of Sarawak across the South China Sea. The dam is 75 m in height and encloses a reservoir with an active storage volume of just over 50 million cubic metres. The power station, which is in an underground cavern, has an installed capacity of 600 MW – again not large by the standards of these other hydro projects. Four turbines of 150 MW each are powered by water entering from the reservoir through a 2 km tunnel. There is also a flow capture scheme comprising a 24 km tunnel that transfers water from adjoining catchments into the reservoir, and this flow is enhanced by a pumping station at the start of the tunnel. A re-regulating pond below the power station controls the outflow into the Pergau River so as to avoid flood surges downstream. There is a control building and switchyard with a short length of transmission line to interconnect with the national grid.

The reservoir, known as the Kuala Yong, has become a minor tourist destination for fishing, boating and wildlife watching. Cradled amidst forested mountain slopes, it has a serene beauty. When I visited it one late summer evening in 2011, there was a rainy mist coming down from the mountains and there was a lone fisherman out in the lake. On the path leading towards the water intake tunnel, there was the fresh footprint of an elephant. The contrast between this beautiful scene and the political controversy that lay behind it – a controversy of which my hosts were largely unaware – seemed utterly incongruous.

The dam itself does not look particularly impressive. Unlike the great concrete dams on the Indus, it is much smaller in height and the grass on the gently sloping earth-fill gives little hint that this is part of a major industrial complex.

By contrast, the cavern that houses the four 150 MW turbines 2 km below the dam and 500 m underground is a great temple of technology. This enormous cave hewn out of the rock is chock full of machinery and, in the hours that the plant is operating, there is the steady, deep thrum of revolving turbines. To a non-engineer, there is an impression of immense, tamed power.

There are 50 employees at Pergau and they are proud of their plant and of the contribution it makes to the Malaysia power system. There is a strong maintenance culture and effective operating procedures, and the plant generally performs well. If it wasn't for the knowledge that the project was seen as extremely costly as against other options for meeting Malaysia's peaking electricity needs in the late 1990s and early 2000s, one's overall impression would be wholly positive.

Pergau is the largest of peninsular Malaysia's hydro stations and is managed along with six others from a control unit at Bursia in the adjoining state of Perak. This is in turn comes under the headquarter dispatch centre of TNB in Kuala Lumpur. Pergau has operational targets that it is expected to meet. Chief amongst these is to maintain availability at over 90 per cent at each of the four 150 MW turbines, and over the past four years it has mostly achieved this.

TNB originally conceived Pergau as a base-load station (i.e. supplying electricity for up to 24 hours a day) with a capacity of 211 MW. In 1987 the Australian consulting company, Snowy Mountain Engineering Corporation, was hired to produce a feasibility study. They reported in April 1988 and recommended that, instead of a base-load station, the scheme should be designed as a peak-load station (i.e. supplying electricity at peak times of day only or to provide emergency supply if one or more base-load stations temporarily fail). Since the water in the reservoir was to be used only for about

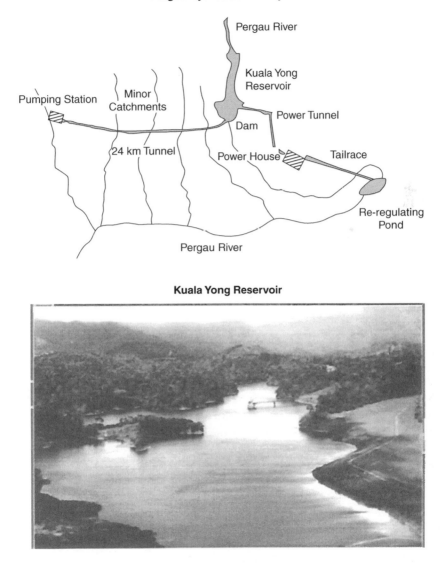

Pergau Hydroelectric Project

Pergau River

Kuala Yong Reservoir

Pumping Station

Minor Catchments

Power Tunnel

Dam

24 km Tunnel

Power House

Tailrace

Re-regulating Pond

Pergau River

Kuala Yong Reservoir

two or three hours a day, it was possible to increase the capacity to 600 MW. SMEC's view was that on certain assumptions regarding energy demand and costs, Pergau could be economic; but as we shall see later, more detailed analysis by Malaysia's own power planners, the World Bank and ODA concluded that the SMEC assessment was far too optimistic. The assessment of all three was that Pergau should be delayed in favour of a gas-fired plant for a number of years, or possibly indefinitely. It was an excessively costly scheme for the amount of electricity it was capable of generating. As one participant commented, "too much cement, not enough water".

The project, nevertheless, went ahead with British aid financing. The client was TNB, which at the time of the financing in 1991 was 100 per cent owned by the Malaysian government. In May 1992, TNB was part-privatised. The aid took the form of an interest subsidy, £234 million in total payable over 14 years, on long-term export credits to cover the UK and EU inputs to the project amounting to £308 million. In NPV terms, the ODA subsidy equated to £133 million. The credits were provided to TNB by a syndicate of 12 British and foreign banks led by the investment bank, J. Henry Schroder Wagg, and guaranteed by ECGD. The financing was approved and guaranteed by the Malaysian government.

TNB paid a fixed annual interest rate of just 0.809 per cent on the credits. In early 1991, sterling interest rates – i.e. the funding costs to the banks – were in the low teens. The banks received two subsidies from the government – the one mentioned above from ODA, and a second one from ECGD. Taken together, these subsidies filled the gap between the 0.809 per cent interest paid by TNB and the banks' funding costs. The ECGD subsidy covered the gap between the banks' cost of borrowing and the rate of 9.65 per cent then ruling under ECGD's Fixed Rated Export Financing (FREF) scheme for which all UK exporters of capital goods were eligible; the ODA subsidy covered the gap between the FREF rate and the rate of 0.809 per cent paid by TNB. The additional subsidy provided by ECGD was estimated at £26 million in NPV terms, making a grand total of £158 million (NAO Report, para. 38).

The actual amount of subsidy eventually paid was complicated and obscured by the fact that TNB in due course pre-paid the credits and by the fact that, following the ruling that the aid was unlawful, the subsidies provided by ODA were henceforth paid by ECGD. No figures are available on the actual subsidies eventually paid by ECGD on behalf of itself and ODA. In return for agreeing to TNB's wish to pre-pay, ECGD was able to negotiate a small reduction in the level of subsidy; but how much exactly is not known. It appears that the subsidy that would have been attributable to ODA probably still amounted to close to £130 million in NPV terms.

The construction was undertaken as a turn-key project by a consortium of Malaysian and British companies, led on the British side by Balfour Beatty and Cementation International. The General Electric Company (GEC) was a principal sub-contractor, and played a major part in the negotiations. There were approximately 170 other sub-contractors in Britain mainly located in the Midlands and in Northern England.

GEC was a major industrial conglomerate. In the mid-1980s it was the largest private sector employer in Britain. It spanned many industries but was particularly well known for its electrical equipment and electronics. Power systems and defence sales were an important part of its business. At the end of the 1990s, the company's constituent divisions were sold off to other companies – notably its Marconi division to British Aerospace. GEC as a company no longer exists.

Balfour Beatty was and remains a major construction and engineering company, involved in numerous infrastructure projects in the UK and abroad. Cementation is also a leading construction business, specialising in ground engineering. Its parent company, Trafalgar House, was taken over by the Norwegian shipping company, Kvaerner ASA, in 1996.

All three companies at the time of the Pergau story were an important part of the UK industrial landscape. As large employers and exporters, they were well connected in Westminster and in Whitehall. Cementation's parent company, Trafalgar House, was a significant donor to the Conservative Party.

The Pergau project was due to be completed in 1996 but was delivered 18 months behind schedule and with a 3 per cent overrun on the original contract price. Neither the delay nor the cost overrun was at all exceptional for a major infrastructure project. Geological conditions turned out to be more difficult than expected, requiring additional steel cladding in the tunnels. The final cost to TNB was RM 1,879.5 million, or £427 million.[6] This was net of RM 24 million in liquidated damages that the consortium had to pay for the delay in delivery. The effect of this was to reduce the profitability of the project to the consortium; and one of the principal companies, GEC, later said that it had made no money on the contract. At the peak of the construction period, about 4,000 workers were employed on the site, of whom around 80 per cent were Malaysians.

In terms of quality, the civil works were considered by TNB to be satisfactory. Likewise, TNB was satisfied with the measures taken by the contractors to minimise the impact on the environment during construction. On the other hand, TNB's project management completion report in 2000 described the performance of GEC-Alstom in the execution of the electrical and mechanical works as below expectation; and numerous defects had to be remedied, which accounted for much of the delivery delay. The need for continuing remedial works after delivery meant that for the first three years of operation, the plant performed poorly – with high unplanned outage and low power availability. The contractors were also criticised for the high level of accidents during construction: 342 in all including seven deaths.

After the teething problems of the first few years, since the early 2000s Pergau has operated well. The energy it produces is not particularly large in national terms – an average of 520 million kWh per year in recent years, about half a per cent of current national electricity generation. But because it is used for peaking and for system security, this is high value energy. Due to the many unplanned outages at other power stations – which included a national black-out in September 2003 – the turbines at Pergau, which can be started very rapidly, have proved useful as an insurance back-up.

There are no published data on Pergau's financial performance. Pergau benefited enormously from the interest subsidy from the British government that it enjoyed on its capital financing. Consequently, in pure financial terms

Pergau almost certainly makes a profit. Whether it makes a profit on a fully costed basis – i.e. including a notional capital charge on capital employed – must be very doubtful.

When the project was at the planning stage, environmental groups expressed concern about its likely environmental impact. However, from an environmental point of view, the Pergau dam was very different from many other dams in Asia and elsewhere. Compared, for example, with the Bakun hydroelectric scheme in Sarawak, which was four times the size in terms of generation capacity, with a dam three times the height, and involving significant population resettlement, Pergau received relatively little attention from environmental lobbyists.

The project only affected an area of approximately 9 square km. Population in the area was sparse and there was no need for any resettlement to make way for the reservoir. The flora and fauna in the area include a number of threatened species; but these have not been put at any significantly greater risk due to the project. The Environmental Impact Statement prepared for TNB in January 1989 concluded that "the environmental impacts are mostly of little to moderate significance and could be effectively mitigated."[7] This was confirmed by an ODA Environmental Adviser who, after visiting the project mid-way through construction in 1994, wrote that mitigation measures, for example in relation to sedimentation, were being effectively implemented, and that the project "will not cause significant long term adverse environmental or social impacts".[8]

In that same year, the environmental campaigning group Friends of the Earth (FOA) presented a memorandum on the project to the House of Commons Foreign Affairs Committee, and a representative, Andrew Lees, gave oral evidence to the Committee. FOA appeared to be more concerned about the poor economics of the project than about the environmental aspects. They did list a number of continuing concerns about the latter but many of these were about process rather than substance. The Committee were not overly impressed and in their report, which was highly critical on so many other aspects of the project, the environment did not get a mention.

4   Politicians and bureaucrats

The fundamental reason why the decision to fund the Pergau project became such a cause célèbre was that it flatly contradicted official policy on development aid. It failed by a large margin to meet ODA's project assistance criteria and it was indirectly connected to a promise of aid in return for a major arms export deal. Public dismay was further fuelled by the court ruling that the decision was unlawful.

That the decision to fund Pergau constituted a major policy failure there can be little doubt. Later chapters will describe exactly what happened. Part of the failure, as we will see, was due to administrative shortcomings that could have been avoided. But there were other reasons, centring on the lack of agreement on policy goals, on which this chapter attempts to throw light.

Political science is replete with theories as to how and why public policy making works in practice, so often falling short of the ideal. Most of them fall within two families. The first is public choice theory, which focuses on the motivations of individual politicians and bureaucrats (ranging from the entirely idealistic to the entirely self-serving). The second is institutionalist theory, which emphasises the continuities and regularities in politics and the inherited and ongoing values and ideologies of different government agencies.[1] And within these two theories, there are numerous sub-theories. No single one appears to be of much help in explaining what happened in the decision making over Pergau.[2]

The theoretical literature does, however, underscore the usefulness of looking at the attitudes, values and motives of the key individual actors (i.e. the ministers and key civil servants); at the attitudes and values of the relevant bureaucracies (i.e. government departments); at the balance of power on the issues at stake between the relevant ministers and between the relevant departments; at the competing role and power of the relevant interest groups; and at how changing styles of public management might have contributed to the difficulties.

For an aid project, an unusually wide array of ministers played a part: five cabinet members, including Margaret Thatcher and her successor as Prime Minister, John Major; and at least five Ministers of State (i.e. deputy ministers just below cabinet rank).

The pivotal figure on the British side was Mrs Thatcher. Although no longer Prime Minister when the final decision was taken in February 1991 to fund the project, her role was critical in two respects. First, she insisted that a mistaken undertaking to provide civil aid in connection with a major defence deal had to be honoured. And second, it was she who made the unqualified offer of aid for Pergau in person to Dr Mahathir in 1989 based on advice from ODA, which she would have known could only be tentative at that stage. It was this initial offer that Foreign Secretary Douglas Hurd and John Major subsequently decided in 1991 could not be reneged on, even though by then it was abundantly clear that the project was uneconomic.

Mrs Thatcher had some superlative qualities. As her Private Secretary for Economic Affairs from 1979 to 1981, I had first-hand experience of these. Most notable were her understanding of the fundamental problems facing the British economy, and her courage and determination in tackling them – insisting on legislation to reduce the excessive power of the trade unions that previous Labour and Conservative governments had shied away from, pushing through other reforms to improve the supply side of the economy, and establishing a medium-term macroeconomic framework aimed at reducing inflation on a permanent basis. In terms of economic policy, Mrs Thatcher pushed back the frontiers as to what was politically feasible. She recognized instinctively what few economists and fewer politicians understood – that without a reversal of the secular decline in the share of national income going into profits, Britain's market economy was doomed.[3] There were some early policy mistakes: chief amongst them was a false obsession with reducing the growth of "broad money", which resulted in excessively high interest rates for too long and an over-valued exchange rate – which in turn caused unnecessary damage to some parts of British industry. But over time Mrs Thatcher's economic reforms laid the basis for Britain's economic revival after the dismal 1970s. Many of these reforms could not have happened without her strong leadership. And her instinct that Britain should stay out of Europe's monetary arrangements was amply vindicated by our forced exit from the Exchange Rate Mechanism in 1992, and again by the Euro crisis of 2010–11. (For Mrs Thatcher, her second official title, First Lord of the Treasury, was far more than just a title, and these were the days before the Bank of England became independent. Her successors would have been amazed at the extent to which she was involved in the decision making on monetary policy.)[4]

However, like all great political leaders – Churchill and India come to mind – Mrs Thatcher had her blind-spots. One of these was her attitude to overseas aid and development. In a letter to his successor as aid minister in 1986, Tim Raison noted that Mrs Thatcher had many qualities but "I can't say that over-enthusiasm for the aid programme is one of them". He warned Chris Patten that "there are those who see the aid budget as simply a big pot to be used for buying business and impressing foreign rulers".[5]

Mrs Thatcher was essentially unsympathetic and uninterested in aid qua development assistance. Under her Prime Ministerial watch, the ratio of aid to GNP roughly halved, whilst the ratio of total public spending to GNP fell by just a few percentage points. She was really only interested in aid to the extent that it might be beneficial for British exporters, might be useful for winning and keeping friends, or for dealing with humanitarian crises. Her ruling that the mistaken undertaking to provide civil aid linked to defence exports must be honoured, and her eagerness to fund Pergau, need to be seen in this context.

She was more than capable of being touched by personal misfortune; but sympathy for the poor en masse, especially overseas, was not within her repertoire. (It was equally the case, though, that she had an aversion in general to thinking about individuals in aggregates – something she associated with totalitarian regimes.) The idea that poor countries had a moral right to aid and the rich had a moral duty to provide it was foreign to her. Mrs Thatcher believed that "charity begins at home"; and at least as far as British tax-payers' money was concerned, it should pretty much end at home.

Like others on the Conservative Right – and some elsewhere in the political spectrum – she had serious doubts about the possibility of doing good in far off countries of which we had limited knowledge, and particular reservations about the efficacy of overseas aid. She had either read or was certainly aware of the writings of the LSE economist, Peter Bauer, mentioned in Chapter 2. Like Bauer, she believed that aid had often bolstered bad economic policies and in that way had a negative impact on economic development. Some of her doubts about aid's efficacy were justified, but they went too far. As numerous studies showed, aid could improve the development prospects of countries and the lives of their peoples. Her negative attitude was heightened by her lack of sympathy, in some cases not without good reason, for many of the governments of the countries that received British aid. She thoroughly disliked the biennial Commonwealth Heads of Government Meetings when she was routinely attacked for her government's policy towards apartheid. It annoyed her that few if any of the Commonwealth leaders ever said "thank you" for the aid their countries received.

Indicative of her attitude to aid was her appointment of Neil Marten, a maverick right-winger with strong anti-EU views, as her first aid minister. He proved an easy target in the face of moves to reduce the aid budget and willingly cooperated in the shift to a more commercially driven aid programme. The appointment of three much more liberal ministers in succession to Marten – Tim Raison, Chris Patten and, finally, Lynda Chalker – was probably due to Mrs Thatcher's realisation that, with ministers such as these, the development lobby in the UK and our development partners overseas were less likely to cause a fuss.

Mrs Thatcher's lack of interest was demonstrated when, soon after taking office, she declined more than one request from Robert McNamara, the then President of the World Bank, to meet her. McNamara had already been President of the World Bank for more than ten years, and was the preeminent leader in the development assistance field. Though in retrospect he was guilty of placing too much faith in the ability of aid monies alone to boost development and too little emphasis on governance and institution building, he was nonetheless someone with whom most political leaders would automatically wish to discuss aid and development issues – with the added interest of his having been Secretary of Defence under Presidents Kennedy and Johnson. Yet Mrs Thatcher could see no point in meeting him. She couldn't see what was worth discussing.

As a scientist, one might have expected Mrs Thatcher at least to have been interested in ODA's scientific work. Not at all: she once expressed astonishment that ODA was supporting research on locusts, a perennial destroyer of crops in Africa. The work of the Anti-Locust Research Centre had a long and distinguished history, but Mrs Thatcher showed no interest in this work.[6]

Other than for humanitarian purposes, she basically took the view that if there had to be an aid programme, it should be used to support the government's political and commercial interests. She saw it as one of her prime responsibilities to "bat for Britain" in expanding exports, and if providing aid could help, so much the better. I know of one example in the 1980s of Mrs Thatcher siding with ODA against the commercial interest – when she backed ODA's objections to an ATP proposal from DTI for an uneconomic power station in Nigeria. But such support for ODA was exceedingly rare.

That her approach to aid might be in conflict with official policy did not seem to worry her. This was not untypical of her approach to policy in general. Rather than seeking a change in policy through formal channels, she often preferred to "make policy on the trot" or simply ignore the official line. She often spoke of "their policies" in relation to a department's policies that she did not like – when the policy in question was the government's official policy.

Mrs Thatcher had mixed feelings about Malaysia – starting off badly and getting warmer as the years went by. In 1981, Dr Mahathir had introduced a policy of "Buy British Last" in retaliation for the huge increase in overseas student fees at British universities in that year. She was infuriated by this action, the more so as there was little Britain could do by way of retaliation. Through her personal intervention with Dr Mahathir, she helped to settle the dispute in 1983.[7] But this didn't put an end to his regular outbursts against Britain and the West. On one occasion at a dinner for her in Kuala Lumpur, he made one such attack that she found seriously offensive – although what he said was typical in her view of what many Commonwealth leaders felt, but didn't dare say so brazenly.

On the other hand, as she got to know him, she admired his no-nonsense political leadership, not dissimilar to her own, and the way he had transformed Malaysia's economy. His methods were of little interest to her, but she was impressed by the results. He was someone she could do business with. The qualities she saw in Dr Mahathir to a considerable extent mirrored her own. She wrote in her memoirs: "I got on rather well with Dr Mahathir and developed an increasing respect for him. He was tough, shrewd and practical.

He had a refreshingly matter-of-fact outlook on everything that related to his country" (Thatcher 1995, p. 502).

There were excellent prospects for British exports to Malaysia, and she was happy to put aside any ambivalence in her attitude towards Dr Mahathir for the sake of British business. Well before the Pergau project emerged, she was taking a keen interest in other projects in Malaysia for funding under the ATP scheme. One such was a rural water supply project for which the contract was won by water services company Biwater. This was achieved with the help of a £59.5 million ATP grant, the largest ATP commitment prior to Pergau. Biwater had close links with the Conservative Party.

Mrs Thatcher had already achieved big success in boosting Britain's arms exports. In 1985 she played a crucial role in sealing the intergovernmental agreement that laid the framework for the Al Yamamah arms deal with Saudi Arabia, Britain's largest ever. That same year she visited Kuala Lumpur for the first time. The main topics for discussion between her and Dr Mahathir were landing rights for Malaysian Airlines at Heathrow, and arms exports and civil aid. This meeting set the scene for greatly increased aid and arms exports to Malaysia in subsequent years. Later, the scent of a major arms export deal easily trumped in her mind the political dangers of aid and arms sales appearing to be linked.

Between July 1987 and December 1989, Mrs Thatcher had bilateral meetings with Dr Mahathir on six occasions.[8] For the two leaders to meet so many times in just two and a half years was by any standards extraordinary. Relations between Britain and Malaysia became very much her personal fiefdom. Others in her close circle were also involved. In a debate on overseas aid in the House of Commons in 1994, the former leader of the Liberal Party, David Steel, pointed out that her public relations adviser, Tim Bell, was also adviser to the Malaysian Prime Minister, as well as to Dr Mahathir's adviser, A. P. Arumugam. Steel also claimed that Steve Tipping, at one time a business associate of Mrs Thatcher's son, Mark, had helped broker the Pergau contract.[9]

In March 1989, when she made the offer of aid for Pergau, Mrs Thatcher was still dominant politically. Within 20 months she would be turned on by her cabinet colleagues and forced to resign as Prime Minister. The unpopular new property tax, known as the Poll Tax, which she had personally championed, was a principal factor; so too was her increasingly maladroit handling of her cabinet colleagues. But at this point in March 1989 she remained all-powerful. Other ministers did not take her on lightly if they wanted to survive or achieve promotion – especially where she already had reached a firm view.

With Thatcher so dominant, and with strong views of her own across the whole range of policy issues, it became all too common in her later period as Prime Minister for officials and ministers to put up advice that they anticipated she would want to hear. It was well known that she had views on Britain's aid and trade relations with Malaysia, which favoured doing all we could with the aid budget to support British exports.

Neither the Pergau project nor the linking of aid to arms exports get any mention in Mrs Thatcher's memoirs. Either they were insufficiently important in her mind to deserve a mention, or else, by the time she was completing her memoirs in 1993, she preferred to steer clear of the controversy that would soon hit the headlines.

The other senior politicians who played significant roles in the Pergau story were, in chronological order, George Younger, Geoffrey Howe, Douglas Hurd and John Major.

Younger was Secretary of State for Defence in 1988, and it was he who signed up to the egregious linking of civil aid to arms sales. For seven years until 1986 he had been an effective, albeit low-key Secretary of State for Scotland. He was variously described as an old-fashioned Tory and an instinctive liberal. Like other Tory moderates, he was in favour of aid for development and not just to promote British exports. But he was a pragmatist with a job to do – one of which was to promote the sale of British defence equipment. By 1991, he was no longer Defence Secretary (or even a member of the government, having retired from front-line politics into business), and so wasn't involved in the final decision to approve the funding of Pergau.

Howe was Foreign Secretary from 1983 to 1989. A free marketer like Mrs Thatcher, he wasn't as hostile to aid as Mrs Thatcher, but he wasn't an enthusiast either. As Chancellor of the Exchequer from 1979 to 1983, it was he who effectively implemented the swingeing cuts to the aid budget in the early Thatcher period; and he saw aid as one of several tools furthering Britain's interests abroad. But as Chancellor he was also exposed to development issues and the needs of poorer countries in his dealings with the IMF and World Bank (he attended their twice-yearly meetings); and unlike Mrs Thatcher, who mostly listened to the aid sceptics, he was better attuned to the views of the pro-aid lobby and to the fact that the "silent majority", whilst not necessarily in favour of larger aid budgets, nonetheless wanted the money spent on what it was primarily intended for – development and poverty alleviation. He was also a careful decision maker – some argued too careful as it often took officials an inordinate time to secure decisions from him. A lawyer by training, he was a stickler for proper procedures being followed – a quality that came to the fore when he learnt that aid was intended to be linked to arms sales.

Hurd was originally on the centre-left of Conservative politics. He started his political career as a close adviser to Edward Heath when the latter was Prime Minister, and like Heath he was a Europhile and an internationalist. As the acolyte of her predecessor as Tory Party leader whom she so thoroughly disliked, Mrs Thatcher took her time in promoting Hurd up the rungs of her government. Like many Tories on the centre-left he had to move to the middle ground in order to prosper under the new dispensation. He was promoted to Home Secretary in 1985 and then in 1989 he became Foreign Secretary, a position for which his temperament and training (prior to entering politics he was a professional diplomat) appeared to make him ideally suited. He was a candidate for the succession to Mrs Thatcher in 1990 but, because of his patrician style and pro-Europe views, was never a serious contender.

The kind of Foreign Secretary Hurd aspired to can be gleaned from his masterly study of 13 Foreign Secretaries (Hurd 2010). Hurd contrasts two types of Foreign Secretary. On the one hand, those who followed Castlereagh and believed in "quiet negotiation, in compromise, in cooperation with other countries", and who "worked for arrangements or alliances which could span an ideological divide, for institutions which combine rules and power to advance peace and security"; and on the other hand, those who followed Canning and preferred "a noisier foreign policy, with an emphasis on independent British action and national prestige, a preference for liberal causes across the world and a willingness to intervene, sometimes by force, to help these causes prevail".

Hurd admires Canning and some of those who followed in his mould, but his sympathy is clearly more with those in the Castlereagh camp – such as Disraeli's Foreign Secretary, the Earl of Derby, Austen Chamberlain and Anthony Eden (until he became Prime Minister and his disastrous Suez enterprise in 1956). Hurd's leaning towards the latter group is reflected in his record as Foreign Secretary. He believed that Britain could simultaneously protect its interests and, without great fanfare, be a force for good in the world – especially by building a stronger Europe as well as maintaining a strong alliance with America. Through expert method – knowing the facts, understanding the character and motivation of others, listening and speaking carefully – and the ability to think on a wider scale (he eschewed the word "vision"), and projecting a certain style, he believed Britain could, as he often put it, "punch above its weight".[10] At the same time, he was realistic about what Britain could achieve on its own and cautious about taking action that might cause more problems than it solved. This caution caused him to be criticised for opposing air strikes against the Bosnian Serbs in 1993 and supporting a continued arms embargo on all combatants in Bosnia – and thereby, his critics claimed, prolonging the conflict there. He was careful not to promise more than Britain could deliver; but equally, he believed it essential that, a promise once made, Britain should stand by it unless there were overwhelming considerations to the contrary. To do otherwise was to compromise Britain's credibility whether as partner or adversary. This, as we shall see, was a primary consideration in Hurd's mind when he came to make the decision on Pergau.

Although ODA had its own minister and its own Permanent Secretary, it was a branch of the FCO and came under the Foreign Secretary's authority. What happened in ODA was ultimately Hurd's responsibility. On taking office, he took little interest in its activities. Unlike Mrs Thatcher, this was not because he was unsympathetic to aid as such: it was simply that he had a vast and all-consuming foreign policy agenda to handle, and the issues around development policy did not greatly interest him. As a former diplomat, he had real empathy for diplomacy whereas aid administration seemed fairly run-of-the-mill and the issues around aid and development did not engage him intellectually. He gave the impression on the infrequent occasions when he was obliged to discuss aid that it was slightly below him and that he did not have time to go into the issues in any depth – a failing that certainly contributed to his over-hasty handling of the Pergau issue in 1991.

ODA in any case seemed to run itself without much need for top-level direction. To the extent that Hurd had views on aid, they were that it could be useful for development, especially if it was technical assistance; and provided its basic purpose of supporting development was kept to the fore, aid could also be useful in serving Britain's commercial and political interests.

On the two significant occasions other than Pergau when Hurd did turn his attention to aid matters, he in fact made important contributions. He was instrumental in creating, in the face of some scepticism in ODA, the successful Know How Funds that provided technical assistance for capacity building in the countries of the former Soviet bloc, which were jointly managed by ODA and the FCO – an example of cooperation between the two that was all too rare in other areas.

He was also the first senior politician in Britain, and amongst the first in any of the donor countries, to raise publicly the issue of corruption as a serious impediment to development. Up until then, unbelievably it now seems in retrospect, it was considered too sensitive an issue for ministers in donor countries to raise in public. Hurd personally inserted a reference to it in a speech he made in June 1990 at a conference on Prospects for Africa in the House of Commons.[11] This was probably the only speech of any significance that he made on aid before he became embroiled with Pergau. Its main theme was that British aid should be used to promote political reform and good governance, both of which were necessary for faster economic progress. Whilst Hurd's speech cannot be said to have been the cause of the growing debate on these issues in academic and policy circles that developed rapidly in the early 1990s, it certainly had some effect. I was with Hurd at this conference. Untypically for him, he punched the air as he left the hall: he knew that in raising the issue of corruption, he had struck an important chord.

When in early 1991 he was obliged to turn his attention to Pergau, he saw it as a foreign policy issue rather than a purely aid and development issue. There was nothing wrong with that; after all, it was his responsibility to weigh all the considerations against each other. But his training, his experience and his intuition made it likely that he would give relatively less weight to the negative implications for aid policy from confirming the funding of the project and more to the negative implications for British–Malaysia relations if it were refused. He knew from the Buy British Last policy of the early 1980s how difficult Dr Mahathir could be if he felt he or his country worsted by the former colonial power.

Officials and junior ministers having failed to reach agreement, it was inevitable that Hurd would have to take over. He had the overarching responsibility for ODA, and he also had responsibility for the UK's overall relations with Malaysia.

For over a year after his becoming Foreign Secretary, the Pergau issue did not engage his attention, and perhaps understandably so. Although his office was kept abreast of the toings and froings on whether the project would or should proceed, at no time prior to the end of 1990 was Hurd asked to consider the matter seriously. As long as the Malaysians and the British companies were negotiating over price, and as long as there was a degree of doubt as to whether the Malaysians wished to proceed with it, the project remained in a real sense hypothetical. In the circumstances, officials were loath to ask Hurd to take on the role of "coordinator" and take a view on the various depart-mental differences. Doing this could hardly rank for his attention alongside the major foreign policy issues of the day – such as the breaking up of Yugoslavia, the collapsing Soviet Empire, the ending of apartheid, the run-up to the first Iraq war. Yet by waiting so long, the political difficulty of withdrawing Mrs Thatcher's provisional offer became all the greater.

Tired and exasperated by the Tory in-fighting and opposition regarding his approach to Europe, Hurd resigned from his position as Foreign Secretary in July 1995. In the week he left office, he gave an interview to *The Independent* newspaper in which he was asked whether he had any serious regrets. He mentioned just two: Bosnia (though he didn't believe the outcome would have been any better had he acted differently) and Pergau.

On the latter, he said: "With the benefit of hindsight I would not have honoured Mrs Thatcher's promise about Pergau. Because I think that didn't do anyone any good. ... at the time it seemed relatively straightforward, with hindsight I wouldn't have done it".[12]

Hurd returned to Pergau in his memoirs when he wrote:

> The Pergau episode vexed me greatly. It spoiled what was otherwise a creditable record which Lynda Chalker with my support had built up on aid. ... Looking back, I can see it was a mistake to act so quickly in 1991. If I had called a meeting and summoned papers, no doubt the temporary link with arms sales would have been revealed. Conceivably FCO legal advisers might then have raised the legal doubts which sur-faced in 1994. I would have had to think more carefully about the cost of keeping Mrs Thatcher's word.
>
> (Hurd 2003, pp. 494–95)

In reality, Hurd was unlucky and didn't deserve the obloquy that he subsequently received. He inherited an extremely difficult dilemma. He had not been involved at all in Mrs Thatcher's offer of aid in 1989, and he had nothing to do with the linking of aid to arms sales. Moreover, as the above quotation from his memoirs indicates and is confirmed by the documentary evidence, he knew nothing about it when in February 1991 he decided to approve the aid. Furthermore, he was not advised that there was any risk of a legal challenge.

John Major succeeded Mrs Thatcher as Prime Minister in November 1990, just three months before the government finally decided to fund the project.

He was consulted by Hurd before the decision was taken, and he approved Hurd's recommendation. So, formally, it was he who had the last word – and much was made of this when I revealed it when I gave evidence to the Public Accounts Committee. Major did know about the aid/arms sales linkage from his time as Chief Secretary at the Treasury and would have been familiar with the Pergau issue when it came to him for decision. He also had first-hand knowledge of Dr Mahathir. For a few months in 1989 he was Foreign Secretary, and in this role he visited Malaysia with Mrs Thatcher for the biennial Commonwealth Heads of Government Meeting (CHOGM). His experience at CHOGM was a bruising one. Mrs Thatcher was incensed by the continuing stand other Commonwealth leaders were taking in favour of sanctions against South Africa, and – to the fury of her Commonwealth colleagues – insisted on putting out a separate communiqué. Dr Mahathir as chairman of the meeting was in typically steely form. I was there as ODA permanent secretary and witnessed how shocked Major was by the unwillingness of Dr Mahathir and other leaders to compromise.

Unlike Mrs Thatcher, Major believed in aid for the good it could do in fostering development and raising living standards. He was genuinely interested in the problems of development, perhaps stemming from his time working as a young man in Nigeria. As was evident from his time as a Treasury Minister (Chief Secretary and later Chancellor of the Exchequer), he was a stickler for efficient and effective use of public money. As Chancellor, he played an important role in promoting debt relief for the poorest countries. I was with him in Trinidad for the Commonwealth Finance Ministers' meeting in September 1990 when he launched his own debt initiative known as the Trinidad Terms, a version of which was eventually adopted by the other main creditor countries. His personal commitment to helping the poorest was evident. All these factors would have tended him to take the side of ODA in the Pergau debate.

On the other hand, having been unexpectedly promoted to the position of Prime Minister, his political position was relatively weak and he would have been reluctant to overturn the advice of his more senior rival for the premiership or be held responsible for the loss of jobs and a row with Dr Mahathir if he were to do so. Equally important, he was Mrs Thatcher's favoured successor and he would have been loath to put at risk so soon into his premiership the relationship with Malaysia that she had done so much to nurture.

The minister in charge of ODA at the time when Pergau was first put forward for consideration was Chris Patten. Patten was perhaps the most talented politician amongst the younger group of Conservative MPs. He had all the attributes – intellectual ability, administrative skill and political acumen – needed in an effective minister. But his liberal views made him suspect amongst Thatcherites, and for this reason he had yet to reach cabinet rank. It was convenient for Mrs Thatcher to have him parked in the political backwater that was ODA where his competence, presentational skills and liberal attitudes could compensate for the modest level of aid spending.

Patten enjoyed the job, was a firm believer in the ability of aid to "do good", and was respected and admired by officials in the same way that Barbara Castle had been in the 1960s. He was frustrated by the pressures to strengthen the links between aid and trade. Yet, he was enough of a pragmatist to know that, with a still-dominant Mrs Thatcher fully supportive of these pressures, there was not a lot he could do to resist them. It is against this background that Patten gave his approval for the initial offer of aid to Pergau in March 1989 even though it was based on a far from satisfactory appraisal, and then felt unable to prevent the offer being confirmed when within a few weeks the cost of the project had mounted by a third.

Patten was promoted to the cabinet later in 1989, and then, under John Major as Prime Minister, to the chairmanship of the Conservative Party. His political career came to a premature end when he was unexpectedly defeated in the 1992 General Election. After that, he was successively Britain's last Governor of Hong Kong and EU Commissioner for External Relations.

Patten's successor as ODA minister was Lynda Chalker. More modest in ability and ambition than Patten, more interested in practical detail and less in policy, she was in different ways an effective and popular minister – especially popular in Africa where the close rapport she established with several political leaders enabled her to be an effective advocate of economic and political reform. Having spent her early career in business, she understood the case for trying to align Britain's aid and business interests. Yet when it came to individual aid projects, especially under the ATP scheme, she was frequently appalled by the tactics used by British exporters to subvert aid in their favour.

Taking over from Patten four months after the Pergau aid offer had been made, she realised that she had inherited a "smoking gun"; but she didn't realise quite how serious it was and, anyway, as a relatively junior member of the government, the possibility of countermanding what had gone before seemed to her wholly unrealistic. However, when in late 1990 the end game approached and the government had finally to decide whether to provide the aid, she advised strongly against. With Mrs Thatcher no longer Prime Minister, this was not the risky move it would have been earlier. Nonetheless, Mrs Chalker showed independence and courage in standing up for the development interest. For doing so, she was pilloried by some in her party and by the right-wing media, though she was eventually vindicated for her stand. Like Patten, Mrs Chalker was also defeated in the 1992 General Election; but she continued as ODA minister until 1997, having been elevated to a seat in the House of Lords.

There were junior ministers in other departments who also played a part in the decision making, but inevitably their personal attitudes and views were less important. One exception was Alan Clark, who between 1989 and 1992 was Minister for Defence Procurement in the MOD. Most famous now for his racy diaries about politics and his personal life, he was an ardent Thatcherite and wholly opposed to overseas aid. He could see nothing wrong

at all in aid being used as an inducement for arms sales. His personal antag-
onism towards aid in general certainly reinforced the MOD desire that the
funding of Pergau should proceed. (We will later see that Clark was involved
in the final decision making, thus further giving the lie to the assertion that
the arms sale and civil aid were not linked.)

Ultimately, amongst the politicians on the British side of the Pergau story,
we come back to Mrs Thatcher as the main mover and shaker. She set the tone
for Britain's overall relationship with Malaysia. Her special interest in promoting British exports to Malaysia, both defence and non-defence, made her
more than receptive to the funding of Pergau; and given her dominance in the
government, it was all too likely that – once she had "spoken" – the funding
would go ahead.

Bureaucrats

It was not just the attitudes and views of politicians that were important in
determining the outcome on Pergau: those of the civil servants in the key
departments also undoubtedly played a part.

Whilst ministers come and go in the British system consequent on their
regular reshuffling at cabinet and sub-cabinet level, government departments
have a life of their own. They have their own attitudes and values that develop
over time and produce in-built policy biases irrespective of the ministers who
are in charge. There exists what is known as the "departmental view".

There were five government departments with a close involvement in the
Pergau and aid/arms linkage issues: ODA, MOD, DTI, FCO and the Treasury.
There was also a sixth, ECGD, whose job was to provide credit guarantees in
respect of export financing with modest interest subsidies frequently thrown
in. ECGD's role was largely a technical one, subject very much to Treasury
control; but their participation was crucial both for the Pergau financing and
for the arms exports.

At the risk of over-generalisation and stereotyping, ODA's culture was
idealistic and professional. Most ODA staff believed strongly in the power of aid
to assist development and reduce poverty. I shared these beliefs. The ratio of
professionals (economists, sociologists, engineers, agricultural, education and
health specialists) was much higher than in other government departments.
The culture was one of openness, challenge and continual learning with a view to
getting policy and its implementation right. Staff were narrowly focused on
aid and development, and had little appetite for the sort of inter-departmental
jockeying that characterised the Pergau story and dealing with the unequal
power relations that ultimately had a large influence on the outcome.

ODA officials may not have been enthusiastic about the ATP scheme, but
they did their best to implement it – striking the difficult balance between the
development and commercial objectives of the scheme. It was only when, as
with Pergau, the development objective seemed to be jettisoned that they
"dug in" against the commercial interest. It was said by ODA's detractors that

the department was in the grip of the development NGOs who hated the scheme. But this was far from the case. Although ODA listened to the views of the development NGOs on a whole range of issues, and on many of them enjoyed their support, the department was not in their hold. For example, the NGOs typically were strongly opposed to ODA's support for World Bank and IMF Structural Adjustment Programmes in Africa. And the amount of British aid that was channelled through UK NGOs was quite small, and far less than they would have liked.[13]

DTI and MOD culture, as it affected Pergau, was one of narrow focus too, but from a very different angle. Their *raison d'être* was to push for the interests of their "clients". Both suffered from "client capture". At times they seemed oblivious to ODA's mandate to fund sound development projects.[14] DTI's overriding interest was to secure orders for British firms. MOD saw aid to Malaysia solely as a potential lever for promoting British defence exports.

MOD officials, who were party to the undertaking to link aid to arms sales, clearly acted outside the bounds of official aid policy. DTI officials involved in co-administering the ATP scheme were all too prone to try to bend the rules of the scheme in favour of British contractors at the expense of aid's development purpose. In their defence it could be argued that both departments were merely acting in accordance with their department's policy agenda as inherited from the past and as projected by their ministers. On the other hand, it is arguable that the "revolving door" phenomenon of both MOD and DTI officials moving to and from their "client" industries could have had some effect on how hard they pressed the interests of these industries. Although personal interests probably only played a limited part, the degree of "client capture" in both departments was remarkable by any standards.

The FCO culture was and is one of mediation and compromise, highly professional and aimed at securing Britain's overall interests. The FCO saw aid as an instrument for promoting friendly relations with Malaysia and the whole range of British interests, including Malaysia's economic development. It was difficult to balance those interests, and this was part of the problem; but typically, ODA's interests came second to most others.

I have little doubt that those involved at the FCO were motivated by what they saw as the public interest. But what was the public interest? How were they to square ODA's interest in funding sound projects with other departments' – and Mrs Thatcher's – determination to win large export orders?

Being a diplomat during Thatcher's premiership was tricky for all sorts of reasons. The FCO was considered soft on the Soviet Union, soft on Europe, and soft on many other things. In regard to aid and trade, the messages coming out of 10 Downing Street indicated a balance of priorities strongly in favour of trade and, if necessary, at the expense of sound aid.[15]

In the case of Pergau, Britain's High Commissioner in Kuala Lumpur, Nicholas Spreckley, correctly read the runes coming from Mrs Thatcher's office, and gave a strong and consistent push for the Pergau project in the face of ODA's concerns. He went along with the willingness of MOD officials and their minister to link aid with arms sales, and for this he was strongly criticised by the Foreign Affairs Committee. Yet, whilst Spreckley lost the confidence of one Foreign Secretary (Howe), he was almost certainly admired by Mrs Thatcher for acting according to her agenda, and respected by another Foreign Secretary (Hurd) for his political judgement.

The Treasury by tradition and practice was concerned with value for money and therefore instinctively supportive of ODA on Pergau. It could have made a serious attempt to block the Pergau expenditure. But Whitehall battles have to be carefully chosen. Despite Treasury civil servants' misgivings about spending tax-payers' money on a seemingly wasteful project, in their hearts they reckoned that a showdown on this issue, which meant challenging both the Foreign Secretary and the Prime Minister, was unlikely to be successful. As we shall see, David Mellor, the Treasury Minister in 1991 responsible for public spending, did send in a stern memorandum of dissent, but he was persuaded by officials to do this more for the record than with any great hope of success. The issue was not judged sufficiently important for the Chancellor of the Exchequer, by this time Norman Lamont, to get involved.

No account of the bureaucracy as it affected the decisions on Pergau would be complete without mention of the Prime Minister's Office. During the Thatcher and Major premierships, the key staff members at 10 Downing Street were nearly all career civil servants on secondment from government departments. Those of us whom she inherited as Private Secretaries from James Callaghan had assumed that political appointees would become much more important under her regime. But with the exception of the economist, Alan Walters, who was her personal economic adviser for two short periods, and from time to time others in the Number 10 Policy Unit, this was not to be. The key staff comprised the Principal Private Secretary and four Private Secretaries and the Press Secretary – all career civil servants. It was only with the advent of Tony Blair as Prime Minister in 1997 that political appointees took on a much bigger role at Number 10.

Apart from their day-to-day administrative function, Private Secretaries at 10 Downing Street have two principal and sometimes conflicting roles. The first is to interpret and articulate the Prime Minister's views on particular issues, and ensure that departmental ministers carry out her wishes. The second is to bring together and put forward in a balanced manner for her consideration the views of the relevant departmental ministers, and ensure that individual ministers are given a fair hearing.

The issue of Pergau fell naturally to the Private Secretary (Foreign Affairs), who from 1983 to 1991 was Charles Powell, a career diplomat. Amongst the many Private Secretaries who worked for Mrs Thatcher, Powell was without peer in fulfilling the first role mentioned above. He was brilliant at articulating her instincts and views and helping to fashion policy and policy decisions so as to reflect them. For this reason, unusually for a Private Secretary, he became a powerful figure in his own right in Whitehall politics. On the other hand, it was a common view in Whitehall, especially in his "home" department, the FCO, that this was too often at the expense of the second Private Secretary role – making sure that departmental ministers' views were fully taken into account.

In any event, on the Pergau issue Powell was seen by ODA – whether fairly or not – as a friend at court on behalf of the commercial and political interest and inimical to the ODA position. Both the companies and the Malaysians used him as a channel to lobby the Prime Minister. With a less influential and effective Private Secretary – effective, that is to say, in reflecting Mrs Thatcher's views – ODA might have been emboldened to put up more of a fight.

In summary, the civil servants concerned with Pergau were far from singing from the same policy hymn sheet. Amongst the five departments, ODA was by far the weakest politically: it was a small department; it didn't have its own cabinet minister; it was not accustomed to fighting battles in Whitehall; and – above all – the government attached low priority to its work. In the absence of a really strong stand by the Treasury, the weight of bureaucratic opinion in the other key departments – FCO, DTI and MOD – in favour of Pergau, bolstered by the knowledge that they had Mrs Thatcher's support, was bound to tell against ODA. In Hashim's words, "decision-making was chaotic and competitive ... Despite control of the ATP funding, ODA could not get on top of the chaos and competition to influence the outcome to reflect official policy" (Hashim 2002).

As for external checks, as we shall see later, neither accountability to Parliament nor the risk of challenge in the courts played any significant role in the period up to the final decision to fund the project – although these both became hugely important in the aftermath.

Interest groups

The unequal power relations between departments were mirrored by the greater strength of the export lobby *vis-à-vis* the development lobby.

The political sociologist, Mancur Olson, long ago showed that governments are more likely to listen to small lobby groups with narrow demands than to larger groups with more diffuse demands (Olson 1965). A small producer group can point to identifiable benefits whilst the costs of favouring the group are typically borne by a much wider group – i.e. taxpayers – and are not as easily identifiable as the benefits to the producer group. Overseas aid is an extreme example of this unequal equation because the costs of giving special preferences to a producer group are not felt in a material way by taxpayers at all: the cost is borne by the recipient of the aid in terms of higher costs. Another reason why some interest groups, according to Olson, are more powerful than others is that they have more relevant information at their disposal.

The export lobby represented a narrow producer group for whom the likely benefits from their lobbying relative to the costs of lobbying were high and the costs of their succeeding would be diffused and virtually invisible to the British public at large.

GEC, Trafalgar House and several other companies bidding for the Pergau contract also had an interest in the defence package. Just as there was a blurring of the aid and defence interest in government, so too was there a blurring amongst the companies. Although British ministers might have formally delinked the promise of civil aid from the defence package, those companies with defence interests would have known that in Malaysian eyes there was a linkage.[16] For these companies, it was therefore doubly important for them that ODA's funding for Pergau should be agreed. Thus, there was – as Hashim puts it – the "covert encroachment of arms salesmen into the ATP sector" (Hashim 2002, p. 152). If Pergau fell by the wayside, then the prospects for defence sales would be diminished. This dual interest meant that, for these companies, the Pergau stakes were that much higher, and it made them all the more determined to win. By the same token, it made those in government with an interest in the defence package, most notably MOD, the FCO and Mrs Thatcher, the more receptive to this lobbying.

The NGOs by contrast were effectively an interest group on behalf of two very diffuse groups – the Malaysian consumer and those in Britain who wanted aid spent for development. The benefits from their lobbying, if successful, would be virtually invisible to the public at large. From a purely political point of view, these contrasting positions were likely to make the exporters the more compelling lobby group.

Furthermore, there was asymmetry in terms of the information that was available to the two groups. The exporters – or at least some amongst them – knew about the Defence Protocol long before the NGOs did,[17] and of course they were party to the details of the Pergau contract and had a great deal of background information relating to it. By contrast, the NGOs did not have access to information on the contract and its financing until well after it was signed. It was only in the light of the NAO report in 1993 that the NGOs really found out about the project. Because of the secrecy surrounding the initial consideration of the project, the NGOs were unable to mount any serious critique before the initial offer of aid was made or during the two years that followed before the aid was finally confirmed. They lobbied intermittently against the ATP scheme in general but did not have the data on which to lobby against Pergau; and like MPs, although they suspected some double-dealing in regard to arms exports, they didn't have firm information. It was only much later in 1994 in the light of evidence given to the Public Accounts Committee and to the Foreign Affairs Committee that the World Development Movement had the information on which to mount their legal challenge.

New public management

The competition between departments over Pergau was largely a product of divergent and unresolved departmental interests. It is arguable that this was also reinforced by the shift that started in the 1980s to a more individualist style of public management, sometimes known as the New Public Management. This put greater emphasis on results and less on process; it gave scope for and encouraged individual civil servants to operate in a more entrepreneurial, results-oriented manner and to pursue their departments' goals with greater vigour (performance pay was introduced as part of this). It put less emphasis on the collective good and on reaching collective decisions on the basis of well-understood general rules and structures. There was reduced emphasis on hierarchy and on coordination, and there was less mediation and smoothing out of differences by Permanent Secretaries – which traditionally had been at the heart of Whitehall practice. The Whitehall "Village Life", which the political scientists Heclo and Wildavsky described and admired in their 1974 classic, was definitely on the wane (Heclo & Wildavsky 1974). Policy was more likely to be decided by departmental self-interest, with outcomes both less predictable and more dependent on the vigour with which the competing agenda were pursued and on the relative power of individual ministers and their departments.[18]

This style of government, as Christopher Hood has argued, was particularly vulnerable to unresolved arguments and feuds, with collegiality descending into mere coexistence. Policy coordination was lacking yet all the more needed. For too long in the case of Pergau, there were too many parties "doing their own thing" when coordination and resolution of differences was needed. Coordination has an opportunity cost, especially for senior ministers: dealing with one issue means devoting less time to other, seemingly more pressing issues. Yet the failure to coordinate at a political level until very late was one of the reasons why the outcome was so unsatisfactory.

5   Dr Mahathir and the politics of Malaysia

It takes both sides to tango for an aid project to be undertaken. So why did the Malaysian government want Pergau so badly when, both to ODA's economists and engineers and to the power planners in Malaysia, it appeared seriously uneconomic; and why did the Malaysian government insist on the linkage between aid and defence sales?

As to why the Malaysians wanted to make their purchases of defence equipment conditional on the provision of civil aid, this was all of a piece with Dr Mahathir's determination to drive a hard bargain with foreign suppliers, and especially the British with whom he had a love/hate relationship. If he was to direct such a large part of his defence budget to procuring equipment from Britain, for his self-esteem and to protect his own back politically, he needed a quid pro quo from Britain. He and his advisers would have been aware that any linkage between defence purchases and civil aid was not allowed under international rules, but they may have judged that Mrs Thatcher's determination to promote defence sales and her lack of serious interest in aid matters would make her susceptible to accepting the linkage.

As for Pergau itself and why Malaysia opted for it over other power station options, the basic answer is that Dr Mahathir wanted it and wanted it badly. There were others in Malaysia too who supported it, but without Dr Mahathir's strong support – as with so many things in Malaysia – it would never have happened.

If Mrs Thatcher dominated the political scene in Britain in the 1980s, it was nothing as compared with Dr Mahathir's domination of Malaysian politics. And unlike Mrs Thatcher, his dominance continued well through the 1990s and into the early 2000s. He finally stepped down as Prime Minister in 2003 but continued to wield a great deal of influence behind the scenes.

Mohamad Mahathir qualified as a medical doctor, hence his being known routinely as Dr Mahathir, and he practised for 20 years. But his ambition had always been to go into politics. He entered national politics in the mid-1960s; became a cabinet minister and then Deputy Prime Minister in the 1970s; and finally Prime Minister in 1981.

He was by his own lights, and in the view of many Malaysians, a highly effective Prime Minister, but also – like Mrs Thatcher – a complex and controversial one. His leadership had four principal characteristics. First of all, he was determined that Malaysia should emulate the East Asian "tigers" and achieve rapid economic development. His economic model was that of Japan and Korea – capitalism with heavy doses of government intervention. He saw technology, education and investment as the key growth drivers. His approach to development was guided by political instinct and a desire to develop a fully balanced economy. He was a utopian in the sense that he believed it was possible to improve society through administrative ordering and through the correct application of science and technology. Like other utopians, he liked big projects and took the long view, tending to discount uncertainty and costs.[1] He had little time for economists, especially when they criticised him for promoting grandiose projects. He regarded them as theoreticians, out of touch with the real world. He wanted to reduce Malaysia's economic dependence, but not by cutting itself off from the rest of the world. He welcomed inward investment and foreign aid, but they had to be on terms of Malaysia's choosing. He had a vision of Malaysia as a thoroughly modern nation by 2020.

Second, although only half Malay (his father was of Indian extraction), he projected himself as a radical Malay nationalist, determined to promote the interests of the Malay majority that under the British were politically and economically the backward community – and had remained so for the first decade or so after Malaysia's independence in 1957. He wanted to shift economic and political power away from the Chinese community and from foreign capital; and also away from the conservative Malay royal sultans. In this he was influenced by the terrible riots of May 1969 that he and other Malay nationalist politicians blamed on too much power having been ceded to Malaysia's minority Chinese community. He achieved a major shift of power to the Malay community by affirmative action programmes – the Bumiputera policies.

Third, Dr Mahathir wanted Malaysia to stand tall and be influential amongst not only its immediate neighbours but also amongst Third World nations in general: his ambition was to be their spokesman. He also sought to cut a figure as a leader who could embrace modernism whilst remaining true to Islam. On both counts, whilst routinely embracing Western business interests, he was often sharply critical of Western governments. Unlike his three predecessors as Prime Minister, who had all been educated in Britain and had a certain nostalgia for things British, he had grown up entirely in Malaysia and was determined to break loose from any remaining colonial bonds. He wanted to broaden Malaysia's international relations, particularly with America and Japan. Continuing ties with Britain would be on his terms, not Britain's. He was quick to rise to insult or condescension and was acutely sensitive to any criticism by the former colonial power; yet at the same time, he sought recognition and respect from the British. He enjoyed the attention that Mrs Thatcher gave him and was ready to exploit it to the full.

Fourth, Dr Mahathir was a tough political operator, determined to maintain the dominance of UMNO, and his own dominance within UMNO. He was routinely suspicious of potential rivals and if he scented serious opposition or competition for his position as leader, he took steps to neutralise it. Thus, in the late 1980s he cast aside two of his most capable colleagues – Deputy Prime Minister Musa Hitam, and Trade and Industry Minister (and earlier, Finance Minister) Tengku Razaleigh. Most famously, in 1998 he sacked Anwar Ibrahim as Deputy Prime Minister and Finance Minister and had him expelled from UMNO. Differences over the handling of the economy, which was badly affected by the Asian economic crisis of that year, were partly responsible for Anwar's removal. But Dr Mahathir's desire to forestall any potential threat from an able and popular colleague was widely regarded as the main reason. Anwar was subsequently accused and then convicted and jailed on charges of corruption and sodomy. Many believed at the time that Anwar was the victim of a political vendetta on the part of Dr Mahathir, and Amnesty International adopted him as a prisoner of conscience. The convictions were overturned by Malaysia's Federal Court after Dr Mahathir left office.

Many years earlier in March 1988, Dr Mahathir had first weakened the power of the judiciary by whisking through Parliament an amendment to the Constitution that abolished judicial review by the courts. With the executive already so dominant *vis-à-vis* parliament and the media, this at one stroke removed a key check on arbitrary actions by government.

Then, two months later the Lord President of the Supreme Court, who was also head of the Malaysian judiciary, was dismissed, and another judge appointed in his stead. Formally, the Lord President was dismissed on the instruction of the king (the Sultan of Johore), and that was how Dr Mahathir presented it. However, Barry Wain makes a strong case in arguing that Dr Mahathir was responsible for the sacking (Wain 2009, pp. 72–76). According to the constitution, the king acted on the advice of the Prime Minister and not the other way round. Moreover, the membership of the special tribunal that recommended the sacking was chosen by Dr Mahathir. The tribunal's report was described by the eminent British QC Geoffrey Robertson as "the most despicable document in modern legal history".[2] It appears that Dr Mahathir gave Mrs Thatcher his own version of what had happened: he evidently wanted to persuade her that what had happened was above board.[3]

According to Wain, the sacking of the Lord President, and later of several other senior judges, was motivated by Dr Mahathir's determination to derail a Supreme Court hearing on an appeal by political opponents that would almost certainly have gone against him and led to his resignation. Wain writes that "the assault on the judiciary, as it was ever after known, though motivated by political factors, opened the way for money to seep into the system" (Wain 2009, p. 75).

Dr Mahathir presided over a government in which, amongst its leading members, conflict of interest often seemed more the norm than the exception. This is documented by Wain, and also in a study by Jeff Tan (Tan 2008). Another study cites numerous cases where political patronage played a significant role in the privatisation of state assets (Gomez and Jomo 1999, pp. 75–110). One of the results of the entanglement of private and public interests amongst government ministers and their advisers was that public investment decisions, such as over Pergau, were less likely to follow the objective criteria of public sector economics. (Not that Malaysia was unique in either regard.)

Whilst observing the principles of a multi-party democracy, allowing opposition parties to contest elections and play a role in Parliament, Dr Mahathir was adept at ensuring that his ruling party won election after election. This was not achieved by anything as tawdry or unlawful as stuffing of ballot boxes. His means were twofold. First, he made sure that UMNO was well resourced financially; and second, he made sure the media were supportive – through its virtually 100 per cent ownership by UMNO and UMNO's allies, and by tough controls on press freedom. He abandoned his party's historically moderate position on Islam in order to outflank the Islamist opposition party, Parti Islam SeMalaysia (PAS).

Yet in most respects, Dr Mahathir achieved what he set out to do. Over the period of his premiership, Malaysia achieved an impressive rate of economic growth, and the income and wealth of the Malay community grew disproportionately as he had intended. Despite his anti-colonial rhetoric, Malaysia welcomed inward investment and foreign technology. This, together with sensible macroeconomic policies and the discovery of massive natural gas reserves, made it possible for the economy to be transformed from one dependent largely on natural resource exports into an economy with a significant manufacturing export base. Like Lee Kuan Yu in Singapore and Soeharto in Indonesia – and unlike many African leaders – Dr Mahathir correctly believed in working predominantly with, rather than against, the market.

Malaysia under Dr Mahathir established itself as a significant player in the Southeast Asia region. It earned respect amongst developed countries, especially Britain, as an economic success story and as a market for their exports. And Dr Mahathir's became a strident voice on behalf of the Third World, managing to balance this nonetheless with maintaining relationships with developed country leaders such as Mrs Thatcher.

When the Pergau scheme was recommended in early 1988 by the Australian consulting firm, SMEC, for early implementation, Malaysia was undoubtedly in need of additional electricity generating capacity. Rapid economic growth had driven demand for electricity up very fast. The question was what type of plant or plants should be selected – turbines driven by oil, coal, natural gas or water.

The technocrats in the national electricity company (TNB) basically agreed with the World Bank and ODA that, on the basis of more realistic costings than those used by SMEC, the project was seriously uneconomic – and at the very least should be postponed for a number of years. On the other hand, Dr Mahathir and others close to him favoured the project. The latter included GEC's local representative and minority shareholder in GEC Malaysia,

A. P. Arumugam; the Finance Minister and Treasurer of UMNO, Daim Zainuddin; and the Energy Minister, Samy Vellu.

Arumugam not only acted for GEC; he was also an intermediary for the purchase of technology and equipment across a range of industries, including defence. He was a close confidant of Dr Mahathir and his unofficial adviser on defence procurement. He was therefore a key player on the Malaysian side in respect of both the £1 billion defence deal and the Pergau project. He was also well known and had easy access to Mrs Thatcher's office. In effect, he was the go-between for Dr Mahathir via Charles Powell with Mrs Thatcher. By all accounts, Arumugam became extremely wealthy through his middle-man activities.[4]

Daim Zainuddin was a highly capable Finance Minister – he served twice from 1984 to 1991 and again from 1998 to 2001; and was Treasurer of UMNO from 1984 to 2001. He was also a very successful businessman, and according to Wain, had no qualms about having his own business interests, the interests of the Malaysian economy and the interests of UMNO deeply entangled. In an interview with Wain, he defended his mixing of government and personal business as follows: "If everyone is going to make money, why not? So I see no reason why it is a conflict, so long as everybody declares their interest" (Wain 2009, p. 103).

Samy Vellu was the leader of one of the smaller political parties, the Malaysian Indian Congress (MIC), which was a member of the ruling coalition. He became Minister of Energy, Telecommunications and Posts in May 1989, two months after Mrs Thatcher's offer of aid. He was another who was not above mixing personal and official business. From his time as Minister of Works up until 1989, he had a murky reputation for inappropriate financial dealings, and this reputation continued in his new role as energy minister.[5]

It is no surprise that Dr Mahathir and his team prevailed over the technocrats. But why were they so ready to set aside the economic assessment? In his memoirs published in 2011, a book of over 800 pages, neither Pergau nor any of the controversies surrounding it – such as the allegations of corruption and Malaysia's boycott of British contractors – get a single mention. Whether this is a deliberate omission because he prefers not to mention them (there are many other controversies during his premiership that he ignores or glides over), or whether, midst all the other issues, Pergau does not rank high in his recollection, is not clear (Mahathir 2011).[6] As mentioned earlier, it gets no mention in Mrs Thatcher's memoirs either.

Although Dr Mahathir's memoirs are of no help, we know enough to be able to point to a number of factors. Dr Mahathir had no great regard for economists and would have discounted their views. He liked big projects: he supported others in the industrial sector where the economics were decidedly shaky. Moreover, whereas the ODA looked at the economics of Pergau without the benefit of the aid, to Dr Mahathir's way of thinking the aid would help to make it economic. Furthermore, whatever the economists had to say about the economic advantages of other fuels, he saw the need for a more diversified power generation sector. The expansion of hydro would put off the day when Malaysia's natural gas reserves ran out, and with the right planning, hydro could be better in environmental terms.

The Pergau project was located in a state that had regularly voted for the main opposition party, PAS. In 1989 it was the only state where the ruling party, UMNO, was not in power. It was also the state of one of Dr Mahathir's key political adversaries, Tengku Razaleigh. There was another hydro project, Ulu Jelai, which appeared more promising than Pergau in economic terms and which the British contractors for Pergau had initially been invited to look at. But Ulu Jelai was located in the more developed state of Pahang to the south, and Dr Mahathir favoured Pergau over Ulu Jelai partly because of Kelantan's backwardness. The PAS government in Kelantan had been unsuccessful in attracting foreign investment, and by offering the project to the state Mahathir could show how much better off Kelantan would be if they voted for the ruling party. (UMNO actually lost Kelantan to PAS in the 1990 elections, but Dr Mahathir decided that he did not want to punish the electors by taking Pergau away from them.)

Finally, in a convoluted sort of way typical of Dr Mahathir, there is evidence from the reporting by the British High Commission in Kuala Lumpur that, once he felt sure that the aid package was on the table, he felt a moral duty to reciprocate by delivering the project for the sake of Britain and the British contractors.

Amongst Dr Mahathir's close advisers, Arumugan had personal reasons for backing the project. As GEC's principal representative in Malaysia and minority owner of its Malaysian subsidiary, he potentially stood to benefit personally from it. He and GEC also had an interest in the defence deal, so – insofar as Pergau and the defence deal were connected – this would have been an added reason for his wishing to press the case for Pergau.

Daim Zainuddin may also have had an interest in pushing the case for Pergau, not on his own account but in case there might be a cash spin-off for UMNO. As for Samy Vellu, he may have seen financial advantage for himself and his political party in backing the project. There were later suggestions, though none proven, that he was suborned into backing Pergau; it was also suggested that he and the MIC benefited inappropriately from the privatisation of TNB.

The ODA economist, Alan Whitworth, who conducted the initial appraisal in March 1989, wrote in his report that the decision by Malaysia to support the project was political and he doubted that economic analysis would change this. The British High Commissioner, Nicholas Spreckley, made the same point on numerous occasions. If the ODA as an organisation had fully understood this, and had understood the factors that were driving the decision making on the Malaysian side, we might have taken a firmer view in opposing the project earlier on. Whether this would have affected the outcome, given the other pressures within Whitehall, is perhaps doubtful.

6   Arms and aid entangled

The Pergau story gets off to a bad start with Defence Secretary, George Younger, signing a "Protocol on Malaysia Defence Procurement Programme" with his Malaysian counterpart in Kuala Lumpur on 23 March 1988. The Protocol was intended to pave the way for a more detailed Memorandum of Understanding (MOU) to be signed later in the year in support of sales of defence equipment to the tune of £1 billion over a five-year period.

There was nothing unusual about such a protocol or the intended follow-up MOU: the MOD habitually draws up such documents setting out the terms and arrangements by which it can assist sales of defence equipment by British companies to particular governments. What was unusual, and without precedent, was the inclusion of language that indicated a willingness on the part of the UK government to consider the possibility of providing aid for civil projects as part of the deal. The Protocol included the following undertaking:

> The Government of the United Kingdom will bring to bear the resources of its Ministry of Defence on the overall programme in order to grant certain facilities, but not necessarily limited to:
>
> • aid in support of non-military aspects under this Programme, the type, terms and conditions of which shall be mutually determined by both governments. Her Majesty's Government has taken note of the Malaysian Government's desire that this grant should amount to no less 20 percent of the defence equipment, and that will be discussed in the context of the Memorandum of Understanding.[1]

The Protocol mentioned the following projects under the proposed programme: Tornado aircraft, Rapier missile systems, Martello radars and an integrated command, control, communications and intelligence system. It did not include a value for the overall programme, but the British side estimated it at about £1 billion – with the implication of a possible aid commitment for civil projects of £200 million.

In the late 1980s the UK had the largest military–industrial base in Europe (it still does). Defence suppliers accounted for roughly 300,000 jobs and indirect suppliers accounted for a further quarter of a million jobs. British Aerospace was much the largest single supplier. Other companies that were heavily dependent on defence sales included the three largest companies involved with the Pergau project – GEC, BICC (the parent company of Balfour Beatty) and Trafalgar House (the parent company of Cementation International). They each had major defence businesses.

Defence equipment exports accounted for 3 per cent of visible exports and were vitally important for the defence industry: roughly a quarter of all sales went abroad. But the overseas market was becoming much more competitive. With the Cold War drawing to a close, there was surplus capacity in the traditional exporting countries, especially the US; there was new competition from non-traditional exporters such as South Africa and China; and many developing countries were beset with debt problems that constrained their military spending.

In this environment, the industry had to become much more aggressive in its export marketing to survive. It was helped in this by more active support from the MOD – from MOD ministers (with active involvement and support from Mrs Thatcher herself), from the MOD's Defence Export Services Organization (DESO) and from military attaches deployed in Britain's embassies and high commissions in over 100 countries. DESO had long existed to assist the industry in its marketing, but with Mrs Thatcher's encouragement, DESO in the 1980s stepped up its activities. It was staffed to a large extent by executives on secondment from the defence industry. By convention, it was headed in turn by a senior executive from one of the four principal defence suppliers. In 1988, the head of DESO was Colin Chandler, who had been seconded from British Aerospace and later became chairman of the board of another major defence supplier, Vickers. He and his staff were described by an official who had to deal with them in another government department as "buccaneers". They were better at winning defence business for Britain than in understanding the correct procedures for doing business within Whitehall.[2]

The industry's most famous success in the 1980s was in securing the multi-billion pound Al Yamamah contract with Saudi Arabia. Mrs Thatcher and DESO played an important part in the winning of this contract. It later became mired in controversy when the Special Fraud Office (SFO) mounted an investigation into allegations of bribery on the part of British Aerospace. The investigation was called off in 2006 by Tony Blair on the grounds that it was endangering Saudi Arabia's cooperation on national security issues. A more wide-ranging investigation led by the Department of Justice in the United States resulted in British Aerospace in 2010 pleading guilty, amongst other things, to "mak[ing] false statements about its Foreign Corrupt Practices Act compliance program". For these and other "criminal acts", the company was ordered to pay a fine of £400 million. In the words of the Acting Deputy Attorney General, British Aerospace's actions "impeded U.S. efforts to ensure international trade is free of corruption and to maintain control over sensitive U.S. technology".[3]

Bribery of foreign government officials and ministers was in fact endemic in the British defence industry, as it was amongst most other countries' defence exporters. Bribery was by no means unique to the defence industry, but it was generally much more widespread than in other exporting industries.

In 1977, the United States government passed legislation making bribery by American-based companies operating overseas illegal. It was due to this legislation and subsequent pressure from the American government that other countries began to clamp down on bribes paid overseas. But it took the UK longer than most. In 2001, the British parliament tacked a less than satisfactory anti-bribery clause onto an anti-terrorist bill, and it was under this provision that the SFO initiated their investigation into British Aerospace. Finally, a more comprehensive anti-bribery bill was passed in 2010 shortly before the General Election; it finally came into force on 1 July 2011.

Bribery by defence contractors has proved the hardest nut to crack. It was sufficiently widespread in Europe, notwithstanding legislation in most countries outlawing bribery of foreign officials, that the major European defence contractors were persuaded by anti-corruption pressure groups in 2007 to adopt a voluntary code of practice, the Common Industry Standards for European Aerospace and Defence.[4]

Bribery of course was not the only dubious activity defence exporters were involved in. Exports of lethal weapons, and products that could be used to manufacture them, were subject to official rules as regards what products, and to which countries, they could be exported. Defence exporters were adept at getting round these rules. Most famously, in the Arms for Iraq Affair it emerged that the firm involved, Matrix Churchill, not only flouted the rules but did so with the knowledge of certain ministers.

Malaysia in the 1980s was identified as a key target for expanded defence sales. Good relations had been maintained between the UK's and Malaysia's defence forces, and Malaysia under Dr Mahathir had decided – because of booming revenues – that it was able to spend large amounts on modernising its defence forces. Once Malaysia's Buy British Last policy had been lifted in 1983, there seemed good prospects for Britain's defence suppliers, and particularly so if they had strong political support.

It was against this general background that George Younger sought to advance the industry's Malaysian ambitions. He had consulted Mrs Thatcher about a possible defence protocol. She was in favour "provided it did not impose any financial obligation on us",[5] and the Chief Secretary to the Treasury (at that time, John Major) wrote to Younger that "no doubt [he] would consult colleagues again should it look as if government support would be required".[6]

The Malaysians clearly had their sights on such assistance. On 14 March 1988, the Malaysian Finance Minister, Daim Zainuddin, called on Younger in London. Daim said that he understood that the package was to be supported by a "cash grant of some £60 million." He was told that "aid could only apply to civil projects".[7] Where the figure of £60 million came from is unclear; equally unclear is whether Daim understood from the reply that there could be no linkage between civil aid and defence sales. In any event, during the course of the discussions between Younger and his Malaysian counterpart in Kuala Lumpur on 22 March, the Malaysian side returned to the issue, and the following day – after the Protocol had been signed – Daim wrote to Younger in the following terms: "As indicated to you during our meeting on 14 March, British aid is an important element in this package. ... The signing of a Memorandum of Understanding will only be possible if the Malaysian government is satisfied that this aid is forthcoming".[8]

Significantly, MOD had failed to inform the FCO or ODA of the exchange between Younger and Daim on 14 March. (They only saw the record of the meeting after the Protocol had been signed.) The result was that they had no idea that the Malaysians were looking for aid as part of the package, and therefore they were unable to warn Britain's High Commissioner in Kuala Lumpur, Nicholas Spreckley, that the issue might reappear during Younger's visit. Even after the signing, it appears that Spreckley was still unaware that the issue of aid had been raised by Daim in London the previous week. In a telegram explaining why he felt that Younger had been right to sign, Spreckley wrote: "It would have been much easier if the MOD had agreed a line on aid beforehand. But as the matter had not previously been raised, MOD saw no need".[9]

Why did Younger agree to the language in the Protocol just one week after Daim's request for aid had been more or less rebutted? At the FAC hearings in 1994, Younger said that it was requested by the Malaysians late in the negotiations and he felt it necessary to agree to it in order to secure agreement on the defence package; and in any case, he argued, the language did not involve an absolute commitment. He told the FAC that he was convinced that if he had refused the linkage, the Malaysians would have broken off the discussions.

He, as well as Spreckley, were criticised by the FAC for not alerting the FCO in London to the Malaysian request before he signed. Younger's response was that the timing was such that he had no option but to make a snap decision, and he judged that the language was acceptable in the context of the likely loss of the defence sales package if he had failed to sign.

The record shows clearly that Younger and his team of MOD/DESO advisers, which included Chandler, could have consulted the FCO in London before signing. The request for inclusion of an undertaking to provide aid was made during the discussion on 22 March, and the text was negotiated with the Malaysian Ministry of Finance the next morning. They simply chose not to do so.

Younger and the officials accompanying him were either unaware of the extreme sensitivity of any linking of aid with arms exports, or if they were, they chose to ignore it in the interests of the British defence industry.

Younger later put a rather different gloss on the story when he told *The Economist* that "a verbal undertaking was given by somebody – not myself – to link aid to the defence project. There was pressure from the Prime Minister's side to be pals [with the Malaysians], saying 'what the hell, let's do the deal'".[10] It is not clear precisely what Younger meant. It reads as if, in Younger's view, "the Prime Minister's side" was complicit in the signing. But this seems unlikely, given Mrs Thatcher's earlier stricture that there should be no financial obligation involved. Most likely, he meant that once he had mistakenly signed the Protocol, he believed that "a verbal undertaking ... from the Prime Minister's side" had been given to the Malaysians that his promise of aid would be fulfilled. However, when questioned about this by the FAC, Younger said he had no knowledge of any such promise having been given.[11]

The FCO and ODA were notified of the signing by telegram from the High Commission on 24 March.[12] When told about it, the ODA minister, Chris Patten, was absolutely horrified. And so too was Foreign Secretary Geoffrey Howe when he was informed a few days later.

There was no one at ODA who had a better appreciation of the tough world of international business than its then Permanent Secretary, John Caines. Before becoming Permanent Secretary in 1987, he had made his career – and reputation – at the DTI (and its predecessor, the Board of Trade). He well understood the pressures on British exporters and need for government to assist them in difficult markets, especially where defence exports were involved. A wise and effective operator in the best Whitehall tradition, he was not a man given to over-reaction. All the more telling then was his sense of outrage.

In an internal memo, Caines wrote: "I find myself aghast that a Minister of another department should have apparently signed a document carrying implications for another Secretary of State without their having been any prior discussion". He went on to refer to a "total failure to observe proper standards of conduct of government business".[13] In advice to Howe, he wrote:

> For British development assistance to be seen to be associated in any way with a defence procurement package would be disastrous. It would be totally inconsistent with the general thrust of the government statement of aid policy in its reply to the Foreign Affairs Committee report; it would lead to a loss of confidence amongst aid recipients in our motivation, from which the aid programme might never recover; and it would attract massive domestic and international criticism.[14]

He also pointed out that the £200 million (the amount implied by the Protocol) would be an impossibly large commitment from the ATP budget, and it would seriously distort ODA's allocation of aid worldwide. He concluded by advising that the reference to aid in the Protocol must have nothing to do with ODA and if the reference was to be retained, MOD must find the money from their own budget. In a separate letter to Chandler, Caines wrote: "I see no easy way out of this situation, particularly as the politics of using aid undertakings to secure defence orders are such political dynamite".[15]

Howe summoned Younger to explain. He told Younger that he was

> in no doubt that the Malaysians, given Mr Younger's signature of the Protocol, will now regard it [the aid] as a firm part of the package to be negotiated. They are likely to regard a failure by HMG to agree aid resources of the order proposed in the context of the package as a breach of faith.

He went on to say that "it is illusory to imagine that such a link could be kept secret ... there is every likelihood that it would rapidly become common knowledge. This would place us in an impossible position in Parliament and with our OECD partners."[16] He asked that the linkage with aid should be removed, although he would not object if Younger were to reassure Finance Minister Daim that ODA was willing to consider suitable projects for ATP support as an entirely separate exercise. If the MOD felt the linkage had to remain, then the MOD would have to find the money from its own budget. Younger responded that this was not feasible and that if ODA could not help, the MOD would have to accept that the package would have to be dropped.

Quite coincidentally, Howe had arranged to visit Malaysia a day or two later. He avoided any discussion of the defence package with his Malaysian counterpart, but he took the opportunity – according to another diplomat who was present – to give High Commissioner Spreckley a stern dressing down. Howe was furious that Spreckley had failed to consult London when the aid language was mooted and, according to Younger, had advised him that he could sign. Spreckley was unrepentant, feeling he had done the right thing in the circumstances.

For the next few weeks, there was impasse in Whitehall. The FCO and ODA insisted that the linkage with aid should be removed and the Protocol adjusted accordingly. Caines told Chandler that ministers "must be able to rebut in public with total honesty any allegation that additional aid flows to Malaysia had been promised as an inducement for securing the aircraft sale."[17] MOD ministers and officials for obvious reasons were reluctant to unscramble the link. Then on 6 May 1988, after a further inconclusive meeting between Younger and Howe, Younger's private secretary wrote to Charles Powell at Number 10 setting out the problem but without suggesting a solution.[18] Powell responded on 9 May that Mrs Thatcher's view was that since Younger had signed the Protocol for the government, "the commitment would have to be met one way or another".[19]

In the meantime, Powell – who was clearly more sensitive to the linkage risks than his boss – had spoken with Dr Mahathir's adviser on defence procurement, Arumugam, and explained to him that we "had to avoid any direct or explicit link between ATP and defence contracts". Arumugam had replied that "this point was now well understood in Malaysia".[20] Subsequent exchanges suggest that it was not.

A further month went by with further toing and froing between officials and no solution. Younger wrote to Mrs Thatcher on 12 June reiterating his view that the MOD would likely lose the defence deal unless some reference to aid was retained.[21] Powell responded on behalf of Mrs Thatcher that Howe and Younger must meet urgently with the Treasury's John Major and the DTI Secretary of State, David Young, and come to a conclusion. Her view, he wrote, was that: "it is vitally important that we secure the defence package. Whatever commitment was given by the Defence Secretary in Malaysia must be honoured".[22]

I was deputy head of the Overseas Group at the Treasury at the time. When I heard about the Protocol, I was appalled – like Caines at ODA – that part of our paltry aid budget was to be hijacked to win military orders. I warned John Major, first of all, about the pressure on the Malaysia country limit for export credit cover – which would have to be raised to an unacceptable level if the defence package and likely new civil contracts were to be accommodated. In relation to the Defence Protocol and the aid linkage, I wrote:

> I am deeply concerned about the way in which this whole business has been handled by MOD and FCO. It is an appalling saga of ineptitude which could well in the end create acute embarrassment to Ministers and wasteful public expenditure.
>
> The embarrassment will arise from the de facto linkage of the aid commitment to the defence package. The FCO and MOD are now seeking to break the formal linkage by an exchange of letters with the Malaysians; but this will do nothing to alter the fact – which now seems to be well-known amongst the interested businessmen – that there was a linkage in the minds of the negotiators, both British and Malaysian. I have little doubt that the press will eventually get onto this. Not only is linkage of this kind against all the rules and likely to be condemned internationally; but there are many, including myself, who would regard it as undermining the credibility of our aid efforts.

I suggested:

> [T]he ideal outcome would be if somehow MOD could revert to the original concept of a simple defence deal paid for in cash, or at most with some limited export cover. But that seems, after all that has now passed, an unlikely scenario. The second best option would – I think – be for the whole proposal to collapse.[23]

But in reality there was little the Treasury could do. It was unrealistic to expect John Major, at that stage a relatively junior member of the cabinet, to insist on the substantive revocation of the aid linkage. His only realistic option was to take a restrictive stance on proposals for increased export credit cover, and to block any request from MOD or ODA for additional funding.

Seen from the point of view of aid policy and good governance, it was an immensely depressing situation. I remember having an intuition that this was the first in a chain of events that would eventually lead to a political train crash, though I had no inkling as to quite how bad it would be.

Howe's view that the linkage would become public proved all too prescient. On 10 May David Young reported that Adrian White, the chairman of the water supply company Biwater, was aware that a condition of the defence package was £200 million in aid. Biwater had benefited from the largest ATP grant ever prior to Pergau – £59.5 million in aid for a rural water supply project also in Malaysia. Naturally, White was delighted as it could mean more business for his company. He told Young that he understood the Malaysians were now looking for a higher figure. A month later, the FCO reported that several British companies now knew of the contents of the Protocol.

And it wasn't just the business community that got to hear about it. The Japanese embassy a few months later told ODA that, if £200 million had been offered in the context of a defence deal, this would "have very serious repercussions in the OECD".[24] This was tough talking for a middle-ranking Japanese diplomat.

The four cabinet ministers plus Chris Patten met on 23 June to consider the options. In the light of Mrs Thatcher's ruling that Younger's commitment must be honoured, it was common ground that at least £200 million of aid would have to be found. But the value of the defence package was now estimated at £1.5 billion, and Younger accordingly argued that – in view of the 20 per cent figure in the Protocol – the aid should be increased to £300 million. Both Major and Patten rejected this proposal – the former because it would entail too large an increase in ECGD cover for Malaysia and the latter that it would commit too much of the ATP budget. Patten was keen to ensure, as one senior participant put, to "get the aid programme back on track": he told his colleagues that ATP projects would have to be considered on their merits. Little did he know that within a year ODA would be entrapped into funding a far from meritorious project. Younger conceded that the aid should be in the form of mixed credits rather than straight grant, and the meeting was able to agree that, instead of a £200 million grant envisaged in the Protocol, HMG should offer ATP projects to the total value of £200 million – that is to say, £70 million of grant and £130 million of guaranteed export credit. From ODA's point of view, the potential call on the ATP budget had at least been substantially reduced.[25]

As for the linkage problem, ministers decided that two letters should be sent to the Malaysian government: one from the Secretary for Defence to the Malaysian Finance Minister saying that, because of OECD rules, aid could not be linked with arms sales; the other from High Commissioner Spreckley – again to the Finance Minister – confirming that we were willing to offer "support for contracts (through ATP grants plus normal ECGD export credit cover) of up to a total of £200 million for development projects to be agreed".[26]

Both letters were delivered on the same day, 28 June 1988. It was hardly a coincidence that the very next day, the Malaysians were told that Mrs Thatcher would like to visit Malaysia in August.

This was, to say the least, an imperfect solution to the linkage problem. There can be no doubt whatsoever that the £200 million mixed credit offer was designed to ensure that the Malaysians did not go back on their under-taking in the Protocol to purchase British defence equipment to the tune of £1 billion. Whatever might be said publicly, and even though it was quite possible that there would be ATP projects to this amount over the coming years in Malaysia anyway, this was how it was intended the Malaysians would interpret it. Technically, the decoupling through the parallel letters enabled British ministers to say there was no direct linkage. Geoffrey Howe, who had overseen the exercise, believed that delinkage had genuinely been achieved But his was a legalistic interpretation. The view at the ODA and amongst Treasury officials was that the unscrambling through the two letters was really no more than a smoke screen.

Yet this was the best solution that could be devised, given the overriding objectives, ordained by Mrs Thatcher, of not jeopardising the defence deal and, as Geoffrey Howe later put it, "complying with the expectations of good faith"[27] on the part of the Malaysians. But it was a long way from satisfactory. It was a solution that cut the link in a formal sense but failed to break the linkage in practice. That was the view of the House of Commons Foreign Affairs Committee when it examined the issue six years later.

The Malaysians certainly believed the linkage remained. Indeed, Dr Mahathir and his advisers continued to insist that they needed the commitment of additional aid to justify the arms deal to the Malaysian Parliament. In November 1990 as the moment of final decision on the financing of Pergau was nearing, High Commissioner Spreckley advised the FCO that if the aid for Pergau was denied:

> [W]e could not expect the Malaysian Prime Minister and government to stick to the defence MOU with any great vigour. ... It is possible that the Malaysian Prime Minister would remind us of the undertakings which were given before signature of the MOU about availability of aid for civil projects. I cannot imagine that anyone on our side wants this whole painful subject reopened. And there would be complaints that we were not measuring up to our undertakings by refusing aid for Pergau.[28]

The Malaysians were not the only ones who believed the linkage had not been broken by the "disentangling" exercise. In January 1989 the interdepartmental "case paper" on Pergau had opined that the funding "would go a long way to meeting our commitments under the Thatcher/Mahathir Defence Agreement". Clearly, the DTI drafter knew nothing of the "disentangling" exercise; or if she did, she thought it was meaningless.[29]

Chancellor of the Exchequer Nigel Lawson had become increasingly alarmed by Mrs Thatcher's rush for arms sales. He was principally concerned about the risks for the Treasury arising from ECGD's export credit guarantees connected with arms sales, and by the pressure to increase ECGD's exposure in markets such as Malaysia. Offering aid to help secure arms deals, besides being wrong in itself, would only add to these pressures. At a lunch with *The Observer*'s political editor in the spring of 1989 Lawson voiced these concerns and confirmed that aid was being used as a sweetener to win arms orders: he clearly had in mind Malaysia. (Lawson would resign later in 1989 over disagreement with Mrs Thatcher over the handling of economic policy.)

But this is to advance the story. Back in 1988 after the two letters had been delivered, the Malaysian response was frosty. Obviously ignoring what Spreckley's letter of 28 June had said (i.e. that the £200 million was a combination of grant and export credits), Finance Minister Daim asked for confirmation that the £200 million would all be in grants. On firm instruction from London – for he had been straining to offer some flexibility – Spreckley told Daim that the £200 million figure meant £70 million in grant and £130 million in export credits.[30]

Dr Mahathir dispatched Arumugam to London to complain. On 13 July Arumugam called at the FCO and at Number 10. He told the FCO that Dr Mahathir felt personally let down by the offer, and the defence deal would be in jeopardy unless the grant was £200 million. He warned that they might have to cancel Mrs Thatcher's planned stopover in Kuala Lumpur in early August unless there was a change of heart. (GEC's Lippitt accompanied Arumugam. According to the record, he accused Whitehall of "ignorance, stupidity and incompetence".)

Arumugam was less threatening with Powell but pressed the point on the grant. He explained that £200 million in grant was the only way Dr Mahathir could justify an exclusive deal with Britain to the Malaysian Parliament. Powell was equally clear in reply that £200 million in grant was not feasible.[31]

Powell, nonetheless, asked the FCO if there was any flexibility in the offer. The FCO said there wasn't but suggested that the Malaysians could be told that ODA would consider sympathetically the possibility of additional support if good progress was made in the utilisation of the aid already promised. Powell agreed but said "he did not believe [the Prime Minister] would absolutely rule out some further concession at the end of the day".[32]

Despite the Malaysian threat of cancellation, Mrs Thatcher stopped off in Kuala Lumpur for a brief meeting with Dr Mahathir in early August. In a follow-up letter, she referred to the £1 billion arms package and confirmed that £70 million in grants and £130 million in export credits were available for civil projects, and she added: "I want to underline that further grant aid will continue to be available on a similar basis for development projects agreed between our two governments".[33] It seems all too evident from this letter that both for her and for Dr Mahathir the link between arms exports and civil aid remained in their minds.

On 27 September, the two Prime Ministers met in London and signed the MOU that the Protocol had foreshadowed. The MOU set out Malaysia's requirements in greater detail and the support that the MOD would be able to provide. This time there was no mention in writing of civil aid, but it promised concessionary interest rates on the financing of the defence equipment exports.[34]

The Malaysian side had been informed that Mrs Thatcher did not normally sign defence sales MOUs – this was for the Defence Secretary. However, Dr Mahathir was very keen that the two of them should sign – such was the importance he personally attached to it – and she agreed to do so.

In a final twist, MOD negotiators had initialled a near-final text of the MOU, which included the undertaking mentioned above that the government would ensure concessionary interest rates on the financing. This had not been cleared with the Treasury. The MOD/DESO negotiators – buccaneers to the end – once again pleaded lack of time to consult. John Major from the Treasury sent a sharp rebuke and demanded that the clause be deleted. This time, however, the FCO sided with the MOD – the date for the signing by the two Prime Ministers was already set and a new spat at this late stage on the financial arrangements could too easily unhinge the whole deal. The final text was signed with the offending clause intact.

At the signing meeting on 27 September, the two Prime Ministers discussed landing rights at Heathrow for Malaysian Airlines. This had been raised by the Malaysian side with George Younger during the negotiation of the Protocol in March, but Younger had deflected it. Mrs Thatcher once again deflected the request but she asked that the Department of Transport should urgently consider it.

Five months later, shortly before Mrs Thatcher's crucial meeting with Dr Mahathir when she offered the aid for Pergau, British Airways agreed to give up one of their landing slots at Heathrow to enable Malaysian Airlines to operate an additional service. This was later described by the British government as a commercial agreement between the two companies, and – though there were rumours that BA had been paid compensation by the government – this was officially denied.[35] Whether BA received compensation from Malaysian Airlines is unknown. But according to one report, the chairman of BA, John King, who happened to be a strong supporter of Mrs Thatcher and she likewise of him, was annoyed at the pressure from the government on the issue.[36] Was this a commercial concession, instigated by the government, to further oil the wheels of the arms deal?

Towards the end of the meeting between the two prime ministers on 27 September 1988, officials on both sides were asked to leave, and no record of what they said is available. It was exactly a week after GEC's John Lippitt had mentioned to DTI that a financing proposal for Pergau was in the offing, and it is tempting to speculate that they discussed the subject. High Commissioner Spreckley certainly believed they had done so. When pressing the case for ODA funding for the project a couple of years later, he wrote: "Dr Mahathir indicated to the Prime Minister in 1988 that if all went well in other fields and ATP was available, Pergau would come to Britain".[37]

Understandably, the British government had every interest in keeping the Protocol and the original aid/arms linkage secret. But already by 1989, the existence of the linkage was becoming more widely known or at least more widely suspected. On 7 May 1989 *The Observer* published a story by Adam Raphael headlined "Thatcher Used Aid to Sell Arms". Raphael wrote that "Mrs Thatcher has personally 'lubricated' a huge £1,000 million arms deal with Malaysia". Referring to the signing of the MOU in September 1988, he wrote that this had "coincided with pledges of a large civil aid package". He went on that the "Foreign Office, Downing Street and MOD officials were unable to explain this coincidence in view of the Government's claim that there was 'absolutely no connection' between arms and aid". He reported Lord Trefgarne, the Minister for Defence Procurement, as saying that "the conjunction between the Malaysian arms deal and the aid package is 'pure coincidence'. The Government is not involved in 'any skulduggery'".

The FCO and others presumably felt able to get away with this because Raphael only made references to the MOU in which there was no mention of aid: he hadn't managed to unearth the earlier Protocol in which there was, or the parallel letters of 28 June 1988.

On 17 May 1989, Joan Lestor MP, the then Labour spokesman on overseas aid, asked the Secretary of State for Defence "whether there was any reference to civil aid in any of the correspondence in 1988 between the two governments on arms sales". In a classic example of deliberate ministerial obfuscation, the minister replied: "All dealings between the two governments on the proposed sale of arms were formalised in the MOU signed in September 1988. No mention is made in that document of overseas aid to Malaysia".[38] The answer gave the impression of addressing the question, but in fact did not do so at all.

To further questions in Parliament and in reply to constituents, Ministers repeatedly denied that there was any linkage. They restated the general policy that any linking of aid to arms exports was impossible and denied there had ever been any such linkage in practice. For example, in a letter to Alan Williams MP on 27 July 1989, John Major, newly promoted to the position of Foreign Secretary, wrote: "There was no link between arms sales to Malaysia and the provision of aid and although the Malaysian authorities had suggested such aid be considered, they had been told this was unacceptable".[39] In June 1989, Chris Patten told the Foreign Affairs Committee: "The fact of the matter is that aid has not been used as a sweetener for defence deals anywhere" (FAC 1993–94 vol. l, p. xx).

Given the existence of the Protocol, and its far from satisfactory correction in the two letters of June 1988, ministers were skating on thin ice. The Foreign Affairs Committee in 1994 concluded that "Ministerial replies to certain questions were literally true, though less open and less informative than the House has a right to expect".[40]

And yet, it is easy to see why ministers were unwilling to explain what had really happened. Had they done so, there was a serious risk of a political firestorm that could in turn have led the Malaysians to abort the arms deal because of the adverse publicity or because British ministers might have been forced to withdraw the aid offer. Ministers would undoubtedly have been mindful of the Jordanian government's cancellation in March 1989 of a deal to purchase Tornado aircraft in the wake of allegations of bribery and over-pricing.

Whilst there were continued rumblings in the press and in Parliament, the de facto linkage only really came back to haunt the government after the National Audit Office published its very critical report on the Pergau project in October 1993. This led to renewed pressure for the government to come clean on whether or not there had been an aid/arms linkage. With questions now being asked as to why such a large and uneconomic project had been supported with British aid, the political fire-storm that some of us had foreseen was now only too likely to happen.

In December 1993 FCO officials advised Douglas Hurd to approach John Major (recently appointed Prime Minister) to secure his agreement that he (Hurd) should make a statement admitting the facts around the 1988 signing and putting as good a face on it as possible. Hurd and Major discussed the matter but decided to defer a decision.

The matter finally came to a head when on 22 January 1994 *The Economist* referred to the signing of a Protocol prior to the signing of the MOU. At this point, Douglas Hurd decided he could wait no longer, and on 25 January in a written answer to a question from the Labour spokesman on Foreign Affairs, Jack Cunningham, he gave a partial explanation of what had happened. He conceded that there had been such a Protocol; that it had included a reference to "aid in support of non-military aspects under this programme"; but that the Malaysian government had been subsequently told that aid could not be linked to arms sales.[41] What he did not mention was that the Protocol included a figure for the amount of aid the Malaysians wanted as part of the deal (20 per cent of the sale value), and that it included an effective under-taking by the MOD to secure the aid for Malaysia. This had to wait until the FAC inquiry a month or two later.

In subsequent questioning by the FAC, he described the aid/arms sales linkage as a "temporary and incorrect entanglement"[42] that had been cor-rected in the correspondence of 28 June 1988 with the Malaysian government. He stuck doggedly to the line that, once the Protocol had been corrected by this correspondence, the two policies (arms exports and aid) proceeded strictly in parallel and any conditionality suggested in the Protocol no longer existed.

As already mentioned, not many people really believed that the linkage between aid and arms sales had been broken. Some ministers or officials, such as Geoffrey Howe, may have genuinely believed that the linkage had been broken. If they did, they suffered from what the distinguished psychologist, Daniel Kahneman, has called "the illusion of validity" – the continued belief in something even though it is contradicted by evidence.[43]

There is little doubt that the aid language in the Protocol played a key part in enabling the MOD to secure Malaysian agreement to the defence exports package, thus paving the way for the massive orders that ensued. We can deduce this from the fact that Younger told the FAC that, if he hadn't signed, the Malaysians would have walked away. On 10 December 1990, the Malaysian Defence Secretary General signed an agreement worth RM 2 billion (about £500 million) with British Aerospace for the purchase of 28 Hawk fighter jets, and other orders followed. Between 1989 and 1993 new defence equipment contracts were signed totalling £1.3 billion.[44]

From the point of view of aid policy, the inclusion of the aid reference was highly regrettable. As in the Arms for Iraq Affair, the government had breached its own stated policies.[45] Aside from the potential political embarrassment if it became public, it created an expectation on the part of the Malaysians that there would be aid that British ministers felt they had to honour. Equally, it meant that there would be pressure on ODA from Number 10 and others in Whitehall to move speedily to commit aid money to ensure that the Malaysians implemented their planned purchases of defence equipment. It could well have been a factor in Mrs Thatcher's eagerness to fund Pergau. The Protocol as such could not have influenced Douglas Hurd in his decision in 1991 to confirm the funding of Pergau since – extraordinary as it may seem – he was not aware at the time of the Protocol's existence. But what is indubitable – as we shall see – is that Hurd was concerned about the potential loss of defence equipment exports, made possible by the promise of aid in the Protocol in the first place.

A final irony is that ODA really didn't have to provide aid for Pergau in order to fulfil the £70 million ATP grant undertaking. Over the period November 1988 to September 1993, ATP grants for projects in Malaysia other than for Pergau totalled £49.8 million,[46] and it is more than likely that much better projects than Pergau in the power sector could have filled the remaining gap. But this is to discount Dr Mahathir's keenness on Pergau, the pressures from the British contractors, and the reluctance in Whitehall to disturb the Thatcher/Mahathir relationship by going back on the offer once it had been made.

7 Mrs Thatcher's offer

By 1989, Malaysia was a middle-income country and therefore no longer eligible for British aid other than for technical assistance and assistance under the ODA's Aid and Trade Provision (ATP).

As explained in Chapter 2, ATP was a scheme introduced by the Labour government in 1977 to enable British companies to compete in developing country markets where other OECD governments were offering mixed credits or soft loans.

Malaysia was the largest recipient of ATP aid in the 1980s. Prior to Pergau, there had been 17 ATP projects in Malaysia, mainly in the power, transport, telecom and water sectors. There was nothing particularly unusual therefore when, on 28 October 1988, DTI sent to ODA a proposal for the funding of the 600 MW hydroelectric scheme on the Pergau River.

TNB, Malaysia's electricity utility, had taken a provisional decision to implement the scheme provided it could secure the necessary financing. The leading British contractors, Balfour Beatty, Cementation International and GEC had become aware of the plan and in early October 1988 had proposed it to DTI as a candidate for ATP funding. They wished to put in a pre-emptive bid to head off potential competition from Japan, Continental Europe and possibly India.

DTI accepted their case for ATP support on the basis that it would create a substantial number of jobs in Britain and could lead on to other contracts in Malaysia. High Commissioner Spreckley from Kuala Lumpur lent his support, and in a telegram sent on 28 October, commented that it was reasonable to assume that the contract would go to the British consortium, citing the role of Tan Sri Arumugam who was both GEC's representative in Malaysia and also coordinator on the Malaysian side for the Defence MOU signed by the two Prime Ministers the previous month. Spreckley believed that Arumugam would make sure the contract went to the British consortium. In view of the potential competition from elsewhere, DTI pressed for an initial response from ODA by 31 October, just three days later.

ODA economists had some knowledge of the Malaysian power sector already, based on earlier ATP projects in the sector and studies carried out by the World Bank. Even at this stage, they were not convinced that Malaysia needed Pergau for at least another ten years – and the more so since the consortium's preliminary costings were considerably in excess of the cost estimates in the SMEC feasibility study. But without more time and discussion with the Malaysians, they could not say definitively at this stage that it was a bad project.

Dick Jones, ODA's senior power engineering adviser, commented that the request for a quick response for a project of this size and complexity was "entirely unrealistic", and he believed that DTI had in fact known about it for some time. Nonetheless, under pressure from DTI and the consortium, on 10 November 1988 – just two weeks after first hearing about it – ODA issued a "comfort letter" to the consortium, which indicated that it was willing to consider ATP support for the project subject to a satisfactory appraisal.[1] The consortium was naturally pleased, and so were the Malaysians. Arumugam told Spreckley in Kuala Lumpur that he reckoned the letter, though cautious in tone, "conceals one hundred per cent support".[2] Unless he knew something that ODA didn't know, his optimism was surprising so early in the process.

The next day, the consortium submitted a formal application for the funding of the project with estimated "total contract costs of £315 million". The British and EU content was estimated at £200 million for which ATP funding in principle would be eligible. On 30 November, DTI sent a message to the High Commission in Kuala Lumpur saying that "ODA do not believe that an appraisal mission will be necessary though they reserve judgement until their desk appraisal is completed".[3]

DTI were already jumping the gun. ODA's economic staff had many questions to ask about the project. They were particularly concerned about SMEC's demand forecast for electricity, which seemed wildly optimistic, and they also needed to review SMEC's cost assumptions. It looked very likely that a visit to Malaysia would be needed.

By coincidence, the economist conducting the initial work, Alan Whitworth, was going to be in Malaysia on leave with his Malaysian wife for much of January 1989. He offered to undertake the further investigations while he was there. However, the consortium was strongly opposed for fear that it might, as Whitworth put it, "rock the boat". Bowing to pressure from the consortium, DTI and the High Commission, ODA agreed to defer Whitworth's investigation. The consortium later denied that they had put any pressure on ODA: they may not have done so directly, but the evidence shows that they certainly did so through DTI and the High Commission.

During February, Whitworth consulted the World Bank. The Bank's view was that Pergau might be viable at the capital costs assumed by SMEC. But this needed checking through TNB's planning model, and the Bank was by no means sure that the capital cost SMEC had assumed was realistic. Whitworth concluded that an appraisal visit to Kuala Lumpur was now imperative.

Earlier in January, DTI had prepared a "case paper" covering all the main aspects for the interdepartmental committee that considered ATP proposals at the preliminary stage.[4] In this paper, DTI had presented the industrial and commercial benefits that would arise from providing ATP support for the Pergau. It would help to ensure that large contractors like Balfour Beatty and Cementation would maintain a presence in more difficult markets, and thus "provide a platform for the export of related goods and services", at a time when they were pulling back from such markets. And the work involved in manufacturing the turbines, generators, switchgear and other equipment would help to preserve capacity and jobs in these sub-sectors that were under pressure from a falling off of business and that were in areas where jobs were generally scarce. The paper estimated that the work would provide for 9,800 man-years of employment. In early March, the consortium informed DTI and ODA that they needed to put in a formal proposal to the Malaysians by 4 April; otherwise, so the consortium had been told, the Malaysians would go for an open tender (i.e. go to international competition with the serious risk that the Japanese would come in with a lower price). The consortium said that, for their offer to be credible, they would need written confirmation of aid from ODA.

Under OECD rules, intended aid offers in connection with mixed credits had to be "pre-notified" to other OECD members 20 working days before a formal offer was made. To meet their 4 April deadline, the consortium pressed ODA to "pre-notify" OECD immediately. ODA had always taken the view that it would only "pre-notify" after ministerial approval since – if the minister failed to approve the aid later – it would be difficult, if not impossible, to take the "pre-notified" aid off the table.

For once in this story, ODA dug in and said it would not "pre-notify" until the aid offer had been approved. ODA also finally insisted (at a meeting with the consortium on 7 March) that it could not recommend aid for Pergau without an appraisal visit to Kuala Lumpur.[5]

ODA economists had confidence in the planning model used by the electricity utility, TNB. With the work they had by now already done, ODA felt that a two-day mission – to check on the assumptions being used in the model – should be sufficient. The consortium's representative from Balfour Beatty reluctantly accepted this but not without writing the next day: "Regarding the doubts expressed by ODA concerning the viability of Pergau, we would like to advise that any approaches by ODA at this late stage are likely substantially to reduce confidence in our offer".[6]

ODA was unable to control events for long. On 9 March, it learnt that Dr Mahathir would be visiting London for medical treatment the following week. Not surprisingly, the consortium had also heard of Dr Mahathir's visit, and there followed a classic Whitehall "bounce". ODA had hoped to advise Mrs Thatcher to say to Dr Mahathir that the aid proposal was being urgently considered and a decision would be taken shortly: in other words, after additional analysis of the economics of the project.

But this was not to be. On 13 March, two letters reached the Prime Minister's office. The first was from William Barlow, chairman of Balfour Beatty's parent company BICC. He wrote that "the prospects for winning the order ... seemed excellent provided that a definitive government to government aid offer could be made quickly". A parallel letter from John Lippitt, GEC's International Director, complained that the ODA was dragging its feet unnecessarily. He wrote:

> The difficulty in Mrs Thatcher giving a firm assurance that ATP support will be available to the Malaysian Prime Minister when they meet tomorrow arises from the fact that ODA have suddenly decided they require more information about the project before they can come to a firm decision; this despite the fact that they had a full feasibility study well before Christmas and could have made the necessary enquiries well before now. In fact, as a result of promptings from Balfour Beatty and ourselves, they have sent a team to Kuala Lumpur this weekend to do the work.[7]

Lippitt was a key figure for the consortium. A former civil servant at DTI and exemplar of the type of entrepreneurial official whom Mrs Thatcher admired, he had made a reputation for himself in the 1970s in helping to implement Labour's interventionist industrial policies. When he moved to GEC, he applied a similarly vigorous approach to winning business for his company and to extracting support from government. It was under his watch that GEC acquired the alternative title in Whitehall of "Get Every Concession". The company was by far the largest beneficiary of ATP grants (£130 million between 1978 and 1990, with Balfour Beatty the next largest at £63 million).[8] Lippitt's approach with Pergau was typically robust in pressing for the aid – he knew exactly which buttons in Whitehall to press and how to press them.

In the meantime, Whitworth had reached Kuala Lumpur on Sunday, 12 March. The British High Commission in Kuala Lumpur was unhappy that he had come. On his arrival, one of its staff members told him that HMG could not now back out of its "offer". The diplomat in question was presumably referring to the November "comfort letter", even though the latter had explicitly stated that funding approval was subject to a satisfactory appraisal. Whitworth spent only one full working day in Kuala Lumpur (13 March) since it had been decided that he should speed home to help with the briefing for Mrs Thatcher's meeting with Dr Mahathir.

During his one day, he met with the planning team at TNB and was shown the full feasibility study for Pergau, as opposed to just the summary that he had seen in London. (So much for Lippitt's claim that ODA had had the full study since before Christmas.) From this he discovered that the very high, and in his view unrealistic, electricity demand forecast that he had seen in the summary was actually a mistype: he concluded that the actual forecast was reasonable and he telexed to ODA that, in this respect, he was satisfied. But crucially, he wasn't able in the time available to get information from TNB on how the economics of Pergau would be affected by the contract price (at that stage £316 million) that the consortium were proposing. It was a long way to go just to discover a typing error.

In the event, he got back to London too late to help with the briefing. Robert Graham-Harrison, the ODA official responsible for putting the briefing together, was left with having to telephone the High Commission to ascertain Whitworth's conclusions.

Either the High Commission misunderstood or preferred to put a rosy gloss on Whitworth's findings. Spreckley's deputy told Graham-Harrison on the telephone that he believed Whitworth was satisfied with the economic and financial soundness of the project and would be recommending approval of an ATP offer.

Graham-Harrison had the good sense to be sceptical. Nonetheless, he found himself in a very difficult position. He was obliged to put forward advice on the basis of very imperfect knowledge on whether the project was economically sound, yet he was aware of the pressure being exerted on Mrs Thatcher by the consortium and by her desire to make progress with fulfilling the promise of aid in connection with the defence deal.

Graham-Harrison's submission advised that in normal circumstances he would "not feel able to recommend a formal ATP offer for a project of this size without an adequate economic appraisal, especially as ODA economists up until now had not been convinced of the economic case". But he noted:

> [T]he Minister may feel that the desirability of enabling the Prime Minister to make a firm offer justifies a decision on the basis of the second hand report from our High Commissioner of the appraisal mission's conclusion. The risk is that the High Commission may not have an entirely accurate appreciation of the mission's conclusions and that the mission might have reservations about the project or may have qualifications to suggest should be included in the ATP offer. The Minister may feel, in the exceptional circumstances, that this risk is worth taking.[9]

In other words, ODA knew that Mrs Thatcher wanted to make a firm, unqualified offer – because it would go a long way towards meeting Dr Mahathir's minimum expectations for aid in connection with the defence package. The advice was effectively fashioned to meet her wishes, in the hope – rather than as a requirement – that the project would in due course be assessed as economically acceptable.

The submission recommended that the Prime Minister should make an unconditional offer of £68.25 million, representing 35 per cent of the value of the estimated UK and EC content of the project based on a total contract price of £316 million.

Permanent secretary John Caines reluctantly endorsed the advice. He noted that "the somewhat unorthodox handling is justified by the unexpected meeting of the Prime Ministers tomorrow". He also pointed out that an offer on Pergau would help put aside a hopelessly uneconomic project – a tourist road connecting three hill stations – which Dr Mahathir was known to be personally keen on.[10]

On something of such potential significance, it would have been normal for the aid minister to have held an office meeting before the advice went forward to Number 10. Unfortunately, however, on that same day, 14 March, when economist Alan Whitworth was also in mid-flight from Asia, Chris Patten was on his way back from Japan. As a consequence, he only saw the Pergau papers in his car on his way into London from the airport very shortly before they were due to be submitted to Number 10. He too knew which way the political wind was blowing on Pergau and the arms deal, and Caines and Graham-Harrison were officials whose judgement he particularly trusted. Unable to give the submission more than a cursory look, he endorsed the recommendation. It was an endorsement he would later bitterly regret.[11]

As was the convention, all advice emanating from ODA to Number 10 had to go through the Foreign Secretary's office. It would only be shown to the Foreign Secretary if his private secretary deemed it important enough. On this occasion the pressure of time probably made it impossible – when questioned by the Foreign Affairs Committee five years later, Howe had no recollection of having seen the papers. Accordingly, ODA's advice went forward to Number 10 via a letter from Howe's private secretary. He wrote that "the Prime Minister can now tell Dr Mahathir that HMG will be able to offer a package of financial support for the offshore component of the project with a grant element of 35 percent up to £68.25 million".[12]

Mrs Thatcher duly saw Dr Mahathir on 15 March and made the aid offer as advised. Dr Mahathir would have reasonably construed that – since the offer was made without any qualification – he had a firm grant commitment up to at least £68 million. (In a wide-ranging discussion, Mrs Thatcher said that she "hoped that rapid progress could now be made on implementation of the defence sales package".)[13] On the same day, ODA "pre-notified" OECD of the decision, so that the offer could be put in writing to the Malaysians on 11 April.

A dominant Prime Minister not much interested in aid as a tool for development but very interested in it as a means of promoting exports, a determination on her part to honour the commitment on aid in the Defence Protocol, pressure from major British companies supported uncritically by DTI, a politically weak ODA unable to stand up to outside pressure – these all conspired to set the government on the fateful path that ended in the High Court.

8 ODA entrapped

On his return from Malaysia, Alan Whitworth reported a less promising picture of Pergau than that indicated by the High Commission on the telephone. Although the demand forecast for electricity underlying the case for Pergau now looked reasonable, the case for early implementation rested crucially on the ability to build it at or around the cost (£140 million at 1986 prices) estimated in the SMEC feasibility study. The consortium had indicated a figure of £316 million in current prices (i.e. allowing for future cost escalation), which – on Whitworth's calculation – worked out at 48 per cent higher than the SMEC price. SMEC had done a sensitivity analysis, which showed that, with a 20 per cent higher price, Pergau would remain economically viable. Whitworth was doubtful whether, with a 48 per cent higher price, this would still be the case; but without more analysis and direct access to TNB's planning model, he was unable to give a firm view. He noted that there was a wish on the part of the Malaysian government on security grounds for some diversification away from fossil fuels. Some extra cost for hydro might be tolerable on these grounds – but only within a limited range.[1]

Very quickly, this all became academic because on 31 March 1989 the consortium notified the DTI and ODA that they now estimated the total contract price at £397 million (later it was to rise further to £415 million). To ODA this came as a complete bombshell. The consortium recognised the embarrassment that this would cause since it would require increased ODA funding; they explained that it was only now, in the light of the detailed design work, that it had been possible to provide final estimates.[2]

It was more than an embarrassment. ODA had with reluctance – and essentially on political grounds – made a positive recommendation to the Prime Minister based on a wholly misleading cost estimate. Their firm impression from the consortium and DTI was that £316 million was a maximum price. The project was now, at the higher price, without question uneconomic. Officials felt that they had been out-manoeuvred by the companies "at pistol point" (as Permanent Secretary John Caines complained) into offering premature advice to the Prime Minister. He commented that the case "shows just how undesirable it is for us to allow ourselves to be pressured by companies to act contrary to the procedures for appraisal and assessment that Ministers have agreed".[3]

At this point, ODA would have liked to have taken the offer off the table altogether, but concluded that "despite the economic arguments, it would be extremely difficult for us not to support the project if the UK consortium succeeds in its negotiations". ODA officials therefore recommended keeping Mrs Thatcher's offer on the table, leaving open the prospect of additional aid once negotiations between the Malaysians and the consortium had been completed, but hoping – vainly as it turned out – that the price would come down. If the worst came to the worst, and ODA ended up having to provide aid at the inflated contract price, the ATP budget would not be able to support the grant element on a mixed credit; so the excess over the original price would have to be covered by a soft loan, which would be much cheaper in the short run and spread the attendant grant out over many more years.[4]

Patten accepted this advice very reluctantly. He was already furious with GEC's Lippitt for misleading Number 10 into believing that ODA was responsible for the delay in appraising the project. The day after he returned from Japan, he had written to Lippitt's chairman, Jim Prior, who had in earlier years been an adversary of Mrs Thatcher in her cabinet, with the parting shot: "You don't need me to tell you that it hardly helps me or my Department for people to write totally unfounded letters to the Prime Minister telling her that we are inefficient".[5] The upping of the contract price so soon after Mrs Thatcher had made the offer was the last straw. He now wrote that "the consortium have behaved intolerably though perhaps predictably".[6]

DTI officials, while also professing embarrassment, had no qualms about arguing for an increase in aid not only for the sake of the contract itself, but they also argued – harking back to the Defence Protocol – that it was "important to preserve in the context of our defence agreement with the Malaysians".[7] The official who wrote this clearly wasn't embarrassed by the aid/arms linkage.

Who was at fault – was it the companies or ODA or DTI, or was it just one of those uncertainties that wasn't properly factored into the decision making? This was a question that the FAC addressed at its hearings. I return to it later.

A formal written offer of aid based on the earlier £316 million cost estimate, with the possibility of more aid to cover a higher contract price, was sent to the Malaysians on 17 April.[8] In the circumstances, the letter was remarkably "forward". It said that "we would welcome the opportunity to discuss. ... the possible need to provide further assistance for this project ... once the final contract price and its composition become clearer". It went on to say: "We are already undertaking a Value for Money investigation and will further consider this alongside the appraisal of the project which we have already carried out". The reference to "the appraisal of the project" was a veiled attempt – too veiled to be understood on any normal construction – to imply that, if the price ended up higher than £316 million, an updated appraisal might deem the project unacceptable. (A value for money investigation was quite different from an economic appraisal: it was to check that the contract price was reasonable, given the costs faced by the contractor, so that the ODA would avoid paying for inflated costs.)

In retrospect, making a formal offer on the basis of an outdated and grossly under-stated price certainly looks bizarre. ODA knew it was far from satis-factory but it didn't dare go back to Mrs Thatcher to advise that the deal was off. Moreover, it harboured the hope that unless the Malaysians were able to secure a significant reduction in price, they (the Malaysians) would back off and either drop the project or turn elsewhere to a cheaper contractor. Experience with many ATP offers was that they eventually came to nothing. This, and the known opposition of TNB's technocrats to the project at the consortium's inflated price, gave some credence to the hope the proposal might go away.

In Chapter 13 I examine the cost/benefit appraisal of Pergau in some detail. Suffice it to say that at this stage in April 1989 the TNB management considered that the economics of Pergau were just about acceptable at a capital cost of around £300 million in current prices (i.e. including an allowance for cost escalation), but at the consortium's much higher price it should be deferred until at least the early 2000s. The High Commission in Kuala Lumpur was clearly worried that the Malaysians would walk away. It recommended that DTI should put pressure on the consortium to reduce its price. DTI and ODA accordingly held a meeting with the consortium on 19 May but the consortium declined to consider any price reduction.

In July 1989 Samy Vellu, newly appointed as Energy Minister, reiterated to the High Commission that the project was only viable up to a capital cost of £300 million. But he also implied that the project might still go ahead at a higher price. Perhaps Dr Mahathir had told him that Pergau would be implemented with the British contractors come what may, but that he should attempt to get the price down. In any event, Vellu said he was happy for the negotiations to proceed. He raised some quite separate questions: had the consortium taken sufficient account of local difficulties such as Thai bandits, communist guerrillas, elephants and tigers? And could the new lake that would be created be used for recreation?[9]

Concerned about Malaysia's rapidly increasing energy needs, the Economic Planning Unit in Dr Mahathir's office invited the World Bank to review the whole energy sector. A World Bank team visited Malaysia in November 1989. In its report the Bank team estimated that, at a capital cost of RM 1.2 billion (£273 million), at 1989 prices (i.e. *excluding* any allowance for future cost escalation), early commissioning of Pergau would involve a cost penalty of RM 400 million (£91 million) compared with alternative investment options. Looking at the capital costs in terms of current prices (i.e. *including* an allowance for future cost escalation), the World Bank recommended that a contract price would only be acceptable up to a maximun of RM 1.2 billion (compared with the consortium offer price in excess of RM 1.8 billion). TNB's planning staff apparently agreed with this conclusion. ODA's chief economist, Jon Wilmshurst, and his staff reviewed the World Bank's findings and could find no reason to dissent from them.

The standard practice for ATP offers was that they lapsed after six months unless extended. This was the case with Pergau. Negotiations with the Malaysians were progressing slowly, and in October 1989 ODA had to decide whether to extend the offer. In theory it could have refused, but this was not a realistic possibility given the decision taken in April to support the project, and it was barely considered. The offer was therefore extended, and with the negotiations still faltering, it was extended once again in April 1990. On neither occasion was the newly appointed Foreign Secretary, Douglas Hurd, consulted. By extending the offer, it made it all the more difficult to renege from it later on. Oddly, when in October 1990 the offer was not extended again neither the consortium nor the Malaysians appeared to notice. No one, it appeared, took the formal lapsing of the offer seriously – such was the political momentum behind the funding. In reality, the offer remained on the table.

As already mentioned, ODA was hoping that the Malaysians would walk away from the project. What no one on the British side, and certainly not in ODA, sufficiently factored in, or realised, was Dr Mahathir's commitment to the project and the consortium's determination to secure it.

In November 1989 the newly appointed Chief Executive of TNB told the High Commission that he was opposed to Pergau, whether it was a negotiated contract with the British or went to open tender. His preference for peaking power was gas turbines; and he probably didn't think Pergau could be built at an economic price. However, he also suggested that Pergau's poor economics might be overridden by undertakings already given by his government both to the British government (presumably he meant Dr Mahathir to Mrs Thatcher) and to the state of Kelantan.

The High Commission reported mixed signals from the energy minister, Samy Vellu. He was in favour of the project but only at a price up to RM 1.25 billion (£284 million). He was presumably referring to the World Bank's recommendation of a RM 1.2 billion maximum at current prices plus a small margin, far below the consortium's offer price.[10]

Dr Mahathir was very keen on the project from the start for the reasons alluded to in Chapter 5. He may possibly have accepted that a gas-fired plant was cheaper to build and more economical over its lifecycle than hydro; but in respect of Pergau, it seems he didn't believe that this mattered because ODA would be providing a large subsidy.

This last point was entirely at odds with ODA's approach to assessing the economic viability of projects. Aid was intended to add resources to the recipient country; it was not intended as a subsidy for a particular economic activity unless there were good economic reasons for this. Projects had to pass the economic viability test on the assumption that there was no aid. It was for this reason that ODA normally insisted, and certainly for commercial activities, that the grant element in any mixed credit should remain with the recipient government and the project itself be funded on commercial terms. This approach by ODA was consistent with standard textbook economics and with international aid best practice.

For the Malaysians, if they could persuade ODA to allow the grant element to be passed on, it was actually not illogical to regard the aid as a subsidy for the project. From their way of looking at the matter, the ATP grant *enabled* the project to become economically viable. The ATP grant was in effect a subsidy that cost Malaysia nothing. They regarded the ATP grant as a bonus specific to Pergau that would not be available for anything else.

Thus, there were two perspectives and both of them were in their different ways correct. But it is likely that neither side fully understood that of the other. Otherwise, ODA would have been less ready to hope that the Malaysians would drop the project; and the Malaysian side would have better understood the reasons why ODA had serious reservations about it.

ODA certainly remained puzzled, in the light of the World Bank's very negative finding, as to why Dr Mahathir continued to be keen to proceed with Pergau – the more so since the World Bank team had been called in by people in Dr Mahathir's own planning unit. High Commissioner Spreckley sent a telegram explaining that the project's "economic viability has little to do with Malaysia's negotiating position. ... The decision will be made on political grounds because: a) it has been promised to our Prime Minister and there would be loss of face if this is not achieved; b) it has been promised to Kelantan, which is an important element in the forthcoming elections".[11] ODA seemed to be in a double bind: Mrs Thatcher had promised Pergau to Dr Mahathir, and he had promised it to Mrs Thatcher.

Dr Mahathir was not the only one who either didn't understand or didn't sympathise with ODA's approach. For example, as if to justify the aid, the High Commission in Kuala Lumpur commented that "aid is of course crucial to the economics of the project", thereby conceding by implication that the economics of the project was poor.[12] The same went for others in DTI and amongst the consortium and their advisers.

Of course, it would be better for both ODA *and* Malaysia if ATP funds of a similar amount could be applied to projects that *were* economically viable. But for the Malaysians, there was no guarantee that the funds offered for Pergau would be transferred to other more viable projects. They preferred what they saw as the certainty of the aid for Pergau assuming a price could be agreed.

In April 1990, after a year in which the negotiations remained stuck, TNB's position began to shift. First, TNB made an offer of RM 1,350 million. The consortium flatly rejected this. In response, TNB upped its offer to RM 1.5 billion. But the consortium rejected this too. The two sides were still a long way apart. Either the consortium were confident that TNB, under instruction from Dr Mahathir and Samy Vellu, would cave in – and crucially, that ODA would be prevailed upon to fund the project at the consortium's proposed price; or else, if necessary, they were prepared to walk away.

There was no question at this point of DTI dropping their support for Pergau. There seemed to be progress on the price negotiations at last. Yet the outcome still remained quite uncertain. In any event, mindful of Mrs Thatcher's mention in her letter to Dr Mahathir in August 1988 of additional aid on top of the promised £200 million, DTI was keen to explore the opportunities for ATP funding for additional projects in the power sector. In June 1990, the Malaysian Energy Minister, Samy Vellu, wrote to DTI asking that UK financial support be considered for a series of named power stations. He was evidently just as keen as DTI to secure aid for other power projects.

In September 1990, therefore, ODA and DTI sent a joint mission to review the sector. In view of the possibility that Pergau might still be presented for ATP funding, ODA decided to send its most senior power engineering adviser, Dick Jones, as leader of the mission. Although not billed as a mission to look at Pergau (it was not mentioned in the terms of reference), its hidden agenda as far as ODA was concerned was to reassess the project's viability in case there was closure on the price negotiations.

Time was now of the essence and the mission produced a comprehensive report – over 100 pages in length – within a couple of weeks of their return.[13] For a team of three to have covered so much ground and so quickly (they were in Malaysia for nine days) was quite an achievement, but it also reflected the fact that there had been a great deal of deskwork over the previous year. The team reported that the TNB planning staff saw no need for new hydro stations until after 2000 and that all new projects in their plan up to 1995 were for gas turbines. Amongst the gas turbine plants, the mission identified several opportunities for British contractors. It also reported that, according to TNB, if the commissioning of Pergau was advanced to 1995, with an assumed capital cost of RM 1,250 million (£284 million) at 1990 prices, there would be a cost penalty of about RM 400 million (£91 million). Since the contract price was likely to be well in excess of the capital cost assumed, the cost penalty was going to be even higher.

The papers that were submitted to ministers in February 1991 to enable them to take a final decision all talked of a cost penalty of around £100 million.[14] However, as will be explained in Chapter 13 and Appendix II, there were already grounds, in the light of the September mission's discussions with TNB, for thinking that the cost penalty could be somewhat lower than this. This was subsequently confirmed in late January 1991 when a new TNB analysis arrived on ODA economists' desks. It showed a cost penalty from proceeding with Pergau of £78 million – lower, but still a very large number.[15]

The updated analysis also showed that, according to the TNB planners' optimal sequencing of new plant, Pergau should not be commissioned until 2008; and then, only after four other hydro schemes. If ever there was confirmation from the TNB technocrats that the construction of Pergau should be postponed, this was it.

The policy department within ODA responsible for preparing the papers for ministers in early February 1991 was advised of the updated analysis from TNB. Surprisingly, given the crucial importance of the economic argument as the basis for the final funding decision, there was no mention of it in the papers that the policy department prepared. The ODA files throw no light on the reasons for the omission. The policy department was frantically trying to secure agreement with five other government departments on the terms of a joint paper, and perhaps it felt that the new cost estimates – coming in so late in the day and not of a game-changing size – would muddy the argument.

As a result, the advice provided to ministers relied on the earlier cost estimates – that is to say, a cost penalty of proceeding with Pergau of around £100 million, and it was this estimate too that appeared in the PAC and FAC reports and in the evidence to these committees. I was not made aware of the lower cost estimate myself (nor when I gave evidence to the PAC in 1994). The estimate was still extremely large and would not have affected the advice I gave that funding the project would be a very bad use of aid money. But it might have strengthened ODA's case if ministers had known of such a very recent confirmation from TNB's planning staff that they recommended that Pergau should be put off until well into the 2000s.

From a different perspective, it is remarkable that the TNB planners sent ODA the new estimate at all – since the Malaysian Cabinet had already decided to proceed with Pergau. Either they had come round to the view that the ODA subsidy could be regarded as a bonus that would outweigh the cost penalty, or perhaps they were just doing their job like ODA's economic and engineering staff – providing the best technical advice they were capable of irrespective of the political decision making around them.

Over the previous year in the British Parliament, there had been continued sporadic interest in Pergau focusing on two aspects. In answer to repeated questions about the alleged link between aid and arms sales, ministers took the line – as we have seen – that there never had been, nor could there be, any such link. They consistently omitted any mention of the "brief entanglement" in the Defence Protocol.

Several MPs also raised questions about corruption. Following a tip-off she had received, Labour MP and official Opposition Spokesman on Aid, Ann Clwyd, on 17 October wrote to the Comptroller and Auditor General (C and AG) in the following terms:

> I am told by a well-informed source that the cost of the £400 million project includes £35 million in bribes (or "fees"). It is alleged that "bribes" and "backhanders" are going to local officials, landowners, politicians and certain members of the Malaysian Royal Family.

Mrs Clwyd was not willing to reveal her source but asked the C and AG nonetheless to investigate.[16]

After consulting ODA, the C and AG replied that ODA had been unable to uncover evidence of any such claim, and there was no evidence of bribery in ODA's books. (But unlike his counterpart in the US, the C and AG is unable to follow public money "wherever it goes", so he had no way of checking on whether bribes had actually been paid.)

It is a fact that we ourselves had no evidence of corrupt payments having been made. We had, however, insisted on a major reduction in the provision for agents' fees in the main contract. During the contract negotiations, ODA had conducted two "value for money" (VFM) investigations into the makeup of the contract price. This was a standard procedure on aid-funded negotiated contracts to check that the contract price was reasonable in relation to the contractor's costs. The second VFM investigation had found that the proposed contract price included £26 million for agents' fees. ODA considered this far too high and insisted on a reduction. The consortium agreed to cut the provision back to £11 million – a figure that ODA considered to be just about acceptable for a contract of this size.

The C and AG told Mrs Clwyd that he was unable to investigate further unless Mrs Clwyd was willing to share her evidence. Mrs Clwyd did not respond – for the simple reason that she didn't have hard evidence, only what she had been told by her informant.

Many years later, I asked Ann Clwyd who had been her "informed source". She was unable to remember. However, her then Deputy-Spokesman on Overseas Aid, Dale Campbell-Savours, told me that the informant had been an anonymous employee of Balfour Beatty.

On 20 March 1991, a Malaysian MP called on Campbell Savours and asked him to instigate an enquiry into the arms deal and into kickbacks that he alleged had been paid by the arms contractor and the contractors for Pergau.

At a DTI reception in 2000, the chairman of one of the companies involved in the Pergau project was overheard boasting about the cheque he had handed to the responsible Malaysian Minister.[17]

In early 1994, a former Malaysian Foreign Minister told journalists in Kuala Lumpur that the aid for Pergau involved "gross irregularity" and was "undeniably linked" to the defence deal.[18]

None of this represents hard evidence, and it is unlikely the truth will ever be known. All one can say is that some Malaysian ministers – though not Dr Mahathir personally – had a reputation for asking for back-handers for themselves, or to swell the finances of their political parties, when major contracts involving foreign companies were involved. Bribery in order to win contracts in overseas markets at this time was still not illegal in Britain. Many British contractors, even though they preferred not to do it, were not averse to offering enhanced agents' fees, which would then be paid on as necessary if absolutely required. In the case of Pergau, it has been noted already that ODA managed to secure a reduction in the provision for agents' fees, so there may not have been any fat in the contract to pay for back-handers to Malaysian ministers. But it is also possible that the companies involved may have found other ways of making "special payments" that were not reflected in the contract price. (In that case, there would at least be comfort for ODA that the aid budget was not being used to fund any such payments.)

In March 1994, the leader of Malaysia's opposition Democratic Action Party, Lim Kit Siang, called for an investigation into claims that some of the defence equipment supplied by British companies under the defence package was seriously overpriced, to the particular benefit of GEC, its Malaysian subsidiary and the latter's minority owner, A. P. Arumugam.[19] It was suggested that the overpricing had enabled bribes to be paid.[20] Since some of the companies involved in Pergau were also involved with the defence deal, it is possible that – if there were bribes in relation to the defence deal – these could have been paid in part for the award of the Pergau contract.

But this is admittedly all speculation; none of it has been proven. When asked by the Foreign Affairs Committee in 1994 if they had been asked for bribes, the representatives of the three lead companies on Pergau denied it.

Towards the end of 1990, the negotiations on the Pergau contract suddenly speeded up. The consortium had stuck to their original offer price. After repeated attempts by TNB to achieve a lower price, in early November – presumably under instructions from Samy Vellu and ultimately Dr Mahathir – TNB caved in and accepted the consortium's offer. It is tempting to suggest that it was not a coincidence that the acceleration of the negotiations came at just about the same time as Mrs Clwyd received information from her unnamed source about bribes having been paid; but to repeat, we have no hard evidence for this.

On 8 November 1990, the Malaysian Cabinet gave the project the formal go-ahead provided the financing from Britain was confirmed.

The ODA's worst fears had come to pass. The Malaysian government had decided against what seemed clear economic logic to ODA and World Bank economists – as well as to Malaysia's own power planners – in favour of this very costly scheme.

9 Crunch time in Whitehall

It was now crunch time in Whitehall. The proposed price of the project was now £417 million, of which the value of goods and services eligible for UK financing was £308 million. If it were to be a mixed credit, this would require an ATP grant of £108 million. The government now had to decide whether or not to confirm this grant. Formally, the offer had lapsed on 17 October; but there was nothing to stop it being reinstated if ministers so wished.

In a late – in reality, much too late – attempt to find a way of deflecting aid away from Pergau, ODA proposed – in the light of the September ODA/DTI sector review – that aid should be provided for combined cycle gas turbines instead. They hoped that an offer of finance for alternative projects could provide a "soft landing" if the offer for Pergau was now withdrawn. Ironically, considering how consistently supportive they had been in favour of the consortium for so long, DTI lent its support to this new approach. I return to this below.

The High Commission in Kuala Lumpur and FCO officials in London were adamant that a "soft landing" was impossible at this late stage. The High Commission wrote that it might have been possible to withdraw in July 1990 when the Malaysians were still not certain they wanted Pergau, but not now. The offer of aid had been based on "properly conducted studies" and Dr Mahathir had "redeemed an undertaking given to the Prime Minister [Thatcher] to award Pergau to the UK". His political position would be undermined if we backed out since he had told his cabinet after his party's election setback in September that Pergau would go ahead. He would see rejection "not just as a slight but as a deliberate attack". Rejection would lead to serious knock-on effects for British exports. "ODA had renewed the original offer twice and could not be allowed, having passed up all opportunities to reconsider the situation, to withdraw it at the last moment."[1]

The High Commission had a point about the twice-renewal of the offer: ODA had failed to revisit the whole issue seriously when on two occasions they could in principle have refused to renew the offer. But it was absurd to say that the "offer was based on properly conducted studies" when the initial appraisal that led ODA to recommend the offer to Mrs Thatcher was based, as the High Commission knew full well, on a contract price one-quarter lower than now being contemplated. Furthermore, British Ministers were now being led to believe that Dr Mahathir was doing the UK a favour by wanting to go ahead with the project rather than the reverse. The High Commission conveniently forgot that it had been relentlessly pressing the case for Pergau from the very start and had never been at all sympathetic to ODA's concerns. Why had they consistently taken the part of the consortium and of those who favoured the project in Malaysia and pressed for closure of the deal when the negotiations seemed to be faltering? If there was an opportunity for withdrawal in July 1990, why didn't they draw this to ODA's attention?

A more charitable view is that the High Commissioner understood ODA's concerns and his reporting was not entirely one-sided: for example, he had reported that "many Malaysians shared ODA's views". But he correctly saw which way the wind was blowing in Whitehall and was trying to protect Britain's overall interests as he interpreted them to be. At various stages, he took a position that was well ahead of the FCO's and ODA's ministers' views, but on each occasion he was vindicated by political decisions at a higher level. He would have been aware of Mrs Thatcher's general attitude (she was still Prime Minister until 22 November 1990); he would have known that Dr Mahathir's adviser and GEC representative, Arumugam, was in regular contact with Mrs Thatcher's Private Secretary, Charles Powell; and he would have been aware that one or two ambassadors and High Commissioners had had their prospects blighted when they had incurred her displeasure.

On 31 January 1991, High Commissioner Spreckley called on Douglas Hurd in London and advised him that HMG was on the verge of a nasty row with Malaysia: if we now told them that they had their sums wrong after it had gone to their cabinet, they would think it a gross impertinence reminiscent of our dealings with them in the early 1980s. The previous week Spreckley had written in the context of Malaysia's attitude to the impending Gulf War: "Is this the right moment to upset the government of a Muslim country under considerable pressure to turn against us?"[2]

As Permanent Secretary, I had been regularly briefed on the progress (or non-progress) with the project. Like my colleagues, I had hoped that the Malaysians would bid the price down; or if not, break off negotiations with the British companies and go elsewhere. I now had to decide, given the very negative views of ODA's economists, whether I could reasonably – as ODA's Accounting Officer – "sign off" on the expenditure if ministers decided to confirm the Pergau funding.

As Accounting Officer, I was required under formal Treasury rules, applicable to all Accounting Officers, to ensure, first, that all ODA expenditures were incurred in accordance with "regularity and propriety"; and second, that all expenditures were incurred with regard to "prudent and economical administration, efficiency and effectiveness".[3]

"Regularity" refers to whether proper procedures have been followed: obtaining Treasury consent and whether the expenditure falls within the "ambit of the Vote" (Parliament's annual expenditure authorisation for the department concerned). "Propriety" refers to whether the expenditure is undertaken for the purpose or purposes authorised by Parliament. This meant in the case of Pergau that the expenditure had to comply with the terms of the Overseas Development and Cooperation Act 1980 – which required that it had to be "for the purpose of promoting the development or maintaining the economy of a country or territory outside the United Kingdom, or the welfare of its people".

The other requirement that the expenditure should be "prudent and economical" was not defined. By long precedent and one that the Treasury and the Public Accounts Committee expected spending departments to follow, it came down to ensuring that, for a policy purpose for which a department was authorised to undertake expenditure, spending aimed at that purpose should be undertaken in the most economical and prudent fashion available.

If the Accounting Officer considers that the expenditure fails to meet the regularity, propriety or economy tests, they are required to advise their minister accordingly; and if the Accounting Officer's objections to the expenditure are overruled, they have to request a written instruction from the minister before the expenditure takes place. In this way, the Accounting Officer is absolved of any blame with the Public Accounts Committee and Parliament.

I discussed the issues over several weeks with ODA's Principal Finance Officer, Barrie Ireton. He was the guardian of ODA's overall finances, and he also had line responsibility for all ATP projects. He was an economist by training and had more than 20 years' experience at ODA in aid policy, programme management and finance.

Economy and effectiveness

It was hard for us to see how, given the very negative economic assessment, the expenditure on Pergau could possibly fulfil the economy test. We were of course aware that there were examples in ODA, and in all government departments for that matter, where spending proposals were of dubious merit in terms of economy or effectiveness. But the economics of Pergau seemed unambiguously bad and, what is more, on a very substantial scale – since according to the economists, Pergau's generating capacity could be replicated by gas turbines to the tune of £100 million more cheaply in present discounted value terms.

It is rare for an Accounting Officer to seek a formal instruction from a minister if his advice is overruled. Although it later emerged that there had been other cases that had received little or no publicity, at the time we were only aware of a couple of cases in the 1970s that involved the Labour minister, Tony Benn, overruling his Permanent Secretary. So we appreciated that requesting an instruction on Pergau would be a very significant step indeed.

There were clearly thought to be political and commercial benefits from proceeding with the aid for Pergau, but these considerations were outside the purposes in the Act and therefore could not be prayed in aid in judging whether the expenditure met the economy test. Whether or not the aid was an economical and effective use of public money had to be judged in relation to whether or not it contributed to the development of the Malaysian economy. If the expenditure was investigated by the National Audit Office and by the Public Accounts Committee, as I was certain it would be, I did not see how I could possibly defend it as Accounting Officer.

So, in my advice to Lynda Chalker and Douglas Hurd, I decided I had to request a formal instruction if I was overruled. When it all came out later, I was praised by several commentators for my "courage" in doing so. The reality was different. I was certainly determined to stand up for prudent financial management and to achieve the best results in terms of development from our limited aid budget. But equally, I was protecting my back against what I foresaw would be sharp criticism by the Public Accounts Committee. I was not willing to take personal responsibility for this use of aid money if ministers decided to proceed. Asking for a ministerial instruction absolved me from this responsibility. At the back of my mind also was my sense that in recent years ODA had been pushed around too much by other government departments and by business interests into financing projects that were developmentally at the margin or worse; and that it was time to "draw a line in the sand". After all that had gone before, I did not seriously think that the government would decline to fund the project; but I felt it necessary to make ODA's and my own opposition to it absolutely clear – both so that ministers were aware this was no ordinary case, and for the record if, as I expected, there would be a parliamentary inquiry later.

In a House of Commons debate on Pergau in 1994, Richard Needham, by then the Trade Minister, said that "accountabilityitis" had come to me rather late in the day (FAC 1993–94 vol. ll, q. 940). He was right in a way: if I was going to insist on a ministerial direction, I could have made this clear earlier. This might have alerted ministers sooner to the seriousness of the issue. Ministers in all the Whitehall departments that had an interest were well aware (or should have been) of ODA's strong objections; yet, if they had been warned earlier that I would insist on a written direction, they just might have stepped back and decided on the withdrawal of the offer. But I doubt it. And it would have been highly unusual as it were to "threaten" ministers in this way in regard to a project that remained somewhat hypothetical until towards the end of 1990.

Regularity and propriety

The question of whether Pergau met the regularity test was straightforward: the expenditure was clearly within the ambit of the Vote, which only referred to mechanisms for giving aid, not to its purposes; and we had followed proper procedures with regard to the Treasury.[4]

The propriety test was trickier. Whether the aid would be *ultra vires* – that is to say, outside the authority of the Act – was more problematic. On the face of it, if cheaper alternatives for generating power in Malaysia were available, then it was questionable whether the financing was contributing to Malaysia's development. On the other hand, Ireton pointed out to me, it had always been the view in ODA – and it had never been challenged in court – that if ministers *believed* an expenditure was assisting a recipient country's development, then it was within the terms of the Act. Here was a project that was technically sound. We were satisfied that it would serve the purpose for which it was intended. It would produce electricity for which there was going to be demand. It might not be the most efficient way of meeting that demand, but ODA financing of Pergau would certainly expand Malaysia's electricity-generating capacity to meet a real need. We were not throwing money at Malaysia for no good purpose at all. In that sense, it wouldn't be altogether unreasonable for ministers to take the view that the aid was assisting Malaysia's development; and on that basis, the expenditure would not be *ultra vires*.

I did not find this line of reasoning altogether persuasive. If the investment was sub-optimal and there were more economical ways of meeting Malaysia's electricity needs, I found it hard to see how we were really assisting Malaysia's development. If one of the basic principles of economic development – both in theory and in practice – was that resources should be used as efficiently as possible, how could aid for a palpably inefficient project be considered as being for the purpose of development? The Secretary of State might believe that the aid was assisting Malaysia's development, but would this be a reasonable view given that there were much more efficient ways of expanding Malaysia's generating capacity?

Ireton advised that it had long been custom and practice at ODA that what mattered from the point of view of the law was what was in the Secretary of State's mind when he took the decision. Provided he took the view that the project was helping Malaysia's development – and provided there was some rationale for this as there was at least in a physical sense – then the provision of aid was within the law. It was the subjective view on the part of the Secretary of State that ultimately mattered.

I accepted his advice. Yet given my doubts, we should have checked it with legal advisers. As it later turned out, Ireton's view was shared by most in the legal profession, and it came as equally a great surprise to them as to ODA that the judge rejected it.

Our failure to seek formal legal advice was partly a symptom of the non-legal culture of the British civil service, which at the time gave primacy to political accountability over the law – and to a considerable degree still does. Few senior civil servants had formal legal training and while we were all aware that we and our ministers had to operate within the law, we tended to be a good deal less attuned than in the US and on the Continent to the risk of legal challenge. Whereas most of us typically had developed strong political antennae, we tended not to have anything like the same sensitivity in relation to the public law.

I had found when I was in the Treasury in the 1970s dealing with public expenditure a somewhat haphazard and occasionally casual attitude to the law. This was possibly encouraged by the legal convention that one-off expenditures could be authorised, even where there was no relevant enabling legislation, by invoking the so-called Appropriation Act. Very few Treasury officials had more than the most basic training in public law, and although legal advice was always available from the Treasury Solicitor's Department and often taken, there were occasions when it was not sought as it should have been.

In the early 1980s I played a part in the Treasury's decision to allow local authorities to undertake interest swaps in order to minimise their cost of borrowing. This made perfectly good economic sense, but in giving our consent we did not as I recall seek legal advice as to whether interest swaps by local authorities were legally permissible. Had we done so – even though the legal issue was really for the local authorities themselves – we might have been forewarned of the legal risks that later emerged with a vengeance when the High Court and then the House of Lords in 1989 ruled that such swaps were unlawful.[5]

By the late 1980s, the culture was starting to change as citizens and pressure groups increasingly sought protection through the courts as a means of checking an over-mighty executive when Parliament was seemingly unable to fulfil this role. The ability to seek judicial review of government decisions had been made easier by the passage of the Supreme Court Act 1981, and the 1980s and 1990s saw a dramatic increase in the number of applicants for judicial review. Moreover, judges for their part became more willing to intervene to determine whether ministers and civil servants – in the formulation of policy and by their actions or inactions – were complying with the law. Civil servants were meant to be made aware of this growing "judicial activism" by the publication in 1987 by the Treasury Solicitor of a booklet entitled "Judge over your Shoulder", though – perhaps because of the slightly jokey title – many regarded this with a degree of amusement rather than with the seriousness it deserved.[6]

In 1991, not much of this awareness had filtered through to ODA. Even by the standards of Whitehall, we were not a "lawyerly" department. Unlike most departments, ODA had no in-house legal adviser and there was little tradition of seeking legal advice from outside the department except in the drawing up of aid contracts. This was very different from the Department for Education, where I was subsequently Permanent Secretary and where we were frequently consulting our in-house lawyer on what could and could not be done in terms of the law. The received wisdom in ODA, in keeping with Ireton's advice to me, was that as long as ministers had it in mind that they were helping the recipient country's economy or its people, they had wide discretion within the law to do what they wished with the aid budget.

Whether taking legal advice would have made any difference is rather doubtful. When the Pergau decision was later challenged in the courts, it was the view of most legal authorities that it was what was in the Secretary of State's mind at the time he took the decision that was important: that is to say, the "subjective" view of the Secretary of State that the aid was for a valid development purpose would prevail over the "objective" view of the experts, unless his decision could be shown to be manifestly unreasonable or perverse. But how certain could we be that, even if it was what was in the Secretary of State's mind that mattered, that the decision would meet the "Wednesbury reasonableness" test?[7] As it turned out, the Court took a different approach altogether and ruled that the Secretary of State's "subjective" view was irrelevant: what mattered was the "objective" view of the experts that the project was economically unsound.

Had formal legal advice been taken, it seems more than likely that Hurd would have been advised to indicate that the prime purpose of the aid was development – over and above any political or commercial purpose. Instead, he and fellow ministers were too ready to admit that politics and commerce were the predominant considerations. In the run-up to the court case, there was concern that the apparent subordination of the development purpose to these other considerations would swing the case against the government. As we shall see in Chapter 11, this was not the reason why the case was lost   the reason was that, according to the presiding judge, the project didn't stand up in development terms; but the failure to play up the development case may possibly have made the court less sympathetic than it otherwise might have been.

In any case, given that the court ruled against the government, the failure to take formal legal advice made Hurd's decision to fund the project even less defensible and added to his political difficulties.

Why didn't we dig deeper into the legality issue? I have already mentioned the ODA's received wisdom on what was legally acceptable and the lack of legal antennae. There was another unsaid factor too: a certain desire not to rock the boat at this late stage. It was one thing to object on grounds of economy and request a formal instruction on those grounds; to go further and raise serious legal doubts might have seemed like sabotage by the civil service when no one had ever mentioned the possibility of illegality earlier.

In the event, none of the advice that went forward to Lynda Chalker or to Douglas Hurd contained any reference to possible concerns about the legality of the aid. They were simply left to assume that the aid was legal even if it was a seriously uneconomic use of the aid budget.

Final decision

In the first week of February 1991, I submitted two memoranda to ODA Minister, Lynda Chalker.[8] In the first, I advised that on the basis of the considerable analysis by ODA economists, whose conclusions were shared by TNB's own analysts, Pergau was an extremely costly project in terms of cost–benefit and could not be justified for ATP funding. I advised that, although it was somewhat obscure, the formal offer letter to the Malaysians of April 1989 did not constitute a cast-iron commitment. I suggested that the aid mooted for Pergau should be redirected to other more viable power projects in Malaysia. I recognised that there were political and commercial arguments in favour of the aid for Pergau, but I pointed out there were political and commercial downsides as well: the exclusion of more worthy projects from ATP funding; the fact that Mrs Clwyd's allegations of corruption might be substantiated; ODA's credibility as a donor; and the likely criticism in Parliament and amongst the wider public.

In my second memorandum written two days later I explained why – in the light of my Accounting Officer responsibilities to ensure that aid funds were spent in a prudent and economical manner – I would require a written instruction if the government decided to approve the funding. I wrote:

> I have looked again at the papers to see whether there are any material counter arguments to be set against the clear economic case against the project, such that reasonable individuals could agree to disagree about the balance of argument with regard to the intrinsic worth of the project. It will not surprise you when I say that I see no serious counter arguments ... The single most striking feature of the project that must weigh heavily in my mind, and which sets it apart from other marginal projects, is that the cost penalty to the Malaysian economy of building Pergau now, rather than installing gas turbines, could well exceed the amount of the grant aid of £108 million we would need to commit to it. Supporting the project with aid funds would not be consistent with policy statements by Ministers to Parliament about the basic objective of the aid programme and the way aid funds are managed, which is also the context in which Parliament votes aid monies. Nor does the project meet well established criteria by which public investments should be assessed and which are the subject of Treasury guidance to all spending departments, and against which the PAC would expect an investment to be primarily judged.

The next day, Lynda Chalker – at Hurd's request – convened a meeting between ministers from the interested departments to try to hammer out an agreed view. In view of the disagreements that had gone before, this was a vain hope.

Five Ministers of State – Malcolm Caithness for the FCO, Alan Clark for the MOD, Tim Sainsbury for the DTI, John Maples for the Treasury, and Lynda Chalker for ODA – met on 8 February 1991 to try to resolve the issue. (The fact that Alan Clark was present, representing the defence sales interest, gave the lie to any suggestion that there was no link with arms sales.) They were unable to reach agreement. Caithness and Clark – reflecting not just the defence interest but also no doubt his personal view that ODA was inhabited by arrogant and misguided do-gooders – argued that the offer should be confirmed. Chalker, Maples and Sainsbury argued against and that ODA should try to switch the aid to other projects in the power sector. Sainsbury's opposition on behalf of DTI – a Damascene conversion after DTI's previous vigorous support for the project up until then – was probably due to the appointment in July 1990 of the neoliberal Peter Lilley as DTI cabinet minister. Lilley was ideologically opposed to industrial subsidies. Had he been in post 18 months earlier, it is possible that the aid funding would have been stopped in its tracks before any commitment was made. Lilley made clear his personal opposition to the project in a letter to Treasury ministers.[9] In the view of Dick Jones, the leader of the September 1990 appraisal mission, the DTI change of view was also due to DTI's representation on that mission and their being belatedly persuaded that support for gas turbines would be a better bet for Malaysia and for British contractors.

Reporting on the meeting to Hurd, Chalker summarised the views of the other ministers. She also set out her opposition to the funding in forthright terms. She wrote:

> Going ahead with this completely uneconomic project would be the worst possible outcome ... We would expect adverse publicity, high profile allegations of corruption and a field day for investigative journalists and the Opposition ... It would do us no good domestically. ... it would seriously damage support for the aid programme. I fear too that that its repercussions would be likely to be seriously damaging for our relations with the Malaysian government.

She said it would "cost the Malaysians £100 million more than the best alternative option".[10]

A striking omission in both Chalker's and my own memoranda was any mention whatever of the Defence Protocol and the aid/arms sales linkage. I was certainly conscious that the linkage, if it was ever revealed, would make a decision in favour of Pergau look a lot worse. But ministers, including Lynda Chalker, had been so robust in their public denials of it that I felt it would be churlish for me to remind them of the problem. (Or perhaps the "illusion of validity" had even seeped through to me.) Moreover, I was confident that Hurd would have been briefed on the Protocol by his own officials when he became Foreign Secretary.

This turned out to be incorrect. Extraordinarily, at no time between his becoming Foreign Secretary and his decision on Pergau was he made aware of the Protocol or of the ineffectual "disentangling" exercise that followed.[11] As the chief drafters of the "disentangling", FCO staff may have persuaded themselves – like their former boss, Geoffrey Howe – that the issue was dead and buried. Coming to it fresh, had Hurd been told about it, it is possible that he would have taken a different view, and spotted the added political dangers involved in approving a large and unsatisfactory aid financing. He finally became aware of the Protocol in October 1993.

Hurd was faced with an obvious dilemma. ODA, the lead department for which he had overarching responsibility, with backing from the Treasury and now DTI, was advising against the project. For ODA to finance an evidently uneconomic project was highly undesirable. In briefing the new Prime Minister, John Major, for the latter's first meeting with Dr Mahathir in mid-December,

Hurd had written in his typically understated way that Pergau "is not an attractive proposition". On the other hand, he had to weigh against this the commercial (including defence sales) and political arguments.

It did not take long for Hurd to make up his mind. He decided that – whatever the caveats in the original offer letter – the Malaysians would have had every reason to regard Mrs Thatcher's offer as a firm commitment, and above all other considerations, this commitment had to be honoured. Regrettable though this was from ODA's point of view, the financing package had to be approved if we were to avoid grievous damage to our political and commercial relations with Malaysia. We had no choice but to proceed for the sake of the good faith of Britain and of Thatcher.

Hurd felt the decision was sufficiently important – and the more so since there were dissenting ministerial views – to require John Major's approval. In his memorandum to Major, he wrote: "The ODA assessment is the project is not economic and would cost the Malaysians at least £100 million more than the best alternative option. ODA, and specifically the Accounting Officer, are concerned that ATP support would be a serious misuse of aid funds – and lead to criticism from the PAC". On the other hand, he went on to say:

> It is very late in the day to pull out … Mahathir believes he had a firm commitment from Mrs Thatcher … Backing out could have grievous consequences for our very substantial commercial interests in Malaysia … Mahathir could take drastic action against our interests if he thinks we have let him down … Although it goes against the grain to support an uneconomic project, we face a test of Britain's good faith and Mrs Thatcher's in particular … We must honour Mrs Thatcher's word … So we have no choice but to proceed.[12]

Unlike Hurd, Major was aware of the aid/arms linkage problem from his time as a Treasury Minister; and so of course was Powell. Major evidently set the problem aside, and gave his approval very quickly. Powell transmitted Major's approval back to the FCO and other departments the very next day (a Sunday). This was too quick for the Treasury. The Treasury minister now in charge of public spending, David Mellor, was furious. His private secretary, Jeremy Heywood, telephoned Hurd's private secretary to say that the way in which the proposal had been handled and approved, without Treasury ministers being given the opportunity to comment first, was "outrageous" and "disgraceful".[13] Treasury Permanent Secretary, Peter Middleton, wrote in equally colourful language to his FCO opposite number, Patrick Wright. But it was hardly the fault of the FCO that Major and Powell had acted so swiftly. The Treasury's complaint should have been directed at Number 10. That it was not was probably a symptom of Powell's preeminent position in Whitehall at this time.

The decision was put on hold for a few days to give other ministers a chance to comment. Mellor then submitted a scathing critique, pointing out amongst other things that Mrs Thatcher's offer had been for a grant of less than £70 million whereas the grant that was now proposed was for £108 million – in which case, why was it necessary to honour her offer? And that the ECGD guarantee for the credit portion of the offer would crowd out other more worthy projects.[14] But to no avail. Major reconfirmed his approval.

Significantly, in view of the intense parliamentary interest in the issue three years later, the government was able to approve the aid without the explicit approval of Parliament. This was because the ODA Vote (i.e. Parliament's annual appropriation of money for overseas aid) was widely drawn and Parliament in effect delegated decisions on the allocation of aid to ODA. Because of its large amount, the aid did require approval by the Treasury. But to the Treasury having lost the battle at ministerial level, this was a mere formality.

So ended a further chapter in the Pergau story but not without some recriminations. Even before the decision to approve the aid had been taken, the High Commission in Kuala Lumpur contrived its own anti-ODA version of events.[15] Foreign Office Minister Caithness referred to "the need to organize our system so that we are never again put in this position".[16]

But we in ODA were equally aware that there were lessons to be learnt. These were that we should take greater care over the risk of price escalation; greater caution was needed by ministers in making offers of aid before there had been a proper appraisal; we should avoid "forward language" with British contractors until we were more ready to commit; ATP appraisals should be undertaken at an earlier stage and be more open in their findings; we should be more careful about affordability; and we should be more careful about extending the offer period.[17]

These self-criticisms of course discounted the political difficulties and the business pressures that ODA had encountered. The same thing was to recur with the PAC and FAC inquiries three years later.

Further concessions by ODA

Although the political decision had been taken to support the project, there were several further twists to the funding story. First, it turned out that the ODA could not afford the preferred method of financing – which was to provide a mixed credit. This would have meant a cash grant of £108 million spread over five years, associated with a bank loan on commercial terms repayable over 14 years guaranteed by ECGD. But such a large grant would have squeezed out most new ATP business for the following few years. A soft loan, by contrast, involved an interest subsidy over 14 years (together with a much larger loan), and therefore could more easily be afforded by ODA in the short term. As explained earlier, it had always been envisaged that at least part of the aid would need to be offered in the form of a soft loan. But this had not been properly explained to Hurd: he had merely been advised by Chalker that the aid would be "the equivalent of £108 million".

To achieve the 35 per cent level of concessionality required under the OECD rules, the exclusive use of a soft loan, in place of a mixed credit, would require an interest subsidy from ODA of £234 million spread over the 14 years of the loan. Although the level of concessionality as defined by the OECD was the same as with the mixed credit method involving a £108 million grant, for technical reasons the net present value of the cost to ODA of the soft loan approach was significantly higher – £133 million compared with £84 million for a mixed credit; and taking into account the additional interest subsidy provided by ECGD, the net present value figures for total British government support were £158 million and £102 million respectively (NAO 1990, para. 38). In other words the economic cost to the government of the soft loan, compared with the originally intended mixed credit, was higher by £56 million. By the same token, Malaysia secured a similar increase in benefit from the deal in terms of reduced debt servicing costs. With a headline figure more than twice the figure originally intended under the mixed credit method, this was also far worse from a presentational point of view.

Many ministers would have hit the roof. I was called in by Hurd to explain. He accepted the argument that the original mixed credit proposal would have meant squeezing out other ATP business, but quite reasonably commented that it ought to have been dealt with in the ODA submissions leading up to the February decision, and – with his usual understatement – that the higher figure "might cause trouble". I felt we had let him down by not providing clearer advice.

Parliament's Public Accounts Committee was critical of ODA for proceeding with the more expensive option. The Committee suggested that ODA should have approached the Treasury to "find a way for the least cost option to be chosen" (PAC 1994, para. 57). It is highly unlikely that the Treasury would have been willing to help. They would either have said: "Adopt the least cost option even if it means squeezing out other ATP business"; or they would have said: "It is your decision how much aid you allocate to ATP from the total aid budget". For a department that prided itself on sound economics, ODA should have bitten the bullet and adopted the least cost option even if it meant squeezing the rest of the aid budget.

The second issue that ODA had to contend with was the request from the Malaysian government that the soft loan should be made directly to TNB. As explained earlier, the general policy of ODA was that project entities – where their activity was commercial – should receive funding on commercial terms and not benefit from the subsidy element in ATP soft loans or mixed credits. The subsidy should go to, and be retained by, the recipient government.

Given that the project had been deemed uneconomic by TNB planners, it wasn't a huge surprise when this request was made. From a financial point of view, Pergau was not quite as bad for TNB as the economic analysis suggested: this was because TNB was paying considerably more for its gas from the government-owned monopoly supplier, Petronas, than the true economic value of the gas (see Appendix II). Nonetheless, it was still going to be a considerable liability in financial terms unless they were able to borrow on soft terms. The Malaysian side were particularly concerned that, if TNB were hobbled with having to pay the debt service on a fully commercial loan, this could damage the prospects for its privatisation. (The Malaysian government's advisers on the privatisation were the same firm, J. Henry Schroder Wagg, which was the lead bank on the syndicated credit that funded the project.)

Again, ODA gave way subject to the loan being guaranteed by the Malaysian government. In theory, we could have resisted and told the Malaysians to deal with the problem that was of their own making. But by this time, having lost the main battle in Whitehall, there was little stomach for a further fight over this relatively minor aspect and we didn't wish to be blamed for undermining TNB's privatisation.[18] We comforted ourselves that in theory the subsidy would feed into a higher valuation of TNB and thus could be recouped by the Malaysian government when it sold TNB's shares.

But two factors countered against this argument. First, it ignored the fact that TNB needed to keep at least some of the subsidy to offset the poor economics of Pergau. Second, when the government came to sell 23 per cent of TNB's shares (685 million in total) in May 1992, the shares were seriously under-priced. Sixty million shares were sold by tender; the remaining 625 million, plus options for an additional 58 million for TNB directors and employees, were sold at a fixed offer price. By the end of the first day's trading, the offer price had jumped by 94 per cent – a gain of about £600 million for those lucky enough to obtain shares at the fixed offer price. And by 1994 the price had quadrupled.

Out of the 625 million, 300 million shares were allocated by the finance ministry through a special pool to "approved investors". Principal beneficiaries of these preferential allocations were various private institutions with close links to UMNO and to the government. There was also a three million share allocation to the Malaysian Indian Congress (MIC), which was a minority partner in the ruling coalition. The MIC's leader was Samy Vellu, the energy minister. The MIC's paper profit after the first day's trading was about £3 million, and it was alleged that Samy Vellu personally profited from the sale. In addition, the directors and employees of TNB were allocated 58 million in share options, which instantly made some of them ringgit millionaires. As a result of the under-pricing and special allocations, part of the ODA subsidy in effect went to private beneficiaries of the sale and not to the government.[19]

It is ironic that back in June 1988, ODA had signed an agreement with the Malaysian government to provide technical assistance for the privatisation programme. It can hardly be said that this technical assistance served ODA's interest when it came to the privatisation of TNB. On the other hand, if ODA had had better intelligence on the political economy of Malaysia, it should have come as no surprise that the government would use the privatisation of TNB to favour certain individuals and groups.

It took another five months for the various contracts to be signed. On 8 July 1991, the Financial Agreement on Pergau was finally signed between the British and Malaysian governments. On 12 July, TNB signed a contract agreement with the consortium, and on the same day TNB signed an agreement with the investment bankers, J. Henry Schroder Wagg, on behalf of the syndicate of banks for a loan of £306 million. On 15 July, ODA put out a low-key press notice announcing a £306 million soft loan guaranteed by ECGD and supported by a £234 million interest subsidy from ODA. It stated that the deal would create 29,000 man-months of employment in the UK.[20] This was almost exactly one-quarter of the 9,800 man-years of employment that had been mooted in the "case paper" written by DTI in January 1989. Was this another example of DTI and the consortium having manipulated the numbers in order to win the ATP aid? On conservative assumptions, the ODA subsidy per man year of employment was over £16,000, which must have made it one of the more expensive employment subsidies in modern times.[21]

There was one further humiliation for ODA that went unnoticed in the PAC and FAC inquiries. In 1993, TNB asked if they could prepay part of the loan, whilst retaining the interest subsidy. The reason for this request was that TNB did not wish to be saddled with such a large long-term foreign exchange liability when the future revenues from Pergau were to be in Malaysian currency; and TNB was able to raise the equivalent financing locally to replace the sterling finance. TNB's request made it clearer than ever that its only real motivation had been to acquire the ODA subsidy, which would not have been available if the loan financing had been provided from within Malaysia. Even allowing for the special relationship with Malaysia, it is inconceivable that ODA would have provided the subsidy grant had the loan financing been originally provided locally – since it would have fallen completely outside the ambit of the ATP scheme.

The Treasury were keen on the prepayment idea because it would remove the liability of the ECGD guarantee, and – on account of the way the prepayment terms were worked out – there was a modest public expenditure saving.[22] ODA had no appetite for challenging TNB's request that it should retain the benefit of the interest subsidy. It was clear that, if TNB were to lose the benefit of the subsidy, it would withdraw the prepayment request. There was potential embarrassment for ODA from TNB being seen to be able to "afford" the prepayment. But in the light of the NAO's criticism (see Chapter 10) that ODA had failed to minimise the cost of the Pergau financing, and with the Treasury on the war-path for ODA's profligate spending on the project, ODA was in no position to resist.

After months of negotiation on the details, TNB made a payment of £80 million in July 1994 and, in return, £140 million of loan was cancelled. ODA would continue paying the interest subsidy through ECGD to the banks that had made the original loans, so as to leave them in no worse position financially. Although the prepayment was announced, fortunately for ODA it received little attention in the press: perhaps at last the media was getting bored with the Pergau story. TNB made a further pre-payment of £120 million in August 1995, but by that time – following the High Court ruling – ODA was no longer involved.

10 Parliament steps in

The main contract having been signed, work at the project site started immediately. As explained in Chapter 3, there were various delays on account of unforeseen geological problems and design issues; but construction nonetheless proceeded relatively smoothly.

The same cannot be said of the British government's position. Although there were continued rumblings in Parliament about bribery and the arms linkage, for the next year or so Pergau did not attract much public attention. It was when the National Audit Office (NAO) published its report in October 1993 that the storm broke. Between then and April 1994 there was rarely a week when Pergau wasn't in the news, and much of this centred on Parliament. There were formal inquiries by two Select Committees of the House of Commons, two House of Commons debates and numerous Parliamentary Questions. Parliament's interest lingered on in 1994 and into 1995, with a brief spurt in November 1994 following the High Court ruling.

National Audit Office and Public Accounts Committee

The NAO is Parliament's watchdog for monitoring public spending. Its job is to evaluate spending on specific projects and programmes to ensure that it has been properly authorised by Parliament and to assess whether monies have been efficiently and effectively spent. It is not supposed to comment on policy or policy decisions, though often it is difficult to disentangle the latter from an evaluation of value for money. The head of the NAO is the Comptroller and Auditor General (C and AG) who is appointed by Parliament and reports to the House of Commons Public Accounts Committee (PAC). The NAO has access to most departmental files relating to government spending. Under the general direction of the PAC, it decides on which expenditures to prepare reports. When completed, the PAC conducts a hearing with the relevant Accounting Officer (in the case of central government spending, normally the Permanent Secretary of the relevant Ministry), and it then issues its own report. The PAC is also supposed to confine itself to issues around whether the expenditure has been properly authorised and the money spent economically and effectively, but often veers into policy debate.

Given the size of the Pergau project and the interest that certain members of Parliament were taking in it, it is not surprising that the NAO wanted to see the ODA files. And once they saw the files, they would have quickly concluded that there was plenty enough unusual in it to warrant a report.

The NAO report issued its report in October 1993. It was largely factual and relatively moderate in tone. It noted that ministers had overridden official ODA advice that the project was uneconomic, and that I as Accounting Officer had felt obliged to ask for a formal instruction before any expenditure could be incurred. But they did not comment one way or the other on the merits of the decision to proceed – which they regarded as outside their mandate.

They were, however, highly critical of the funding arrangements – that is to say the use of a soft loan instead of a mixed credit, which, as explained earlier, was likely to cost the government £56 million more in NPV terms.

Despite its low-key language, there was immediate media interest in the report. One reason was that it revealed a disagreement between an Accounting Officer and his Secretary of State, requiring the issuance of a formal instruction. At the time, the issuing of such instructions was rare, and it was even rarer for one to become public. The uneconomic nature of the project, and the fact of my advice having been overridden, led *The Times* to editorialise: "Misuse of aid money does grave damage to Britain's international reputation – and Hurd's bland justification of a patent scandal makes Lady Chalker's [linking of aid to good governance] so much cant".[1] (Hurd was in Cyprus attending the biennial Commonwealth Heads of Government Meeting on the day the NAO report appeared, and had been obliged to answer questions about Pergau in a radio interview.)

Furthermore, the report reignited interest in the rumours that there was an aid/arms linkage. Whilst the existence of the 1988 Defence Protocol was at this stage not widely known outside Whitehall, journalists were closing in on it. In *The Independent*, Adam Raphael wrote that "correspondence between the British and Malaysian governments prior to the signing of the agreement [in September 1988 relating to the defence package] explicitly links the arms deal to the promise of aid".[2]

The PAC hearing that followed in January 1994 and the subsequent PAC report were far more critical. As the Accounting Officer for ODA, I was called to give evidence. I was commended by Labour members of the committee for insisting on a written instruction from ministers.[3] But in other respects I received rough questioning. Why had ODA been so tardy in sending the economic appraisal mission in 1989; why had ODA delayed hiring consultants to appraise the environmental impact of the project until late 1990; why had Mrs Thatcher's original offer been based on a gross underestimation of the eventual contract price; why had it been renewed twice when ODA remained so doubtful about the project; how could the final decision to fund such a patently uneconomic project have been justified; how could ODA have agreed to fund the project through the more costly soft loan method rather than through a mixed credit? Was the expenditure really within the law?

I tried to answer these questions in as open a way as possible. The pressure was intense. And so was the television lighting, leading Alan Clark – now having left the government and writing for the *Mail on Sunday* – to call my appearance "wild-eyed". There didn't seem any point in attempting to cover up what in truth had been a series of mistakes and misjudgements. But contrary to some later press coverage, I was careful not to impugn British ministers or the Malaysian government. I assured the committee that the expenditure was within the law. On the question of why had the appraisal mission gone so late, I somewhat misleadingly said that had been a "lamentable slip-up". It was indeed lamentable, but it was not really a slip-up: it was a conscious decision – ODA having given in to outside pressures – not to send the mission earlier.

MPs attempted to get me to accept that the decision was linked to arms sales. Although it was clear to me that Mrs Thatcher's initial offer and the final decision to confirm it were indeed motivated to a considerable extent by the wish not to disturb the arms deal, I declined to be drawn down this path. ODA had looked at the project exclusively from an economic and technical point of view. Whether or not there was linkage to the arms deal in their thinking about the project was a question for ministers to answer.

Several MPs were determined to discover who had taken the final decision. There is an unwritten convention that officials appearing before parliamentary committees should not answer questions on whether one or other minister was involved in a particular policy decision. I stonewalled but under pressure conceded that John Major had taken the final decision.

I spoke frankly about the project being "unequivocally unsound" and agreed with Denzil Davies MP that its funding was an "an abuse of the aid programme". It was his phrase rather than mine though inevitably the press attributed it to me. Had I had any idea then that Pergau might end up in the courts, I probably would have spoken with greater caution.

The reference to "abuse" and the revelation that the Prime Minister had taken the final decision created newspaper headlines. The newspaper *Today* (long since defunct) had a headline: "Top Civil Servant blasts Major on £234 million aid scandal". (However, I received a message from Number 10 the next day that John Major did not blame me at all for the revelation.) In an editorial entitled "Dam Deceit", *The Times* wrote: "The abuse of British aid money to finance the Pergau dam is a patent scandal which seriously damages Britain's hitherto high reputation for sound aid policies".

The PAC report itself, when it came out in March 1994, was equally trenchant, but it did at least concede that, in the final reckoning, ODA had given clear advice to ministers about the economics of the project and that I had been right to require a ministerial direction before incurring any expenditure on it. The report did not attempt to delve into the arms linkage issue, which by this time was exercising the Foreign Affairs Committee.

The PAC had only learnt about my having been overruled by the Secretary of State because the NAO chose in 1993 to conduct an investigation. Had the

NAO not investigated, my objection would have remained buried. If the NAO had been informed of it in 1991 immediately after the financing decision was taken, the PAC would also have learnt of it then rather than in 1993. It is just possible that earlier disclosure would have made ministers more wary of proceeding. In any event, in the light of the Pergau experience and in the interests of greater openness and better Parliamentary oversight, the PAC recommended – and Treasury ministers later accepted – that in future, whenever an Accounting Officer is overruled on a matter of prudent and economical administration of funds, this should be automatically communicated to the C and AG at once so that the PAC could be alerted to the fact much earlier. Accounting Officers were already required to inform immediately the C and AG if they were overruled on a matter of propriety or regularity. The PAC recommendation extended this requirement to the issue of economy and prudence.

On the raw facts, the PAC was right to be critical of ODA. But what their report signally ignored was the political context in which ODA was operating. From the very start, ODA was under immense pressure from other parties within Whitehall and from the British contractors – to speed up, slow down, cut corners, compromise. That ODA did all of these things went completely against the professional ethos of the organisation, and can only really be understood in terms of the political environment in which it found itself working. With so many others in powerful places working to a different agenda with regard to the project, it was extremely difficult for ODA to apply its usual standards. There was no recognition of this in the PAC report.

Foreign Affairs Committee

Whereas the PAC has been in existence for well over 100 years, the Foreign Affairs Committee is one of the several House of Commons Committees that were established in the late 1960s. Unlike the PAC, the remit of these committees is to examine policy issues.

Under increasing pressure from the press and from MPs, Douglas Hurd informed Parliament on 25 January 1994 about the Defence Protocol and the "temporary" linking of aid with defence sales. In the light of his admission, the FAC quickly decided to conduct its own inquiry.

This inquiry covered some of the same ground on the funding of Pergau as had the PAC, and came to similar conclusions. But it went much wider and in particular it looked at the linkage between aid and arms exports in the Defence Protocol. It also looked at the role of the British companies involved and at whether the ATP scheme should be scrapped.

Unlike the PAC hearings, ministers were called to give evidence, as were representatives of the consortium and of interested NGOs. Four development NGOs gave evidence: Oxfam, Friends of the Earth, ActionAid and the World Development Movement (WDM). WDM was the least well known of the four, but its role in the end proved much the most significant.

The FAC spent a great deal of time trying to discover how the wording linking aid with arms exports in the Defence Protocol had arisen, and whether this wording influenced the decision making on Pergau. On the former, it took evidence from Geoffrey Howe (Foreign Secretary at the time of the signing of the Protocol), and from George Younger who had signed it and High Commissioner Spreckley who had been present at the signing.

Howe explained his dismay about the Protocol and the reference in it to aid, and the failure of Younger and Spreckley to consult the FCO before signing. He then went on to defend the de-linkage exercise that he had effectively overseen. As regards Mrs Thatcher's offer of aid for Pergau in March 1989, he could not recall having been consulted before ODA's advice reached Number 10 (he referred to the three boxes of papers he had to read each night, six days a week for six years, as Foreign Secretary). But he was unapologetic about the decision to fund the project – saying that "one cannot make it [developmental value] of overriding importance in a world where there is competition taking place for a dam that is going to be built anyway".[4]

Younger told the Committee that he felt he had to sign in order to avoid losing the defence deal; that he knew that linkage was contrary to official policy, but that he didn't believe the wording represented a real commitment. Notwithstanding the pressure he felt he was under to avoid losing the defence deal, the Committee concluded that the "form of words was wholly inappropriate in as much as they were capable of an interpretation quite contrary to declared government policy on links between aid and arms". Younger and Spreckley were criticised for not consulting the FCO before signing.

Douglas Hurd told the committee that his decision to override ODA's advice had been "entirely in terms of ATP and the wider British interest".[5] He accepted that what he called the "brief entanglement" between arms sales and aid in the Protocol was wrong, but this "entanglement" hadn't affected his decision. He effectively blamed it on George Younger – and shortly afterwards in a BBC interview, Younger accepted that he had been at fault. Hurd repeatedly asserted before the Committee that the "brief entanglement" was corrected by the two letters written to the Malaysian government in June 1988; that aid and defence sales were thereafter pursued separately and in parallel; and that it was perfectly legitimate for the UK government to pursue both policies in Malaysia – just as with other countries that qualified for aid and had a legitimate need to purchase defence equipment. Hurd vigorously denied that the defence package was in any way conditional on the provision of aid. He told Mr Denis Canavan MP that neither the parallel letters of 28 June 1988, nor Mrs Thatcher's letter of 8 August that year to Dr Mahathir in which arms sales and aid were both mentioned, amounted to a "nod and a wink" that there was some linkage.[6]

Yet in saying that he took into account the "wider British interest", Hurd was implicitly acknowledging that defence sales were one of the factors he took into account – since arms exports were such an important part of Britain's relationship with Malaysia. This was effectively confirmed when Lynda Chalker told the committee that "the defence sales relationship was one of the wider factors" that Hurd had had to consider.[7]

Hurd explained that the overriding factor in his mind was the need to honour the political commitment given by Mrs Thatcher – whatever the reasons for it – when she made the initial offer to her Malaysian counterpart in March 1989 and the need to maintain good relations with Malaysia across all fronts. He said there had been a "clear undertaking at the highest level. ... We had given our word, and it matters if you break your word. ... I cannot accept that we should have gone back on our word and disregarded the interests of British companies and British workers".[8]

The Minister of Trade, Richard Needham, put it more colourfully when he later told the committee:

[It was not] realistic in February 1991 to go back to the Malaysians and say, "Sorry, two years after all this, and renewals and whatever, we now have to tell you that we think you don't know what you're talking about, you don't need this dam. What we'll do is give you a gas-fired power station instead". They would have said, "Thank you very much. Goodbye," and phoned up the Japanese.[9]

In his memoirs Hurd was more open about how the situation had arisen in the first place – i.e. before he had to rule on whether Mrs Thatcher's word should be honoured. He wrote that "the promise of finance for Pergau had been linked, in conversation and correspondence, with a negotiation conducted in 1988 by Margaret Thatcher and George Younger which included an undertaking to buy defence equipment" (Hurd 2003, p. 548).

The FAC agreed that "the maintenance of good relations between the UK and Malaysia required the approval of the project", though it was highly critical of how the government had got itself into the position of having to approve a project of "questionable developmental value ... on the basis of inadequate information" in order to achieve this. It concluded that the Protocol created a "moral obligation which, upon reflection, the Government had to address"; but it fell short of saying it created a moral obligation necessarily to fund Pergau.[10]

The WDM representative, Ben Jackson, argued the aid for Pergau had undoubtedly been linked to the arms deal. He suggested that Malaysia was not the only country where aid and arms exports were linked. (To my personal knowledge, Malaysia was the only country where there was any serious evidence of a causal linkage.)

Newspaper coverage after Hurd's FAC appearance concentrated on his admission of the "incorrect" aid/arms entanglement and his "naming" of Younger as the cause of it. *The Sun* carried a headline: "It's your dam fault, Hurd tells Younger".[11]

Other issues that the FAC focused on included: ODA's failure to engage adequately with TNB and the Malaysian government on its reservations about the project; the rushed appraisal before Mrs Thatcher met Dr Mahathir in March 1989; the role of the consortium in securing the aid; the increase in costs very soon after the initial offer was made and ODA's failure to anticipate them. On all these points, the FAC's report that came out in July 1994 was highly critical. It also mentioned the issue of legality – though for obvious reasons it did not give an opinion – since by then WDM had been granted leave to challenge Douglas Hurd's decision in the High Court.

The FAC was right to focus on the question of why the cost estimates for the project escalated from £316 million to around £400 million within two weeks of Mrs Thatcher making the initial offer. For it was this increase that created many of the difficulties that later followed.

In evidence, the companies claimed that the £316 million had been only a very preliminary estimate; and they denied that it had ever been a "maximum" price. They explained that the £316 million price was an estimate based purely on the SMEC feasibility study, though in fact the figure – even after adjusting for inflation – was significantly higher than SMEC's. They said they had been in intensive discussion with TNB for several months and it was only after Mrs Thatcher and Dr Mahathir had met that they had finally been able to firm up the cost estimates. They claimed they had made it clear all along that they would not be ready with a firm figure – and even this would be subject to negotiation with the Malaysians – before the end of March, and that they had only been looking for Mrs Thatcher to make a "provisional commitment subject to an appraisal to be undertaken in detail by the ODA".[12]

The committee was not convinced by the companies' explanation and preferred to accept ODA's evidence that the £316 million had been presented as a maximum figure. The consortium could not "have it both ways". If it was a "very preliminary" estimate, they should not have pressed the government to make an offer based on it.[13]

The reality surely is that if the £316 million estimate was, in their words, "very preliminary", they had no interest in informing ODA of this. They were desperately keen for Mrs Thatcher to make a firm offer, and any indication that the estimate was "very preliminary" would have made this more difficult. As the FAC put it, they encouraged Mrs Thatcher "to give an oral commitment on the basis of information which was incomplete". The tactic paid off.

On the other hand, DTI and ODA had been naive in thinking it could be a maximum figure since the design specifications were still being worked on and the advice to Mrs Thatcher should have reflected this. This was all of a piece with DTI, on whom ODA had to rely for advice, in being all too willing to accept uncritically information from their "clients".

The Committee also took evidence on whether the ATP scheme should continue. Following the tightening up of internationally agreed terms for tied aid credits in the Helsinki Agreement in 1991, ODA had conducted with other government departments a review of the ATP scheme. Lynda Chalker, the aid Minister, had announced in June 1993 improved procedures, as well as a tightening of eligibility so that in future ATP funding would only be available for countries with a per capita income of less than $700.

The consortium representatives who gave evidence, backed up by written evidence given by others in the capital goods and construction industries, were most unhappy with these changes. They argued that they would be put at a severe disadvantage compared with their competitors overseas. By contrast, the representatives of Friends of the Earth, Oxfam, ActionAid and WDM – with supporting written evidence by Professor John Toye of the Institute of Development Studies at Sussex University – argued for ATP's complete abolition. The FAC took refuge in the ODA-led review and endorsed its conclusion – that the scheme should be continued, but in modified and more restrictive form.

The Committee invited Mrs Thatcher (now Baroness Thatcher) to give evidence. Citing long precedent that former Prime Ministers do not appear before parliamentary committees to account for their actions in office, she declined. Whether fair or not, *The Times* later carried a story headlined "Thatcher refusal rekindles Pergau dam suspicions".[14]

All in all, the FAC did an excellent job in exploring the issues. Unlike some select committee inquiries, it did not split on party lines. One of the most pressing critics of the government and of the companies was the Tory MP John Stanley, and the Labour Chairman, Peter Shore, was non-partisan and even-handed in his questioning. The Committee's report makes compelling reading.

Parliamentary debate and questions

In each Parliamentary session, the Opposition parties are allotted a certain number of days when they can choose the subject for debate. For their allotted day on 1 March 1994 the Liberal Democrats chose to debate Pergau. The debate motion censured the government's handling of the whole issue from the Defence Protocol signing through to the final decision to provide the aid. The debate was led off by the former Liberal leader, David Steel, and 35 other MPs spoke. The ODA Minister, Lynda Chalker, was unable to lead on behalf of the government because, having lost her House of Commons seat in the 1992 General Election, she was now a member of the House of Lords. Instead, the FCO Minister of State, Alastair Goodlad, responded for the government, and the DTI Minister of State, Richard Needham, spoke at the end of the debate. Tom Clarke, who had taken over from Ann Clwyd as Labour spokesman on aid, was one of the many Labour members who spoke.

The Liberal Democrats were, unsurprisingly, highly critical. On the Conservative side, however, there was a closing of ranks – with many MPs defending the aid programme generally, rationalising the decision to grant the aid for Pergau on "wider grounds", and deploring the effect of the row over Pergau on relations with Malaysia and the potential loss of UK jobs. It was unsatisfactory, though perhaps convenient for her, that Lynda Chalker – the minister directly responsible – was unable to participate. Douglas Hurd opted to let his junior colleagues take the flak for the government. The motion was rejected by a large majority – 305 to 159.[15]

The debate allowed MPs to vent their opinions but it threw little new light on the issues. Government ministers and many of their supporters gave every impression that nothing much had gone wrong at all. Richard Needham mounted a spirited attack on *The Sunday Times* and its editor, Andrew Neil.[16] The voting outcome was meaningless insofar as it bore no reflection of opinion in the media and the wider public – nor did it reflect the privately held view of many Tory MPs.

Following the debate, several Tory MPs made further attempts to blame Labour and the Liberal Democrats for the rift with Malaysia – by putting down Early Day Motions deploring both parties' pronouncements on the Pergau issue.[17] But again, these were pretty meaningless. They were a vain attempt to recover some of the lost political ground.

On 2 March, there was also a debate on aid in the House of Lords in which Pergau featured strongly. In the second chamber, Lynda Chalker was of course able to speak for the government. Popular with other peers, she wasn't given too much of a drubbing; but several of them spoke trenchantly about misuse of the aid programme – including Frank Judd, the former Labour MP and aid minister in the 1970s. Judd reminded his fellow peers that Barbara Castle's White Paper in 1964 had said that "the basis of the aid programme is a moral one".[18] Under Labour and Conservatives, this seemed to have become a distant aspiration.

On 25 January 1995 there was one further debate in the House of Commons on Pergau. This was shortly after the High Court ruling that the aid had been given unlawfully. The Labour Opposition took the opportunity to have a final go at the government. For the Conservatives, it was more like a wake than a debate. Michael Jopling, a former Chief Whip who was a member of the Foreign Affairs Committee, took the House through what he called the "whole sorry saga". He criticised almost everyone who had touched it: our High Commission in Malaysia, the MOD, the FCO, ODA and the contractors. A junior Foreign Office Minister, Tony Baldry, had the unhappy task of replying to the debate. Wisely, he made no attempt to defend the government's actions on Pergau and instead talked about the aid programme in general. Since it was an Adjournment Debate, there was no vote.[19]

Over the seven years from 1988 to 1995, MPs asked more than 100 oral and written questions, on a total of 80 days, about Pergau and the aid/arms linkage. These reached a crescendo in 1994 when there were questions on 54 days. These were mainly asked by Opposition members.[20]

Hard though Ann Clwyd and other Labour MPs tried, they had great difficulty in eliciting information. This was partly because of the government's insistence on secrecy in respect of the Defence Protocol and the commercial negotiations, and a degree of dissembling on the part of ministers of which the FAC was critical. It was also a function of the government's unwillingness – a common enough feature at all times – to admit mistakes and accept that actual policy had seriously diverged from official policy until it was absolutely forced to do so. The fact that MPs were unable to unpick what had occurred – despite plenty of rumour and circumstantial evidence that several things had gone badly wrong – until the NAO had reported five and half years after the start of the saga was an example of the limits on the executive's accountability to the legislature in the British system.

On the other hand, whilst Parliament was unable to provide any real check on the executive prior to the final decision to fund Pergau, the system of accountability ex post arguably worked well. This at any rate is the view of the distinguished Canadian political scientist Charles Franks, who for a long time has campaigned for Canada to adopt the British system of separate and distinct accountabilities for ministers and Permanent Secretaries (Deputy Ministers in Canada). Commenting on the Pergau case, he wrote:

> The system of accountability through accounting officers worked well; an important question of economy and propriety in public expenditure was brought to the attention of Parliament; responsibility for going against the established standards for financial management was squarely placed with the ministers; the conduct of both officials and ministers was reviewed by parliamentary committees; and the electorate was allowed to make an informed judgement on the government's conduct of public business.
>
> (Franks 1997, p. 637)

11 Legal challenge

Those of us who were close to the issue in ODA and also in the Treasury had expected sharp criticism from the PAC, the FAC and the media; but none of us had expected that Pergau would end up in the courts. Yet this is what happened.

I have already explained in Chapter 9 ODA's views on the legality of the expenditure. Although we regarded the expenditure as a very unsatisfactory use of aid funds, we did not believe it was unlawful.

The campaigning organisation, the World Development Movement, had argued in their evidence before the FAC that the aid for Pergau was unlawful. Yet it still came as a considerable surprise when they announced that they would be seeking a declaration of unlawfulness from the courts.

WDM was a small organisation with just 13 staff, an annual budget of £500,000, and 13,000 registered supporters. For some time they had been campaigning against the ATP scheme; against the linking of aid to arms sales, which they believed existed not just in respect of Malaysia but with other countries too; and against subsidisation of arms exports more generally.[1] The publication of the NAO report on Pergau and the rumours of an explicit arms link gave them the perfect opportunity to raise the tempo of their campaign and actually bring about a change in policy – and all the more so after they received informal legal advice that it might be possible to convince the courts that the funding decision was unlawful.

But such an outcome was far from certain: WDM's lawyers put their chances of success at no more than 50/50; and the potential costs – £60,000 or more if they lost – were daunting for such a small charity. The decision to mount a legal challenge was therefore a big one and a brave one for WDM's trustees. They first had to satisfy themselves that they were permitted under Charity Law to mount the challenge. Having done so, they launched a special appeal and printed 120,000 leaflets. WDM were fortunate in being able to persuade the leading law firm, Bindmans, to take on the case at relatively low cost. But the successful outcome for WDM also owed a lot to the extraordinary work of two young WDM staff members, Ben Jackson and Harriet Lamb.[2]

Whether or not they were able to convince the court that the aid for Pergau was unlawful, WDM believed that public opinion was behind them. An NOP poll that they commissioned in 1994 revealed that 60 per cent of those polled agreed that "helping poor people in poor countries is the most important reason for giving aid". Only 17 per cent agreed that it was to "win arms or other contracts for Britain".

The focus of the WDM challenge was Section 1 (1) of the Overseas Development and Cooperation Act 1980: "The Secretary of State shall have power, for the purpose of promoting the development or maintaining the economy of a country or territory outside the United Kingdom, or the welfare of its people, to furnish any person or body with assistance, whether financial, technical, or any other nature".

In their evidence to the FAC, WDM had argued that the decision was unlawful on two grounds: first, Pergau was not a sound development project and therefore could not genuinely have as its purpose the development of the Malaysia economy; and, second, the decision to provide the aid had been taken for political and commercial reasons, not for developmental reasons. On 29 March 1994 Geoffrey Bindman wrote to Hurd elaborating further on why the grant was unlawful. He demanded on WDM's behalf the immediate stoppage of payments, or else WDM would make an application for judicial review.

Douglas Hurd was briefed on the challenge by my successor as Permanent Secretary, John Vereker, on 7 April 1994. (Vereker had been Principal Finance Officer at the beginning of the Pergau saga in 1988, but then spent the period 1988–94 at the Department for Education.) Hurd was deeply dismayed, pointing out – correctly – in his memoirs (2003) that this was the first time any legal point had been raised with him by officials. Hurd had never criticised me for the advice I had given against approving the project and insisting on a ministerial direction. His words to me had been when the controversy blew up in late 1993: "You did your job; I did mine". But he was understandably critical that I had not mentioned possible legal concerns.

Given the ODA view that the Pergau grant was within the law, and ministers' staunch defence of the decision, there was no question of giving way to the WDM demand that payments in support of the project should be stopped. The WDM challenge was obviously unwelcome since it meant continuing publicity around the whole affair. Nonetheless, once the FCO legal advisers had been briefed on the issues, there was reasonable confidence that – if WDM were given "standing" and allowed by the court to pursue their case – their challenge would be quashed and the Secretary of State's position upheld.

WDM first had to obtain leave to present their case for judicial review. Their counsel had to persuade a judge that there was a significant point of law that needed to be decided. FCO lawyers saw no point in trying to challenge WDM at this stage, and on 24 June 1994 a judge ruled that WDM could present their case. The actual substantive application for judicial review of the Pergau decision was heard five months later in the High Court on 10 November before two judges, Lord Justice Rose and Mr Justice Scott Baker (R. v. Secretary of State 1994).[3]

Rose and Scott were both considered relatively conservative judges. Neither would have thought that they were doing anything other than deciding whether the facts fell within the statute or not. Neither would have seen themselves as candidates for the role of "judicial activist", out to constrain an over-mighty executive. WDM could not expect any favours from these particular judges: everything would turn on whether their lawyers could persuade the court that the facts of the case fell outside the statute. In this they were helped by having a brilliant counsel in Nigel Pleming. But Stephen Richards, counsel for the Secretary of State, also had a formidable reputation.

In making their application, WDM faced two barriers. First, they had to persuade the court to grant them "standing" for judicial review; and second, if "standing" was granted, they had to persuade the court to overturn the Pergau decision.

Under English law, an individual or group has "standing" for judicial review only where in the opinion of the court they have "sufficient interest" in the subject matter to which the application relates, as prescribed by S.31(1) of the Supreme Court Act (1981). Compared to a more orthodox judicial review (e.g. where an individual's property rights are threatened by a planning decision), the WDM's interests were seemingly quite remote from the granting of aid to the Pergau project.

Citing an earlier case in which the applicant had been denied "standing" because his interest was simply that of an interested taxpayer, Richards argued that WDM's position was no different and therefore should likewise be denied "standing". Pleming countered by citing other cases where the applicant did not have a strong direct interest, yet – because of wider legal considerations – had still been granted "standing".

Fortunately for WDM, and unfortunately for Hurd, the court adopted the more liberal approach. In justifying the court's decision to grant "standing", Rose noted that the test for "standing" was becoming more liberal. He went on to say that he had had regard to the merits of the WDM's challenge, the importance of vindicating the rule of law, the likely absence of any other responsible challenger, and the prominent role of the WDM in giving advice relating to foreign aid. The decision to grant WDM "standing" was considered significant at the time. The authors of one of the standard textbooks on public law wrote: "The case relaxes the rules of standing further" (Harlow and Rawlins 1997).

Having ruled that WDM did have "standing" in the case, the court then considered the substance of the application itself.

Pleming contended that the power given to the Secretary of State to provide assistance for the purpose of promoting development meant that it had to be for "sound development". Projects that were unsound could not be considered to be contributing to a country's development. Pergau had been deemed economically unsound by ODA and this had not been disputed by ministers. Consequently, the granting of aid to this project was ultra vires.

Richards duly argued that the Secretary of State had not overstepped his statutory boundaries. In reaching his decision not to withdraw the offer of aid, he had had to weigh the political and commercial implications of withdrawing it and the damage that would be incurred for British–Malaysia relations. In his deliberations, he had always regarded Pergau as a development project. It would be of benefit to the people of Malaysia since it would help meet the need for electricity. Sir Tim Lankester's concerns raised "important questions of the economy and efficiency of public expenditure", but the project was still in the Secretary of State's view of undoubted benefit for the development of Malaysia. The cost of Pergau did not give rise to a cost penalty for the Malaysian consumer since ODA's grant bridged the gap between the cost of Pergau and other cheaper means of generating electricity.

It was the Secretary of State's thinking, Richards argued, that was of "decisive importance" in determining the purpose of the aid and therefore whether furnishing the aid was within the statute. The sole purpose of the assistance for Pergau, in the Secretary of State's mind, was the developmental purpose. The political and commercial considerations that he had taken into account in reaching his decision were not "purposes" for which the assistance was furnished but were "considerations" that the Secretary of State was entitled to take into account.

Rose, in his judgement, wrote that the Secretary of State was fully entitled to take into account political and commercial considerations; but the aid had to be for the purpose of development. He took the view that the expansion of Malaysia's electricity capacity was insufficient on its own, when there were clearly more economical ways of developing this capacity than the investment in Pergau. He agreed with WDM that the intention of the statutory power was to provide only "sound" economic assistance. He wrote in his judgement: "If Parliament had intended to confer a power to disburse money for unsound developmental purposes, it could have been expected to say so expressly". It was essentially a matter of practical common sense that Parliament only intended that aid should be used in an economically sound manner. Rose was

> comforted in this view by the way in which the successive ministers, guidelines, Governments and White Papers … have, over the years and without exception, construed the power as relating to economically sound development. That also, judging from his minutes, was the view of Sir Tim Lankester in 1991.

He concluded:

> Where the contemplated development is, on the evidence, so economically unsound that there is no economic argument in favour of the case, it is not, in my judgement, possible to draw any distinction between questions of propriety and regularity on the one hand and questions of economy and efficiency of public expenditure on the other.

In other words, if it failed to meet the economy test, it automatically failed to meet the propriety/regularity tests too. In reaching this conclusion, Rose disagreed with Richards' view that it was for the Secretary of State to determine whether the purpose of the aid was within the statute. He wrote:

> Whatever the Secretary of State's intention or purpose may have been, it is, as it seems to me, a matter for the courts and not the Secretary of State to determine whether, on the evidence before the court, the particular conduct was, or was not, within the statutory purpose.

Having dismissed the aid as having a development purpose, he didn't need to address the other WDM argument that development had not been the dominant purpose.

In short, Rose concluded that, whatever the Secretary of State's personal view, the aid for Pergau could not objectively, given the economic analysis, be considered to be for the purpose of development. He could not accept that expanding Malaysia's power generation capacity per se amounted to development. Consequently, the aid was unlawful. The other judge, Scott Baker, concurred – agreeing that "the Secretary of State's power to provide assistance under Section 1 (1) of the 1980 Act was not triggered".

Needless to say, the judgement was greeted as a great victory by WDM and other development NGOs. But it came as a big shock to ODA and the FCO and its legal advisers. It also surprised the legal profession. There were reasonable grounds for appealing the decision in the Court of Appeal. However, following extensive discussions, Douglas Hurd decided not to appeal, fearing that an appeal – and the more so if it failed – would further inflame the Pergau row.

Away from the fray – for by now I was Permanent Secretary in another government ministry – the judgement seemed to me to make a good deal of sense. It coincided exactly with my instinct prior to the approval of the aid but which I had failed to test with the lawyers: namely, that project aid aimed at a specific economic goal such as power generations could not be regarded as furthering a recipient country's development if there were much more efficient ways of achieving the same goal.

But there was disappointment amongst some in the legal profession who felt that the judgement was wrong and needed to be overturned in order to reestablish the principle that it was the "subjective view" that mattered. Derry Irvine, later to be Lord Chancellor in the Labour government of Tony Blair, wrote in relation to judicial review in general: "The want of parliamentary control over the executive in recent years has been, to an important degree, mitigated by the rigours of judicial review" (Irvine 1996, p. 59).

But he went on to say:

> The court must not substitute its opinion for that of the decision-maker; the court must rule only upon the legality of a decision and not upon its correctness; the court will concern itself with the manner in which a

decision is reached rather than with the substantive merits of the decision itself.

(ibid., p. 60)

And in relation the specific case of Pergau, he wrote: "The court glossed the statute by inserting the word 'sound' before 'development purpose' in the statutory provision. ... Whether [the grant of aid] was sound was for the Secretary of State to decide, not the court". The soundness or otherwise of the project was a relevant consideration that the Secretary of State needed to take into account in reaching his decision; it was for him "on all the facts to decide, subject to Wednesbury, whether the proposed development was sound". The court should have understood the case not as a matter of statutory interpretation (i.e. what does the state mean) but rather as a matter of discretion. The court went too far in "curbing a valuable and legitimate facet of administrative autonomy" (ibid., p. 69).

Irvine did leave open the possibility that the decision might have failed on the "Wednesbury reasonableness" test because – on the facts – it could be argued that the Secretary of State had acted perversely; but the court had not ruled against it on these grounds.

Irvine was not alone in criticising the judgement. Academic lawyers, Carol Harlow and Richard Rawlins, wrote that "this judgement is hardly tightly reasoned", and raised similar issues to those touched on by Irvine (Harlow and Rawlins 1997, p. 594).

Whilst the judgement was on a point of law specific to Pergau, it can be seen as part of the trend of growing "judicial activism" in the 1980s and 1990s. It came a day after the Court of Appeal had ruled against the Home Secretary, Michael Howard, on an issue regarding compensation for the victims of violent crimes. The previous year, the High Court had ruled against Howard's predecessor, Kenneth Baker, in an asylum case – which, according to one legal scholar, Diana Woodhouse, was a "trend-setter for judicial-executive relations over the next few years. It demonstrated ministerial arrogance with regard to the courts and a judicial determination to rein back the powers of an over-mighty executive" (Woodhouse 1997, p. 129).

Many years later in 2011, Jonathan Sumption, soon to take up his seat as a Supreme Court judge, delivered a lecture in which he took a similar line to that of Irvine 15 years earlier. He criticised the growing tendency of judges, as he saw it, to trespass on "the proper functions of government and the legislature" (Sumption 2011). Judges, he argued, were increasingly ruling on matters of policy and efficiency that were the responsibility of Parliament and the government, and not that of the courts. One of the reasons for this was that judges, in interpreting the relevant legislation, were asking themselves what a "good and wise Parliament" would have wanted to achieve. In doing so, they were effectively imposing their own personal views.

As an example of this, Sumption cited the Pergau case and the fact that Lord Justice Rose had taken the view that it must have been Parliament's intention that only economically sound projects could be described as assisting a country's development. According to Sumption, it was really Rose who believed that only "sound" projects could count as developmental, and in this way he had substituted his own view for the discretion of the Secretary of State.

Sumption argued that:

> parliamentary scrutiny is generally perfectly adequate for the purpose of protecting the public interest in the area of policy-making. It is also the only way of doing so that carries any democratic legitimacy. ... To single issue pressure groups, public law is politics by other means. To members of the public who are hung up about dams, development policy or the arms trade, decisions like the one in the Pergau Dam case are admired because they appear to introduce a higher morality into public decision-making, untrammeled by the impurities of the political process.[4]

(Sumption 2011, p. 18)

Stephen Sedley, a former judge in the Court of Appeal, took issue with Sumption on his views on judicial review in general and on the Pergau case in particular. On the latter, he wrote: "The court was doing its job of testing the legality of executive action against the relevant statutory power. It was not, as Sumption openly suggests it was, substituting its own view of policy for the Foreign Secretary's" (Sedley 2012).

On Sumption's point about parliamentary scrutiny, there was indeed a great deal of such scrutiny of the decision to fund Pergau. The trouble was – it took place three years after the decision, by which time project implementation and aid disbursements were well under way and effectively unstoppable. Moreover, without the revelations in the media, the scrutiny would have been a good deal less robust. What was seriously lacking was parliamentary scrutiny at the time the decision was taken. Nonetheless, Sumption's implicit question is an interesting one – was it really necessary for the courts to get involved once the two parliamentary committees had conducted their inquiries?

It is very likely that, in the light of the PAC's and FAC's criticisms, there would have been changes in the way the aid budget was spent – in the direction of giving more emphasis to development and less to political and commercial considerations. On the other hand, the judgement did entrench for good the idea that the minister could not set aside the experts' views on whether an aid project was economically sound. It also resulted, as we shall see, in ODA having some of the monies it had already disbursed on the project being reimbursed and its being relieved of further spending on it. The outcome, therefore, in terms of policy and budget effect went much further than it would have done without the court ruling.

In any event, whatever the views of the legal experts both at the time and later, the judgement was a significant milestone in the development of administrative law. Its immediate effect was that ODA could make no further payments towards the project. There was no question of the government reneging on the aid commitment as this would have put it in breach of contract with the consortium of banks that were providing the export credits. But henceforth the monies would have to come from outside the aid budget. It was decided that future disbursements should be made by ECGD (which had the legal authority to do so) and the Treasury committed itself to providing ECGD with the requisite funding.

There was the further question of what should happen to the monies already spent – amounting to £34.5 million in total (£24 million in the two years prior to 1994/95 and £10.5 million during 1994/95). Lord Justice Rose said "unravelling of some sort will be necessary". This was left to be agreed by the various parties outside the court hearing. Separately, the Comptroller and Auditor General qualified ODA's accounts for 1993–94 because, in the light of the court's ruling, the monies spent on Pergau were not a proper charge on the relevant Vote.

The monies already disbursed clearly could not be recouped from the consortium or from the Malaysians since they were covered by a legally binding contract. Robin Cook, the Opposition foreign affairs spokesman, demanded that the aid budget should be reimbursed by the Treasury. WDM argued the same.

Reimbursement was agreed by the Treasury in respect of the £10.5 million for the current year (1994/95), but the Treasury refused for the two earlier years on the technicality that the accounts for these years were already closed; and in any case, so they argued, the original aid budget would have been lower by the amounts disbursed for Pergau if Pergau hadn't been funded, and therefore the monies would not have been available for other projects. Given the way the aid budget was constructed and negotiated, this latter argument was hardly plausible; but WDM did not press the point, presumably realising that they had done extremely well in stopping all future funding for the project from the ODA budget.

ODA immediately put in hand a review of all other existing ATP commitments to see whether any of them might be "caught" by the judgement – that is to say, projects where the economic case was weak and political or commercial considerations had been the dominant consideration. It found three other projects that might be at risk of legal challenge: Indonesia TV Studio (1985), Botswana Flight Information (1988) and Ankara Metro (1990).[5] Each of these projects had been agreed by ODA despite doubts about their economic merits in order to satisfy commercial and/or political considerations. On Hurd's instructions, ODA was to avoid any risk of legal challenge; so it was agreed with the Treasury that ODA's continuing payments would be met by the Export Credit and Guarantee Department, which had legal authority to make the payments.

Douglas Hurd made a statement in the House of Commons on 13 December 1994 covering all of these points. It amounted to a final abject admission that Pergau had gone horribly wrong from the British government's point of view.

Thenceforth, ODA had nothing more to do with Pergau. Its monitoring function, both in respect of the contract and the environmental impact, had to stop. There was an occasional visit to the site by an official from the British High Commission in Kuala Lumpur. The British High Commissioner attended a low-key opening ceremony on 22 August 1997. The FCO wisely gave it no publicity.

For Douglas Hurd, the legal defeat was politically speaking the last straw. In his memoirs he wrote: "It was one thing to have picked a political row with the Labour Party and aid agencies in which I had strong arguments on my side and the [Conservative] party with me. It was quite another to be hauled before the courts on a point of law" (Hurd 2003, p. 495).

12 The British media and trouble with Malaysia

For an aid project, the press coverage in Britain was quite without precedent. From the publication of the NAO report in October 1993 to the publication of the FAC report in July 1994, there was rarely a week when some aspect of the Pergau story wasn't in the news. And the story reappeared in the wake of the court ruling in November 1994. *The Times* printed over 50 articles, editorials and letters on the subject. Not known for its liberal views on aid, it was amongst the most vocal in its criticism. The headline to a lead editorial, "The Pergau curse", summed up its attitude.[1] The *Daily Telegraph* headlined: "Major and Thatcher may face 'Floodgate'".[2] *The Independent* led with an editorial entitled: "The whole dam scandal".[3] Coverage came to a crescendo in February and March 1994 with the FAC hearings and the Malaysian boycott of British firms for public sector contracts. *The Times* called the Pergau dam project "a monstrous exception to the generally taut, targeted and well monitored British overseas aid programme".[4] The story was widely covered in the tabloids as well as the broadsheets.

The reporting was almost entirely hostile in one form or another. Those newspapers or journalists who supported aid strictly for development praised ODA for taking a stand and trying to stop the project, whilst expressing alarm that it had been unable to do so. They criticised the government for misusing the aid programme for political and commercial purposes. The fact that ministers had chosen to override my advice as Accounting Officer was emphasised repeatedly. It was claimed that several of the companies that benefited most from the ATP scheme were donors to the Conservative Party.

Even greater alarm was expressed at the apparent linkage with the arms deal. The government was accused of hypocrisy and worse in the context of its assertion that it was promoting good governance in the aid programme, and the fact that ministers had repeatedly asserted that no such linkage could possibly exist in any British aid project. The respected *Financial Times* columnist Joe Rogaly wrote that Douglas Hurd, in saying that after the "temporary entanglement" there was no link, "was as convincing as a bigamist protesting that his two marriages are separately enjoyed"; and that "such malarkey can spoil a government's reputation". Rogaly went on: "What sticks in the throat is that government broke its own rules and then hid behind half-truths".[5] In a BBC interview, the Labour MP and Foreign Affairs spokesman, Jack Cunningham, said that "it is exactly because this squalid deal [the arms linkage] has unravelled that British trade and British jobs are now at risk and the responsibility lies on the government front bench".[6]

The contrary view, albeit one expressed by only a minority of the press, was that ODA should not have objected to the project. It was for the Malaysians, not ODA, to decide what sort of power station they wanted and ODA should simply have gone along with Malaysian wishes and funded it. It smacked of colonialism for ODA to tell the Malaysians what was good for them. By trying to block the aid, ODA would have prevented British exporters from winning lucrative business. ODA officials were branded as arrogant "do gooders" who had no interest in Britain's real interests. The French were ruthless in using their aid budget to secure commercial contracts; so should we. Writing in *Construction News*, a former director general of Export Group for the Construction Industries called on John Major to sack both me and Lynda Chalker.[7]

In accusing the ODA of "telling the Malaysians what was good for them", these critics missed the point. Far from telling Malaysia what to do, ODA had had precious little direct contact – the FAC complained that there had been too little contact – with the Malaysian government, and it was simply saying that funding Pergau was not a good use of scarce aid funds. It was our job, and my responsibility in particular as Accounting Officer, to ensure that public money was utilised economically and effectively for the purpose for which Parliament had intended it.

Behind this type of criticism of course was scepticism as to the official purpose and value of the aid programme. At the extreme end was the former minister Alan Clark, who believed that, if there had to be an aid programme at all, it should be used to help British exporters and to help Britain's friends.

A third group of critics didn't take a particular view on whether or not the aid programme had been misused. They concentrated on what they regarded as a serious breakdown in efficient public administration. And of course they were right. On this view, the Defence Protocol should never have been signed and the differences over the handling of the aid for Pergau should have been resolved one way or the other early on. Someone in government should have ensured a decision in favour or against which would have avoided such unnecessary public controversy. The implicit, and unrealistic, assumption here was that Mrs Thatcher would readily have agreed to drop the project after she had made her offer; or else, perhaps more plausibly, that ODA should in the end have "rolled over".

Peter Riddell in *The Times* took an altogether more relaxed view. He couldn't see what all the fuss was about. In a piece entitled "No UK scandal lurks in muddy water of Pergau", he argued that the whole issue had been blown out of proportion. In the real world, particularly when arms exports were involved and with Mrs Thatcher "batting for Britain", unsavoury deals were inevitable. No one had accused anyone in the British government of corruption. The Permanent Secretary had been right to voice his objections to the use of the aid budget for an evidently uneconomic project, but that didn't mean Douglas Hurd was wrong to overrule him in the overall public interest.[8]

There was quite separate criticism of the terms of the MOU on the defence equipment sales when it came to light – particularly the subsidised interest rates that the MOD negotiators had agreed to without consulting the Treasury if the Malaysians had difficulty finding the cash for the purchases.[9] The World Development Movement had been campaigning against covert subsidies for defence exports. Here was a clear example. Whether the government was actually called upon to provide these interest subsidies is not publicly documented.

In Malaysia, interest in these arguments and counter-arguments was at first relatively muted. In late January 1994, Lim Kit Siang, the leader of the opposition Democratic Action Party, called on the (Malaysian) government to issue a White Paper on whether there had been an aid for arms deal; and if so, who in Malaysia had benefited. His concern was not that "sweeteners" had been paid by Britain in order to secure the defence deal, but rather that these "sweeteners" might have benefited individuals and particular companies in Malaysia rather than the government. He also wanted to know why the Pergau contract had been let without an open tender, and why the contract price had escalated so dramatically after Mrs Thatcher had promised the aid.[10] But generally, the response in Malaysia to the revelations in Britain was fairly relaxed. The government had secured the funding for the project and project implementation was progressing well. If there was controversy about the funding of Pergau, this was a UK domestic problem.

This all changed dramatically when *The Sunday Times* on 20 February 1994 published a lengthy piece alleging widespread corruption at the heart of the Malaysian government. Its only specific allegation was that in 1985 the construction company, Wimpey, had offered Dr Mahathir a bribe, but it conceded that no money had changed hands. It mentioned Pergau but offered no specific evidence of bribes.

Dr Mahathir's reaction was immediate and furious. And with some justification – for *The Sunday Times* article was a poor piece of journalism that attacked Dr Mahathir by innuendo rather than through evidence. He took *The Sunday Times*' intervention as a wholly unjustified attack on his personal integrity with damaging consequences for his reputation worldwide. He blamed the article on his refusal to allow Rupert Murdoch's Star Television access to Malaysia – though this was firmly denied by *The Sunday Times* editor, Andrew Neil. He was especially upset that they were able to use freedom of the press to "tell lies" about himself and Malaysia, which were then spread around the world, and which Malaysia found itself unable to refute. Dr Mahathir demanded a retraction, and if *The Sunday Times* was unwilling to retract, action by the British government to get them to do so. Far from retracting, Andrew Neil piled on the trouble by indirectly comparing Dr Mahathir with Hitler.[11]

In part, the outburst against Britain may have been designed to switch attention away from Dr Mahathir's own internal political problems. At the UMNO party Congress meeting in November 1993, the rank and file had forced the leadership to take action against "money politics"; his leverage over the party seemed to be on the decline, in particular in relation to the pace and choice of his succession; and he was facing serious electoral problems in Sabah State. Add to this his outspoken criticism of Britain's failing to protect the Bosnian Muslims, a row with Britain served his political purposes quite well at this time.

On 25 February Malaysia's Finance Minister and Dr Mahathir's successor in waiting, Anwar Ibrahim, announced a boycott of British companies for new public sector contracts. In an official statement, Anwar said: "The British media may have their own political agenda but we detest their patronising attitude and innuendoes that the government of developing countries, particularly a Muslim-led nation like Malaysia, are incompetent and their leaders corrupt".[12] Anwar suggested that *The Sunday Times* attack was racially motivated and that the British press in general implied that doing business with "brown Muslims" inevitably involved bribery.[13]

Dr Mahathir told the media that he couldn't understand why there was such a fuss in Britain about the aid for Pergau. The row over the aid and arms linkage was of no interest in Malaysia. British firms had secured their contracts and, he claimed, the financing wasn't really aid at all because it was in the form of a soft loan. He said that the description by ODA that Pergau was a "bad buy" was stupid – given that Malaysia was receiving a grant of £234 million. For Malaysia, it was an excellent buy.[14] (The "bad buy" phrase was infelicitous: it was shorthand for the project's poor economics.) At the same time, he claimed that the aid was really a subsidy to British industry (which of course to some extent it was).

The Sunday Times stood its ground even though it had produced virtually no evidence to back its claims. John Major was unwilling to rebuke *The Sunday Times* or to try to conciliate Malaysia. Dr Mahathir thought that John Major, by not asking them to retract, was tacitly supporting *The Sunday Times*.

The Sunday Times upped the ante further by making fresh allegations – in particular, that the shares sold when TNB was part-privatised in 1992 had been deliberately underpriced, and that the allocation of blocks of shares to Dr Mahathir's associates had created huge windfall gains for them.[15] Dr Mahathir responded with a vituperative letter to the *Financial Times*.[16]

British–Malaysia relations were suddenly back to where they had been in the early 1980s. British exporters were understandably furious and some urged the government to intervene with *The Sunday Times* and ask them to retract. The day before the Malaysian announcement, GEC's chairman, Jim Prior, telephoned the Prime Minister's Office and urged that John Major should telephone Dr Mahathir to try to avert some of the damage. To the fury of the business community, Major declined – no doubt unwilling to plead with a leader who had subjected him to a public lambasting when he visited

Kuala Lumpur over Britain's failure to do more to protect the Bosnian Muslims. Some newspapers and one or two MPs[17] demanded that Britain should retaliate and boycott Malaysian goods. But under the GATT rules, Britain could not lawfully do this – because Mahathir had advisedly restricted the ban to public procurement, which the rules did not cover.

British ministers found themselves in a wretched position. Douglas Hurd later wrote: "I was defending a wasteful project on grounds of good faith and friendship with a man who was busy kicking us in the teeth" (Hurd 2003, p. 495).

John Major wasn't prepared to retaliate. In an interview he said that he didn't believe "what the Malaysian government have done to British companies is remotely justifiable".[18] But he saw no advantage in attempting retaliatory action, and – to Malaysia's annoyance – he refused to tell *The Sunday Times* to retract. All that he and British exporters could hope for was that *The Sunday Times* would "go quiet" and that quiet diplomacy would secure a reversal of the boycott.

On 4 March, Andrew Neil wrote an open letter stating his regrets "if subsequent misreporting … has led the Malaysian Prime Minister to believe he has been accused by us of a charge we did not make". Not surprisingly, it had no effect. Bizarrely, *The Sunday Times* then resumed its attack.

Most newspapers, whilst denying that Malaysia was in any way justified in imposing the trade ban, argued that the government had only itself to blame. In a blistering piece in *The Times* entitled "Why did we give a dam", Simon Jenkins wrote that "the Pergau project was an outrageous abuse of the aid budget in an attempt to win arms contracts from Malaysia". He could not see "one good reason for appeasing the Malaysian leader in his current campaign for press censorship in Britain".[19]

On the question of bribery, Richard Littlejohn in *The Sun* summed up the majority view: "I don't mind British businessmen bunging bent foreign politicians to secure orders, but we shouldn't be bribing them with our [i.e. aid] money".[20]

In the debate on Pergau in the House of Lords on 2 March, Prior said that the affair was "a perfectly legitimate and reasonable cause for enquiry by the press"; but he called the actual press coverage "little short of catastrophic" for British jobs.[21] The *Evening Standard* took this as an attack on the freedom of the press, which, coming from a former Cabinet Minister, was "disgraceful, pusillanimous and dishonest". It called him a "hypocrite, a fool and a scoundrel".[22] The argument with the British press was getting as nasty in Britain as it was in Malaysia.

On 7 September 1994, thanks partly to mediation on the part of Prior himself and by Charles Powell (who by this time had become a director of Trafalgar House, Cementation International's parent company), the ban was lifted and normal trading relations were restored.

Much of the British media blamed the aid for Pergau, and the public row over its handling, for the trade boycott. They were correct in the sense that, without Pergau, it is unlikely *The Sunday Times* would have written as it did.

Some blamed the FCO for a failing to deter the Malaysians from taking such drastic action. Others suggested that British exporters had only themselves to blame in view of their complicity in the whole affair.

Inevitably, there were some who held ODA responsible for the breakdown with Malaysia. If ODA hadn't opposed the funding so vigorously, no one would have been interested in corruption in Malaysia – or so the argument went. Alan Clark, the former Minister of State for Defence Procurement, but now writing for the *Mail on Sunday*, wrote about a

> wild-eyed Permanent Secretary declaiming about what a faraway country does or does not "need" and you have all the ingredients for a prime muddle. Lace this with malice and insults to the customer and it is hardly surprising it should take its orders away. … Civil servants are short-sighted and incompetent enough about what is right for Britain. Why anyone should pay the slightest regard to their opinions about what is desirable overseas beats me.[23]

The next day in *The Times*, Clark wrote: "Why on earth shouldn't an enormous contract for British Aerospace be linked to a civil engineering project from which some payment came out of the aid budget. … What is all the fuss about?" He defended the linking of Pergau with the arms package as a "fantastic deal".[24] *The Spectator* weighed in with the same line and added that ODA should be abolished and its budget transferred to DTI.[25]

Woodrow Wyatt, the former Labour MP but for many years a Thatcher confidant, wrote that "the dambusters forget which side they are on".[26] The *Sunday Express* said it hoped that "Lankester was sleeping easily over [his] role – the fall-out from which would be putting British engineers on the street". It carried a headline: "The Whistleblower who has had his card marked".[27]

How much British exporters actually lost as a result of the boycott is hard to judge. The biggest loss as seen at the time was in respect of work on the new Kuala Lumpur airport: an Anglo-Japanese consortium involving BICC, GEC and Trafalgar House were told they would not be getting any further contracts. The construction firm, John Laing, was also affected. Figures of £2 billion of lost orders and 25,000 job losses were bandied about; but in the end the losses were probably only a fraction of this.

There was a further flurry of press coverage after the highly critical FAC report was published in July 1994. It was greeted with such headlines as: "Damning the Dam" (*Guardian*), "Pergautory" (*The Times*), "Bitter Truths of Pergau Scandal", "A Dam Cover-Up" (*Today*), "Tory Arms Deal Shame" (*The Star*), "Damning Verdict" (*Daily Mail*), "MOD's Dam Deal Shame" (*Daily Express*).

Press coverage returned with a final vengeance when the High Court declared the funding unlawful. The conservative tabloid, *Daily Express*, led its front page with the headline: "Judges attack Hurd's dam aid".[28] *The Sunday Times*, whilst perhaps somewhat biased after the pasting it had received from the Malaysians, from the British business community and behind the scenes from some in the Conservative Party, editorialised that "Pergau should stand as a lasting memorial to how governments should not go about their business. Mr Hurd, who until now has managed to maintain a dignified aloofness from the incompetence and sleaze engulfing most of the rest of the government, has been wounded by the High Court judgement".[29] The *Observer* columnist, Adrian Hamilton, wrote that Hurd, whilst "one of the cabinet's few – perhaps the only – palpably honourable men" should resign as an act of expiation just as Lord Carrington, his predecessor as Foreign Secretary in the early 1980s, had resigned over the Falklands invasion.[30]

There was criticism that neither he nor I had sought formal legal advice.[31] On the other hand, some who had been critical of ODA now said that my formal objection was vindicated by the court's decision (Riddell 1998, p. 93). This was not true in a strict sense. The court did not actually rule on whether I had been right to object on grounds of economy and efficiency. Instead, it had used the economic reasoning behind my objection to rule that the aid had been unlawfully provided. That said, the court's ruling did quieten the ODA's critics and give further strength to the view that ODA had been right to dig in its heels.

This was certainly the view of Ben Jackson who had played a major role in mounting the legal challenge on behalf of WMD. In an article in *The Independent* he wrote: "Such dams will not drain our aid again". He argued that the court decision set two vital precedents: it was a landmark legal challenge to the administration of the aid programme. And in declaring that WDM as a pressure group had the right to bring the case, the court had opened the way for groups of taxpayers to scrutinise and challenge the government's use of public funds more generally. He concluded:

> Set to cost five times more than all Britain's relief for the Kurds, the timing of the [Pergau] decision was a poignant underscoring of this grotesque travesty of aid priorities ... Mr Lankester's frank evidence ... sparked intense probing from campaigners, press and politicians, unmasking the commercial and political pressures on aid.[32]

13 ODA objections

Right or wrong?

ODA's objections to the funding of Pergau rested entirely on the view taken by ODA economists and engineers that, if Britain was to provide aid funds for the development of the power sector in Malaysia, there were far more efficient ways of doing so. In ODA's view, the choice of the Pergau project was seriously sub-optimal in economic terms compared with other potential projects for expanding Malaysia's electricity generating capacity.

The economics of Pergau had to be the overriding consideration for ODA in judging its merits. If the economics of the project were unsatisfactory, then by definition it was unsatisfactory from the point of view of furthering Malaysia's development. Since ODA's overriding mandate in all its client countries was to support development, funding Pergau was a poor use of aid funds. In theory, a negative assessment of the environmental aspects of the project could also have put a stop to it; but in contrast to many other dam projects, because of its small size and location, the environment was never likely to be a serious issue with Pergau.

As explained in an earlier chapter, under the ATP policy ODA was required to give at least some weight to the industrial and commercial benefits for Britain when considering ATP project proposals; and there is no doubt that over the preceding years, many ATP projects were approved where the development benefits were at best marginal, and which probably would not have been approved had the industrial and commercial considerations not been factored in.

With Pergau, however, the economics – and therefore the development case – were *so* bad that ODA's senior management, with the support of the ODA Minister, Lynda Chalker, took the view that – however strong the industrial and commercial case in its favour – they had no option but to oppose its funding. The fact that the projected funding was on such a large scale made it all the more difficult to brush the poor economics aside.

It is rare in government – or at least in British government – for economists to have the final say in whether or not to support a particular item of expenditure. Of course, in the case of Pergau, ultimately they did not – because ODA's objections were overridden by the Foreign Secretary and by the Prime Minister. But within ODA, it says something about the department's culture, and predominance of economics in its approach to development, that the ODA economists' view of Pergau – supported by ODA's engineers – was of such importance and could not be swept aside for the sake of political expedience.

Those within and outside government who felt that ODA "had got it wrong" were not much interested in the economics of Pergau. Their view mostly was that ODA should have subordinated its economic worries about the project to the industrial, commercial and wider political considerations. One line of attack was that ODA simply didn't understand industry and its needs (in fact, we understood its appetite for subsidies too well). Another was that, if the Malaysians thought Pergau was a good project – though as we will see, some Malaysians didn't – then who were officials in ODA to question its economics?

It was on economic grounds that ODA took its stand in objecting to Pergau. With so much of the subsequent controversy – political, commercial and legal – riding on ODA's objections, it seems only right to review with the benefit of hindsight whether ODA's economic analysis of the project was correct.

I am concerned here with the *ex ante* appraisal – that is to say, the assessment undertaken in the period leading up to the decision to fund the project. This is what really matters in judging whether, given the policy framework within which it operated, ODA was right to object to the project. In other words, given the information available – or potentially available – to them at the time, were ODA economists right to oppose the project? Or could a rational observer have taken a different view, given the same available data?

There is a separate question – certainly of interest but less relevant in judging whether ODA "got it right" in 1991 – of whether (or not), in light of the subsequent developments in Malaysia and in world energy markets, Pergau has proved the wasteful investment ODA economists judged it would be. If ODA economists had had perfect knowledge of the future, would their conclusions in 1990/91 still stand? I address this question later in the chapter.

Ex ante appraisal

ODA's appraisal of Pergau did not involve a one-off report. Rather, it took place over a number of stages. The appraisal started immediately after DTI submitted the project on the consortium's behalf in late 1988; this early work took the form of desk studies and culminated in the too late, and too short, mission to Malaysia in mid-March 1989 just before Mrs Thatcher made the initial offer to Dr Mahathir. Thereafter, the appraisal was updated intermittently, taking account of new evidence as it became available and exchanges with the World Bank and the planning staff at TNB. ODA was able to benefit from the findings of a World Bank power sector mission to Malaysia in late 1989, and also from its own review with DTI of Malaysia's power sector needs in September 1990. There was a final flurry of activity just prior to the advice that was submitted to ministers in February 1991 before the final decision was taken to back the project.[1]

There were three main aspects to the appraisal: technical, environmental and economic.

The *technical* assessments carried out by ODA engineering advisers fed into the economic appraisal and effectively were part and parcel of the latter insofar as the economists required information on what was technically feasible and best practice. ODA's engineers had several concerns. One of these was the uncertain geology. This was a risk factor that the consortium explained was one of the reasons for the escalated price between early and late March 1989. As it turned out, the geology was a good deal more difficult than had been assumed in the original feasibility study. Because of this and other unforeseen problems and design changes, there were completion delays – 21 months in the case of the first two 150 MW turbines and 12 months in the case of the second two – and the final cost exceeded the contract price.

Other technical concerns included:

- the fact that Pergau was located in the far north of the country, whereas the peaking demands that it was designed to satisfy were mainly in the south;
- weaknesses in the interconnecting transmission lines, which would have to take the power from Pergau to the south, and inadequate provision for their reinforcement (these concerns were subsequently addressed in the final project design, necessarily adding to its cost);
- the fact that a gas turbine plant could routinely be run for longer periods than hydro in the event of breakdowns at other plants. (This extra security, apparently not factored into the economic calculations, would have further added to the cost disadvantage of Pergau.)

On the *environmental* implications of the project, ODA received a detailed environmental impact statement prepared by the Malaysian authorities in early 1989. This suggested that, compared with many dam projects, including the much larger Bakun dam in eastern Malaysia, the issues were relatively slight. The area affected was quite small, no resettlement of population was needed, and there was already a history of logging in the area so that the additional disturbance would be limited. Given this assessment, ODA did not feel the need to undertake its own environmental assessment ahead of the initial aid offer in March 1989. In 1990 ODA commissioned a desk study from consultants, and following the receipt of their report in December of that year and with the final decision on the funding of the project impending, ODA finally commissioned a consultant to visit the project area.[2]

At the PAC hearing in 1994, I was challenged to explain why it took so long for anyone to commission this visit. I had no satisfactory answer. The delay was probably a product once again of hoping the project would "go away" and not wanting to disturb the commercial negotiations.

The consultant sent in an initial report in early February 1991, days before the final advice going up to ministers. He was not quite as sanguine as the Malaysians had been in their earlier assessment. He was concerned about the depletion of forest resources and soil erosion, encroachments into ecologically sensitive areas (with the possible presence of the rare and endangered Sumatran rhinoceros) and heightened risk of disease. But none of these problems were in his view insurmountable. He recommended various actions to mitigate the project's environmental impact. These were accepted by the Malaysian government, which undertook to prepare an environmental management plan for the area.

Friends of the Earth, in written evidence to the FAC, complained about the late and cursory nature of the ODA consultant's report.[3] They claimed that the environmental problems were rather greater than he had advised and that the suggested mitigation measures were inadequate. But compared with their concerns about dam projects elsewhere in the world, their critique on Pergau was not especially aggressive. (Their evidence was somewhat undermined by their admission in evidence to the FAC that it was based partly on a visit to the project area by an investigative journalist without any professional environmental qualification.)

Once the construction of Pergau began, ODA appointed an environmental consultant to undertake regular monitoring. His reports show that he had to do a fair amount of "chasing", but up to the end of 1994 when the monitoring ceased, he was satisfied that the various issues were being adequately dealt with.

I now turn to the *economic* appraisal that comprised the nub of the ODA's objections to Pergau. The key questions are whether the methodology was sound and whether, given the knowledge available to ODA at the time, the assumptions that were fed into their assessment were as good as they could have been.

The original feasibility study carried out by the Snowy Mountain Engineering Corporation (SMEC) had recommended a 600 MW power station on the Pergau for commissioning in 1995, assuming capital costs of £140 million at 1986 prices. The consortium's initial price (i.e. the one available to ODA at the time of the Thatcher/Mahathir meeting on 15 March 1989) was £316 million at current prices, an estimated 48 per cent increase in real terms compared with the SMEC assumption. The ODA economist Alan Whitworth, who visited Malaysia just before the Thatcher/Mahathir meeting, reported that – on SMEC's analysis – at a 20 per cent higher capital cost, Pergau would still be viable for early commissioning, but at a price anywhere near the consortium's price, its viability was at best uncertain. However, when two weeks later the consortium price escalated to nearly £400 million, Whitworth firmly advised that Pergau "was no longer a marginal project" and its early commissioning would involve a heavy cost penalty.

Through the remainder of 1989 and through 1990, ODA economists continued to update their knowledge of the Malaysian power sector and to refine the assumptions behind their analysis – with the assistance of the World Bank and the planners at TNB. Throughout this period and up to the time that I advised ministers in early February 1991, the economists' view remained that early implementation of Pergau would be a far more costly way of meeting Malaysia's growing power needs than installing additional gas-fired generation.

As already mentioned in Chapter 8, a World Bank team visited Malaysia in late 1989, at the request of the Economic Planning Unit in Dr Mahathir's office, to advise on power generation priorities. It concluded that, at a capital cost of RM 1.2 billion (£273 million) at 1989 prices, the cost penalty from the early commissioning of Pergau would be approximately £90 million compared with alternative investment options. Superficially, at the consortium's offer price of around £400 million, the cost penalty would be that much higher. However, it later emerged this price was to include £92 million for future cost escalation.

In their analyses, ODA economists drew on the same standard methodology used by power system planners worldwide, including the World Bank and the TNB planners. This methodology is described in greater detail in Appendix II. Basically, for a given projection of electricity demand, it produces a least cost system of power generation looking ahead over a number of years. This will include different types of power station (thermal, hydro, etc.), their size, location and phasing. Through computer modelling, the planner is able to compare the costs of different combinations of candidate power plants so as to deliver a least cost, ideal expansion plan. Future capital and operating costs are expressed in terms of their "present value" by applying an appropriate discount rate so that different combinations of immediate and future fixed and variable costs can be compared on the same basis. The key variables that go into the modelling are:

- forecast of electricity demand, both in total and at peak, over the planning period;
- estimated capital costs of candidate generating plants;
- estimated operating costs, especially fuel costs, of both existing and candidate plants;
- estimated costs of reinforcing and expanding the transmission system to accommodate demand growth and the connection of increments in generating capacity.

Typically, hydroelectric stations have high capital costs and low operating costs; thermal stations (i.e. those that burn a fuel – gas, coal or oil to raise steam to turn the turbines that drive an electrical generator) have lower capital costs but considerably higher running costs. The choice between hydro and thermal plant essentially comes down to the capital cost of the plant, the cost of capital, the cost of fuel and the ratio of actual electricity generation to maximum potential output (known as the "capacity factor"). Hydro typically has a much lower "capacity factor" than thermal. This is because, as in the case of Pergau, the amount of water in the reservoir is often only enough to allow electricity to be generated for a few hours a day over the year. In other words, the ability of hydroelectric plants to generate is limited not by their installed capacity in MW as in a thermal plant, but by the amount of water the associated reservoir can hold.

Other things being equal, the lower the economic cost of fossil fuel, the more likely it is that thermal plant will be favoured over hydro. If capital is cheap and fossil fuels are expensive – and if the reservoir can hold plenty of water to drive the turbines for a significant part of the year – then the economic case for hydro will be that much stronger. A crucial factor also is the choice of discount rate. A low discount rate favours technologies such as hydro, which involve high initial investment and low operating costs; a high discount rate will favour technologies such as gas turbines that have relatively low initial investment costs and higher operating costs.

ODA economists were familiar with the computerised planning model used by TNB's planners and, like the World Bank, had confidence in their ability to use it to generate an optimal power plan for Malaysia. They were also reasonably knowledgeable, from their work on other power projects in Malaysia, about the Malaysian power system. Their appraisal work therefore focused on the main assumptions – for electricity demand, fuel prices and the capital and operating costs of the various candidate plants – which the TNB planners were using in their model.

Pergau was designed to be a peaking station – that is to say, operating a few hours a day to meet peak demand. For the near term, a gas-fired plant for peaking was clearly a less costly option than hydro, given the availability of gas locally; but as Malaysia's own gas reserves began to run down, hydro was likely to become increasingly competitive compared with gas to provide peaking energy. When ODA's economists had first looked at Pergau in 1988 and early 1989, they had taken the view that it wasn't a question of whether Pergau could be justified, but when. Within the range of likely construction prices, at some point Pergau would be required for commissioning as part of peninsular Malaysia's least cost system. The problem was that the capital costs of Pergau very soon escalated, with the result that, at best, its construction needed to be delayed by a number of years and if its construction was advanced to the 1990s, there would be a large cost penalty involved compared with the cheaper gas turbine alternative.

Robin Biggam, the then chairman of BICC, Balfour Beatty's parent company, told the Foreign Affairs Committee that Pergau was "good value for money in terms of capital cost per kilowatt". In a supplementary note, he added that the capital cost of Pergau, "at about \$1,000/kilowatt, as a fixed price contract, falls very much at the bottom end of the range of world prices".[4] This was factually correct: in terms of capital cost per kW of installed capacity, it was indeed at the lower end of the range. What he omitted to tell the committee was that in terms of the cost of electricity generated (per kWh), the capital cost was far from low by international standards. This was because Pergau was designed with a "capacity factor" of only 10 per cent. There wasn't enough water in the reservoir or from the adjoining catchments to allow the turbines to operate more than two to three hours a day. By contrast, the average "capacity factor" for hydro-stations worldwide is of the order of 40 per cent. Adjusting for its low "capacity factor" – which was at the low end even for a power station intended for peaking – would have put Pergau nearer the top end of international prices in terms of capital cost per kWh. In short, for the energy it was going to produce, Pergau was an expensive project by international standards.

But this in itself – bearing in mind that peaking electricity is typically more costly (and more valuable) than base-load power in all power systems – would not necessarily have ruled Pergau out on economic grounds. The question was: could the same amount of peaking energy be produced in Malaysia more cheaply? The answer, for the TNB planners and for the World Bank and ODA economists, was a resounding "Yes" on account of the availability of cheap Malaysian gas.

Malaysia had huge reserves of off-shore gas, some of it offshore peninsular Malaysia and in even larger quantities offshore eastern Malaysia (Sarawak and Sabah). Production from the latter fields enabled Malaysia by the mid-2000s to become the second largest exporter of liquefied natural gas (LNG) in the world. The gas offshore peninsular Malaysia at the time of the Pergau appraisal was piped onshore exclusively for Malaysian domestic use. There were no gas liquefaction facilities that could have enabled it to be exported as LNG, nor were any planned; and the onshore peninsular pipeline did not extend beyond Malaysia's frontiers. Consequently, there were only two foreseeable options for offshore peninsular gas: either pipe it onshore for electricity generation and other domestic use or leave it in the ground for future use.

To decide whether to use this gas now for electricity generation, or instead opt for other fuels such as hydro or coal, required the planners to determine an economic value for the gas. When a product is freely imported or exported, its economic value (or opportunity cost) is the price the country pays or is paid for it. But in the case of peninsular Malaysia in the late 1980s when the TNB planners were doing their modelling, there were neither exports nor imports of gas either currently or in prospect against which they could establish an appropriate valuation; and they assumed that, as and when indigenous gas supplies eventually peaked, peninsular Malaysia would rely on other fuels – principally imported coal and hydro. They therefore applied the rather more complicated and uncertain procedure of valuing offshore peninsular gas at its cost of extraction and delivery plus a "depletion premium". (The depletion premium concept is explained in Appendix II: it essentially ensures that, as finite reserves of indigenous gas are progressively depleted, the cost of replacing indigenous gas with an alternative fuel at some future date is factored into its current valuation.)

Even with the addition of a depletion premium, peninsular Malaysia's off-shore gas looked extremely cheap. The TNB planners used projections agreed with the World Bank. These projections assumed that the economic value or cost of peninsular Malaysian gas in 1990 in terms of energy content was about one-third that of oil and two-thirds that of coal. The value of indigenous gas was projected to rise by two and half per cent a year in real terms until it converged with the price of coal in 2015 when the supply of indigenous gas was assumed to plateau. The price gap between Malaysian gas and internationally traded oil was assumed to widen. On these projections, gas-fired generation would be the cheapest amongst the thermal options for Malaysia for many years to come, and – given the estimated capital costs of various prospective hydro plants – cheaper than hydro too for many years to come.

The ODA economists' appraisal of the case for Pergau culminated with the ODA/DTI mission that visited Malaysia in September 1990.[5] As was so typical of the whole Pergau saga, the mission was not sent specifically to appraise Pergau. That would have looked like too much of a challenge to the commercial negotiations, which were at that point coming to a head. Instead, the mission's terms of reference were to review the power sector as a whole with a view to indentifying the scope for possible UK assistance for the sector. The terms of reference contained no specific mention of Pergau. ODA was genuinely hoping that the mission would identify new projects in the power sector for ATP financing that were economically sound and for which financing could be offered in place of Pergau. But it also provided an important opportunity to conduct a final review of the arguments for and against Pergau. The mission worked closely with the TNB planning team, and its report was effectively the basis for the ODA's final advice on the project. The mission was led by Dick Jones, ODA's most senior power engineer.

The mission's report described the results of the most up-to-date TNB model run. Most worryingly, Pergau did not appear at all in the least cost development plan for new projects in the 1990s. For most of the 1990s, the plan indicated dependence entirely on new open-cycle gas turbine (OCGT) or combined-cycle gas turbine (CCGT) plants.[6] With the economic cost of gas projected to rise, the model showed hydro becoming gradually more competitive, and therefore hydro plants began to appear in the plan for later years.

Pergau did not appear in the TNB model for commissioning until 2005. The penalty for bringing Pergau forward for completion in 1997 was reported by TNB to be about RM 400 million (£91 million) at 1990 prices (a similar penalty to that estimated by the World Bank a year earlier). TNB's estimate, however, assumed a contract price of RM 1,250 million at 1990 prices, which was RM 170 million (£37 million) below the actual contract price (RM 1,420 million excluding provision for price escalation) that was in the course of being agreed with the consortium. With the higher contract price factored in, the cost penalty was well in excess of £100 million; and it was on this basis that ministers were variously advised that the extra cost of Pergau would be about £100 million.

The timing of the mission's visit was unfortunate because the model run referred to above, with its estimate of the £91 million cost penalty for Pergau, was already somewhat out of date. TNB were at that moment in September

1990 working on a new plan based on a revised forecast of electricity demand. But the new demand forecast had yet to be officially agreed, and results from the new modelling were not available to the mission.

However, the mission was shown the revised demand forecast that was likely to be adopted. The new forecast for peak load showed a 9.3 per cent average annual increase for the period 1990 to 2005 – a considerable uplift on the existing official forecast of 7.6 per cent. The effect was to increase peak load in 2005 by 3,000 MW – an increase the equivalent of five plants with the generating capacity of Pergau.

The mission was doubtful about this new forecast. According to their report, they thought it was over-influenced by the extremely rapid growth in demand over the previous two or three years, which had coincided with an acceleration in Malaysia's economic growth; and they were unsure whether the assumed continued rapid growth of GDP was realistic. The mission did not attempt to estimate the effect that the higher demand forecast, if it materialised, might have on the economics of Pergau. We return to this below.

Strange as it may seem in these more "open" times, neither the consortium nor their advisers were given access to the mission's report. But they were aware of some of the assumptions behind the report's findings on Pergau. Then and later, they raised several objections.

First of all, they argued that the analysis was biased against Pergau because of the use of a 10 per cent discount rate for comparing the various types of plant. It would have been more appropriate to have used a 5 per cent rate, so they argued.

ODA economists dismissed this out of hand; 10 per cent was the rate recommended by the World Bank and favoured by TNB, and it was the rate that was commonly used for evaluating power plant options in many developing countries. The consortium's advisers were on weak ground in suggesting that a lower rate than 10 per cent should be used specially for evaluating hydro investments: whatever was the appropriate discount rate for the Malaysian economy should be applied to all investment proposals irrespective of the technology or sector. Nonetheless, as Appendix II explains, ODA should not have been quite so dismissive: there *was* a case for using a lower discount rate alongside the 10 per cent.

The choice of discount rate depends partly on the methodology used. The 10 per cent assumption was based on the social opportunity cost of capital – the rate of return that could be achieved on alternative, well-chosen investments. The justification for this approach was that if the discount rate used was lower than the opportunity cost of capital, it would be likely to lead to investments yielding less than the best returns available elsewhere in the economy. The rate of return generally available on well-chosen investments in Malaysia was at least as high as 10 per cent: hence the need for a 10 per cent discount rate.

There was an alternative methodology, however, based on social time preference – the premium that society places on consuming resources now rather than in the future. This has a more solid basis in the theoretical literature but is hard to estimate. After many years of debate, it is the methodology that the British Treasury adopted for calculating the discount rate to be applied in public sector project evaluation. Typically, the discount rate so calculated is lower than with the opportunity cost of capital approach. We estimate that in 1990 the discount rate in Malaysia based on social time preference might have been approximately 7.5 per cent.

In any event, it would have been useful for ODA – and indeed the World Bank and TNB – to have tested the case for Pergau against more than one discount rate. Given that cost–benefit analysis is an inexact science subject to much uncertainty depending on the assumptions made, this could have helped to confirm (or otherwise) the strength of the case against Pergau. Other agencies like the International Energy Agency routinely evaluated alternative technologies using a range of discount rates. ODA could and should have done the same.

To provide an idea of how much difference it would have made, in Appendix II we have done our own rough calculation. This shows that, on the other assumptions used by TNB regarding fuel prices and other costs, the cost of generating Pergau's output of electricity over a 50 year period would have been cheaper by £71 million on a net present value basis if a combined-cycle gas turbine plant had been built instead. This is on the assumption of a 10 per cent discount rate. If a 7.5 per cent discount rate had been used, the cost advantage of CCGTs would have been £57 million. In short, with a lower discount rate of 7.5 per cent, gas turbines would still have looked more cost-effective by a considerable margin.

A second argument advanced against the ODA's preference for gas-fired plant over Pergau was that the latter was inherently preferable for meeting peak demand. However, there is no a priori reason for such a preference: it all depends on comparative costs, and these would have been captured in the TNB model. There are plenty of examples of hydro being used quite satis-factorily to meet peak demand. But from a technical standpoint, gas turbines are no less suited for peaking duty: they are flexible, reliable and can be started quickly when the need arises.

The consortium also suggested that Pergau was preferable to a gas-fired plant on environmental grounds. No attempt had been made by TNB, ODA or anyone else to compare in any systematic way the social costs of the environmental impact of Pergau with the social costs of the carbon emissions from gas turbines. Friends of the Earth in their evidence to the FAC actually claimed that gas turbines were better environmentally. The promoters of Pergau in Britain and in Malaysia claimed the reverse – and probably cor-rectly so. But it was early days for quantifying the cost of carbon emissions and neither ODA nor anyone else attempted it in evaluating the alternatives to Pergau. Gas turbines were relatively minor polluters compared with coal and oil, and the social costs were unlikely to be sufficient to tilt the argument in favour of Pergau – or so the ODA economists implicitly believed. We return to this below.

At the FAC hearings in 1994, it was further suggested that the economic analysis was biased against Pergau because it assumed that the project would have a life of only 35 years – whereas hydro projects typically had a life of 50 years or more. But this was a simple mistake in the NAO report. In fact, the NAO were wrong. The TNB model on which ODA relied had explicitly assumed a 50 year life for Pergau.

Lastly, the consortium argued that ODA was too conservative on the likely growth of electricity demand in Malaysia. Here, they were on stronger ground, and on the face of it this should have improved the case in favour of the early commissioning of Pergau.

But this was not to be. In late January 1991, very shortly before the final ministerial meetings to decide whether or not to approve the funding, ODA received from TNB an up-to-date sensitivity analysis that incorporated the updated demand forecast, now officially endorsed by TNB and the Malaysian government. It also incorporated a contract price close to that about to be agreed between TNB and the consortium. The analysis showed that, far from bringing Pergau forward in time, it should be put back even further – to 2008.

On the other hand, this late analysis indicated a somewhat lower cost penalty if Pergau were to be commissioned in 1996 instead of 2008 – £78 million compared with £91 million in TNB's earlier model run. However, this still meant that Pergau was a very poor investment compared with alternative gas turbines.

Ex post evaluation

Coming now to the second question: is it possible to say whether, in the light of *actual* developments since 1991 in Malaysia, in world energy markets and in our knowledge of environmental issues, the ODA appraisal was broadly correct? Or was Malaysia right from an economic and social point of view to implement Pergau when it did even though, excluding the benefit of the ODA subsidy, the TNB planners and ODA economists expected that doing so would mean incurring a substantial cost burden? On account of unforeseeable events, or simply good luck, was it right to build Pergau in the 1990s after all?

The technical issues, particularly over the geology, which bothered ODA's power engineers, were eventually dealt with, albeit at significant extra cost; and transmitting Pergau's electricity to meet peaking demand where it is mainly located – in the south of the country – has not proved an issue.

Plant performance during the first three years of Pergau's operation was poor, with high unplanned outage rates and low availability. This was due mainly to equipment failures. Once these were corrected, operational performance became satisfactory. The power station has reliably generated electricity and dealt with peaking power demands pretty much to plan. It has also at times been a useful backup when there were unforeseen breakdowns at thermal stations.

Likewise, the rather minor local environmental issues at the beginning were effectively addressed; and Pergau is rare amongst dams in respect of which environmental groups appear to be generally satisfied.

The main question therefore turns on whether the economics of the project turned out better or worse than expected.

We have already seen that the Malaysian government, if not the TNB planners, viewed the economics of the project through a rather different lens compared with ODA. This was because the principal players, especially Dr Mahathir and his Energy Minister, Samy Vellu, regarded the aid from ODA as a subsidy that enabled the scheme to become economic, whereas the ODA approach was to determine whether the project made economic sense without any subsidy. In this evaluation, we stick to the ODA and TNB planners' approach of ignoring the subsidy.

For the purpose of *ex post* evaluation, we need to check whether there were significant variations from the originally projected costs and benefits. We take as the base case the TNB analysis that was forwarded to ODA in January 1991. In this, the cost penalty for Pergau was £78 million. It assumes a 10 per cent discount rate. We estimate that, with a 7.5 per cent discount rate, the same analysis would have produced a cost penalty of £60 million.

Three key developments over the past 20 years in the Malaysian power sector affect the results. The first is that electricity demand did not grow as rapidly as projected and too much new generating capacity was built – with the result that by 2010 there was a relatively extravagant, and costly, reserve margin of 40 per cent in the system. Pergau contributed to this excess expansion. Second, supplies of gas from offshore peninsular Malaysia peaked sooner than expected – in 2008 rather than 2015 – and by 2011 the power sector was facing severe shortages. Malaysia will be importing significant quantities of LNG from the Middle East by 2013, and TNB and other electricity producers will almost certainly be facing higher gas prices than was assumed in 1991. Third, Malaysia was a signatory to the 1992 UN Framework Convention on Climate Change, and in 2002 it ratified the Kyoto Protocol. In 2009, it announced a voluntary commitment to reduce the intensity of greenhouse gas emissions per unit of GDP by 40 per cent by 2020, compared with 2005. From the point of view of Malaysia and the world community, we need to factor in the social cost of the additional carbon emissions if gas-fired plant had been built instead of Pergau.

In Appendix II we describe in detail how we have estimated the effect of these three factors on the economics of Pergau *ex post*. Our estimates are summarised below. Figures are all at 1990 prices as in the original appraisal. Consistent with our view that the appraisal should have used more than one discount rate, the adjustments for capital cost overrun, lower electricity demand and higher gas prices incorporate discount rates of 10 per cent and 7.5 per cent (shown in brackets). For carbon emissions, we use just the one 7.5 per cent discount rate.

The social cost of carbon emissions is extremely difficult to estimate and there is a wide range of estimates available. For calculating the effect of the carbon emissions from alternative gas turbine plant, we have instead used carbon values based on marginal abatement costs as estimated by the UK Department of

Energy and Climate Change and by Malaysia's Ministry of Energy, Green Technology and Water. They produce very similar results.

Valuing peninsular Malaysia's gas *ex post* is also not straightforward, and we have done it on two bases – one applying the depletion premium methodology mentioned earlier and the other applying international prices. The estimates below show a range for extra fuel costs that reflect these two approaches.

The following is a summary of our *ex post* adjustments (plus means worse for Pergau, minus means better).

- Higher capital cost: plus £8 million (£9 million).
- Lower electricity demand: plus £6 million (£5 million)
- Higher gas cost: minus £20–42 million (£38–68 million).
- Carbon emissions: minus (£19 million).

The total net effect of these *ex post* adjustments is as follows:

- If we assume a 10 per cent discount rate for the first three items, the cost penalty for Pergau reduces from £78 million to £53 million with the lower valuation of gas, and to £31 million with the higher valuation of gas.
- If we assume a 7.5 per cent discount rate, the cost penalty for Pergau reduces from £60 million to £17 million with the lower gas valuation, and switches to a £13 million cost benefit with the higher gas valuation.

These estimates are necessarily approximate because of the uncertainty about several of the underlying assumptions, and they encompass a range of over £60 million. If anything, they are likely to overstate the worsening of CCGT plant's competitiveness because we have not included anything in our analysis for the possible "displacement" savings from CCGTs releasing less efficient, existing OCGTs for peaking duty. Such displacement would moderate the NPV cost addition for CCGTs in respect of both fuel and carbon emissions.

Nonetheless, there is one reasonably firm conclusion that we can draw from the analysis. This is that, with hindsight, the cost penalty for Pergau was significantly less than that indicated in the *ex ante* estimates in 1990/91.

It is not possible to say with absolute certainty whether in retrospect Pergau turned out to be a worse investment than gas turbines. After making the adjustments for higher gas prices and the social cost of carbon emissions, whether Pergau was more or less costly than CCGTs appears to turn on the choice of discount rate. If we follow ODA and TNB analysts and apply a 10 per cent discount rate, Pergau still looks in retrospect seriously uneconomic.

Applying a 7.5 per cent discount rate, with the lower of the two gas valuations, gas turbines remain the preferred choice. But with the higher of the two gas valuations, Pergau becomes by a small margin the preferred option over gas turbines.

However, to repeat, our estimates probably overstate the deterioration in gas turbines' competitiveness. Taking this into account and looking at the estimates in the round, the balance of probability is that – even with the knowledge we now have – gas turbines would still have been a better investment than Pergau.

Thus in retrospect, Pergau has almost certainly turned out to be significantly less costly than British ministers were led to believe it would be in comparison with other options for producing the same amount of energy. Nonetheless, presented *ex ante* with the *ex post* adjustments enumerated above and ignoring the ODA subsidy, a rational policy maker in 1990/91 would still probably have opted for gas turbines as the more economic choice.

The reasons why Pergau turned out less costly than anticipated is that it was able to generate electricity without causing carbon emissions – the benefit of which was not factored into the 1990/91 analysis; because the valuation of peninsular Malaysia's gas turned out to be an under-estimate; and because the 10 per cent discount rate chosen by both TNB and ODA for evaluating investments in the Malaysian power sector may have been on the high side.

From Malaysia's point of view, the subsidy provided by ODA more than compensated for the *ex ante*, and whatever *ex post*, cost penalties that were incurred. From the point of view of TNB, once the company was assured of receiving the subsidy, the deal was a very good one indeed. And as of today, with the capital costs long ago incurred, and the plant operating efficiently from a technical point of view and with low operating costs, Pergau is a useful and cost-effective component of the Malaysian power generation system. Its value will increase in the years ahead if the cost of fossil fuels continues to rise.

Hindsight, however, is a wonderful thing. If we had known back in 1990 what we know now about climate change and its likely associated costs, and if we had known that peninsular Malaysia's gas would start to run down sooner than forecast, the case against Pergau would not have been so self-evidently powerful. But the project would still probably have failed the test of development soundness.

That said, ODA economists should have paid more attention to the uncertainties surrounding the analysis – it is ironic that our *ex post* results appear to reveal more uncertainty than did the *ex ante* appraisal – and perhaps given more weight to Dr Mahathir's desire for a more diversified energy sector as a hedge against unforeseen developments. As regards the latter, however, it is noteworthy that Pergau was deemed the fifth in line amongst hydro projects in TNB's long-term plans at the time (see Table 4).

Superficially, it may seem a small thing that Malaysia commissioned a particular power station in 1997 when, according to economic rationale as perceived at the time, it should have been built a decade or so later. Politicians in Britain and Malaysia might well ask: what was all the fuss about, especially as it is possible in retrospect that it was not such a bad investment after all? This is a fair question. One answer is that, if Malaysia wished to construct Pergau in the 1990s, there was nothing to stop it from doing so out of its own resources. For all the criticism that ODA was "colonialist" in telling Malaysia what it should do, there was never any question of ODA advising Malaysia what it should do with its own money. Malaysia was not short of finance, but it needed the British subsidy so that the project would *become* economic. If it was an uneconomic project without British aid – as both ODA and the Malaysian side believed it to be – then ODA was right to oppose its funding from the aid budget. And in view of the very large estimate of the cost penalty that would be involved, ODA really had no option but to oppose it vigorously. The pity is that this opposition was not made clearer at any earlier stage.

Finally, if one of the purposes of the aid was to protect British jobs, it was an extremely costly exercise. On fairly conservative assumptions, the subsidy received by the British contractors amounted to over £16,000 per man-year of employment in Britain.

14 A fairish nightmare

The British government used its aid budget to fund the Pergau hydro-electric scheme for reasons other than sound development: the real purpose was to secure Britain's commercial and political interests in Malaysia, including giving a major boost to defence exports and providing orders for civil contractors. The project was grossly uneconomic as judged at the time by ODA, the World Bank and even Malaysia's own power planners. The Malaysian government nonetheless wanted the project because of the subsidy provided from the ODA budget, and because Dr Mahathir wanted a major project for backward Kelantan state and to diversify Malaysia's energy sources. Unsubstantiated allegations of bribery in the British media infuriated him and caused a temporary rupture in trade relations. The decision to fund the project from the aid budget was eventually found to be unlawful.

As far as the British government was concerned, this all amounted to a serious failure of governance. Partly, it was down to pure muddle and bad luck. Mainly, it was down to saying one thing and doing another – linking aid to arms sales and offering aid for a grossly uneconomic project when it was declared policy that we would do neither. Britain's hitherto solid reputation as an aid donor was seriously undermined, and the government suffered reputational damage for the way in which it was seen to have mishandled the whole issue. All in all, as Douglas Hurd told his biographer, the Pergau affair was a "fairish nightmare" (Stuart 2008).

ODA made a number of mistakes and miscalculations. We failed to spot the legal risks or take formal legal advice; and we could have played a better hand more generally. Key examples were failing to take a tougher stand in the early stages, and failing to grasp the nettle as it became increasingly clear that the project fell far below normal standards of economic soundness.

Other departments and their ministers made errors and miscalculations too: most notable was the signing by Defence Secretary George Younger of the Defence Protocol linking civil aid with defence sales. But fundamentally, the bad outcome was due to a clash of competing departmental agendas, aided and abetted by different motivations and attitudes on the part of various key officials and ministers. The situation was made much worse by the failure on the part of some officials to follow proper procedures for inter-departmental consultation.

ODA was the guardian of the official policy on aid but it was a weak department in terms of Whitehall politics, its minister lacked the status of a cabinet minister and it had a culture that was not well suited to fighting Whitehall battles. Although supported by the Treasury, it was unable to stand up to the combined pressures from DTI, MOD, the FCO and the Prime Minister's Office.

For the politicians, the mistaken language linking aid with arms sales and the funding of an unsatisfactory aid project might each have been manageable if it had been just one of them. It was the combination of the two together that made them politically lethal.

It is sometimes argued that there can be a conflict in the British system between civil servants providing robust, objective advice to ministers, and their executing the wishes of ministers if their advice has been rejected (Barker and Wilson, 1997).[1] In regard to Pergau, this problem did not arise. Civil servants in ODA tendered their advice; they recognised that, notwithstanding their view that the funding of Pergau was a bad proposition, it was for ministers to decide; and when the ministerial decision went against them, they implemented the decision without demur. Although I insisted on a ministerial instruction before authorising the expenditure, there was never any question of trying to block the execution of the decision, nor was there any attempt by ODA officials to engage the support of outside lobby groups prior to the decision. ODA staff monitored progress of the project diligently until ODA felt bound to cease having anything to do with it after the court ruling. Thus, the minister/civil servant relationship worked as it was supposed to do.

At a personal level, the origin of the failure rested to a considerable extent with Mrs Thatcher. She too readily entered into a moral commitment to her Malaysian counterpart that ODA would support the project before it had been properly assessed, and she allowed the impression to prevail – when other ministers were trying to do the opposite – that it was legitimate for aid to be entangled with defence equipment sales. According to at least one of her senior ministerial colleagues, she was complicit in linking the aid specifically for Pergau with the defence equipment export deal.

The government was subject to a great deal of pressure from the British companies bidding for the project. Some of them had a dual interest: they wanted the Pergau business, but they also regarded the aid for Pergau as vital if they were to win contracts under the defence package. They exaggerated the employment benefits from winning the contract, and under-played the costs.

The development NGOs were no match for the corporate lobbyists. Their job was made a lot more difficult by the fact that the companies were privy to the proposals from the start whereas the NGOs were not. But they got their own back when WDM took the government to court and won. The court's judgement was – and continues to be – controversial amongst leading lawyers; yet it pleased not only the development community but also those who favoured greater "judicial activism" in providing a check on dubious decision making by government.

We have seen how political accountability was ineffectual *before* either of the two critical events – the linking of aid and arms sales, or the decision to fund Pergau. By contrast, in Diana Woodhouse's words, the legal challenge "demonstrated the effectiveness of legal, as opposed to political, action in securing a change in government policy or action" (Woodhouse 1997, p. 130). Political accountability *ex post* worked quite well. Unlike the legal challenge, it didn't bring about an immediate change in policy; but it succeeded in nailing the government for the mistakes it had made and over the longer term helped to bring about reforms in the aid programme.

Some positive lessons were learnt from the debacle. It led to a rethink of aid policy in both main political parties. In retrospect, Pergau came be seen as a turning point when British aid moved away from being so closely geared to British commercial interests and moved towards becoming today possibly the most highly respected amongst all the donors with a much strengthened focus on poverty alleviation.

John Major's Conservative government tightened up the ATP scheme with a view to avoiding a repetition of Pergau. It became more widely recognised that the scheme was unsatisfactory from a development standpoint and did little that was genuinely positive for British industry. The scheme was abolished by the incoming Labour government in 1997. In 2000 British aid was completely untied, and in 2002 legislation came into force with the new and very important requirement that aid has to contribute to poverty reduction. Serving DFID officials regard this as the key public policy dividend arising from Pergau.

The court ruling on Pergau would make ministers much more careful in future about ensuring that the principal purpose of each and every aid intervention was within the letter and the spirit of the enabling legislation. The inability of the ODA to stand up for itself in the case of Pergau also lent weight to the view that Britain's aid programme would be better protected if it were once again an autonomous government department with its own minister in cabinet – a change that the incoming Labour government in 1997 made.

Another benefit was the improved accountability arrangements to Parliament. In future, if a permanent secretary formally dissented from an expenditure proposal and insisted on a ministerial instruction, this would always be notified to the Public Accounts Committee immediately – and not just recorded on a file to be discovered months or years later by the National Audit Office or not at all. Furthermore, whereas previously permanent secretaries had shied away from asking for a ministerial instruction when they felt unable to take personal responsibility for a particular spending decision, after the Pergau controversy it became much more common. As a result, greater clarity was brought into exactly where responsibility and accountability for controversial spending decisions lay.

Individual politicians suffered reputational damage. When the main story came out in early 1994, Mrs Thatcher was already over three years gone from office; yet for her critics, her involvement in the affair was another blackish mark; and even some of her more stalwart admirers were surprised she had been so cavalier in her dealings.

To his credit, George Younger conceded full blame for the Defence Protocol when he could have shifted some of it onto others; but he had left the government as far back as 1989 to go into business (in 1990 he became chairman of the Royal Bank of Scotland), and his role in the affair was no longer of much public interest.

The biggest loser in terms of reputation was Foreign Secretary Douglas Hurd. When the court ruled against the government, he seriously considered resigning. For all his somewhat lofty and detached attitude to aid in general and even to the Pergau issue itself, he was to a significant extent unlucky. He had no involvement in the early stages of the saga when Mrs Thatcher made the initial offer, nor was he involved at all in the Defence Protocol. He inherited a very difficult hand. Starting from his position that a pledge given by a former Prime Minister had to be honoured, he felt he had no option but to decide in favour of Pergau. Had he had better advice or had more time to consider the issue in detail (the decision point was less than two weeks before the 1991 Iraq war), he might have better recognised the risks. When he took the decision, no one had told him about the Defence Protocol and the dangers it posed if made public: it was only much later after the NAO reported that he learnt about it. He also took the rap over the court ruling, unexpected though it was. Had he been advised that there was a significant risk of illegality, he might well have backed off or sought an alternative way of fulfilling Mrs Thatcher's pledge than through the aid budget – as indeed he had to in the light of the court ruling. Instead, he was accused in the press of playing fast with the law.

The experience of Britain's High Commissioner in Malaysia, Nicholas Spreckley, belied the popular notion that only politicians take the rap for policy mistakes. He was severely, and perhaps unfairly in all the circumstances, criticised by the Foreign Affairs Committee for his role in the signing of the Defence Protocol. It appears he had no warning from London – precisely because the MOD had kept the issue to itself – that an aid link might be requested; and the judgement that he and Younger reached in the heat of negotiations – that the wording did not amount to a commitment – was at least arguable. A more forceful and (in Geoffrey Howe's words) less "laconic" individual might have insisted on consulting the FCO in London first. But for a middle-ranking diplomat to stand up to a visiting Cabinet Minister and his specialist entourage is not as easy as some people might imagine. When it came to dealing with Pergau, though his personal sympathies were clearly more with the commercial than the aid policy interest, he found himself caught between the warring departments in Whitehall. Spreckley took early retirement in 1992 after his Malaysia posting, but was called back in 1994 to give evidence to the Foreign Affairs Committee. He took the Committee's criticism of his conduct – and that by some of his superiors in the FCO – very badly, believing that he had acted in the public interest.[2]

Not everyone suffered. The UK's defence equipment exporters were almost certainly indirect beneficiaries. They achieved very large orders from Malaysia in the years following the signing of the Defence Protocol and Mrs Thatcher's offer of aid for Pergau. Over the period 1989–93, British industry signed defence equipment contracts with Malaysia worth some £1.3 billion.[3] If Hurd and Major had not confirmed the aid offer, it is more than likely that this level of contracts would not have been achieved.

The British civil contractors and their employees were also on the face of it beneficiaries. The subsidy per man-year – over £16,000 – was high by any standards. On the other hand, we don't know what would have been the counter-factual. If the aid had gone instead for other power plants in Malaysia, as ODA and eventually DTI suggested that it could have done, they could have obtained orders from these. In addition, some of the companies later claimed that – because of cost overruns, delays and liquidated damages – they made little or no profit from the project. Criticism of the quality of some of the work cannot have enhanced the reputation of the companies concerned.

But British businesses lost out as a result of Malaysia's cancellation of new public sector contracts in the wake of the bribery stories in early 1994. Even after trade relations were restored, the Malaysian government was probably more wary of doing business with Britain.

As for the Malaysians, they got the power station that their leader so badly wanted. It was not the optimal choice in terms of cost: they would have done better, from the point of view of least cost, to concentrate on gas turbines. But Britain in effect paid for the extra cost through the aid subsidy, which, contrary to normal aid practice, was passed on to the electricity company, TNB. In other words, they were able to build an expensive power station without the company or Malaysian consumers having to bear the extra cost.

Based on the knowledge available in early 1991, ODA was right to oppose Pergau on economic grounds. Gas-fired electricity generation appeared a much cheaper option. With the benefit of hindsight, the case against Pergau is less clear-cut. Because relative fuel prices turned out differently and because of the notional costs now attached to carbon emissions, the cost penalty incurred through the construction of Pergau in the 1990s rather than a decade later has almost certainly been significantly less than the £100 million estimate given to ministers in 1991.

Given the state of knowledge at the time, the overall conclusion remains that some bad decisions were taken that led to a misuse of British aid, compromised the hitherto good reputation of Britain as an aid donor, caused considerable political upset for the government and for at least one of its leading members, and damaged Britain's political and commercial relations with Malaysia.

It is impossible to say that something like this will never happen again with British aid. The debacle over Pergau is sufficiently in the folk-memory amongst current ministers and officials that for the time being it is unlikely. For all that, it will require continuing diligence and self-discipline and parliamentary oversight, as well as consensus across government, to make sure that aid is not again diverted from its fundamental purpose – economic development and the alleviation of poverty. If this book has served one useful purpose, it will have been to warn of the dangers if these conditions are absent. For the sake of the tens of millions of very poor people whom Britain's rising aid budget is designed to help, it will be a sad day if a sizeable chunk of it is once again diverted for political and commercial purposes as it was in the case of Pergau.

Appendix I

Pergau chronology

1988

24 March
: Secretary of State for Defence, George Younger, and Malaysian Minister of Defence sign Protocol on Malaysia's defence procurement, including reference to civil aid.

28 June
: George Younger writes to Malaysian Finance Minister that civil aid cannot be linked with defence sales.
British High Commissioner in Malaysia writes to Malaysian Finance Minister that ATP grants and ECGD cover of up to £200 million will be available for civil projects.

8 August
: Mrs Thatcher writes to Dr Mahathir confirming £70 million of grant aid plus £130 million of ECGD cover for civil projects.

27 September
: Mrs Thatcher and Dr Mahathir sign Memorandum of Understanding on Defence Equipment Procurement.

28 October
: DTI write to ODA that consortium led by Balfour Beatty and GEC will be seeking ATP support for Pergau.

10 November
: British High Commission in Malaysia, on instruction from ODA, writes to Malaysian Finance Ministry that HMG willing to consider ATP support for Pergau, subject to appraisal.

25 November
: Formal application for ATP support received from UK consortium.

1989

21 January
: DTI circulates proposal for ATP support for the project: total contract value of £315 million, of which £200 million is UK/EU content and eligible for ATP support.

13–14 March
: ODA/DTI appraisal mission to Malaysia.

14 March	ODA recommends Mrs Thatcher to make offer of ATP aid based on contract price of £316 million.
15 March	Mrs Thatcher makes offer to Dr Mahathir.
31 March	Consortium informs ODA/DTI that contract price revised to £397 million.
14 April	ODA economists advise that at new price Pergau now clearly uneconomic.
17 April	ODA send formal written offer based on £316 million price with possibility of additional assistance if contract price turns out higher.
27 October	Aid offer extended for further six months.

1990

February/April	ODA economists undertake further reviews and conclude that Pergau for the near term very uneconomic and should be postponed, perhaps indefinitely.
23 April	ODA extend offer for further six months.
September	Malaysia's National Electricity Board corporatised in preparation for privatisation. Renamed Tenaga Nasional Berhad (TNB).
September/October	ODA/DTI joint mission to review Malaysian power sector and opportunities for British contracts. ODA concludes once again that early implementation of Pergau uneconomic, and should be postponed until 2005 at the earliest.
17 October	Aid offer lapses.
8 November	Malaysian Cabinet confirms that Pergau will go ahead, subject to ATP support. Letter of intent issued by TNB to the consortium.
22 November	Mrs Thatcher resigns and John Major becomes Prime Minister.
November/December	ODA environmental adviser conducts initial environmental appraisal.
19 December	John Major meets Dr Mahathir who confirms that Pergau will go ahead subject to ATP financing.

1991

January	ODA sends environmental consultant to Malaysia.
14 January	TNB issue letter of award to the consortium based on contract price of £417 million, subject to ATP financing.
5 February	Tim Lankester advises Lynda Chalker that ODA should not provide ATP support.

7 February	Tim Lankester advises Lynda Chalker and Douglas Hurd that he will need a formal written direction if they decide to proceed with support for Pergau.
8 February	Ministers from key departments meet to try to resolve differences. ODA and Trade Ministers, supported by the Treasury Minister, advise against Pergau and in favour of support for alternative power projects. MOD and FCO Ministers urge support in favour of aid for Pergau.
16 February	Douglas Hurd decides in favour of aid for Pergau and seeks John Major's endorsement.
26 February	John Major endorses the decision.
28 February	Malaysian government informed.
11 April	Malaysian government proposes that ODA subsidy be passed through to TNB. ODA agree.
June	ODA decide to shift from originally intended mixed credit to a soft loan in order to spread expenditure over longer period. This means ODA grant increases from £108 million under mixed credit to £234 million with a soft loan.
4 July	Douglas Hurd issues formal direction to Tim Lankester for ODA to incur expenditure on Pergau.
8 July	Financial Agreement between Malaysian and British governments.
July	Construction work starts at Pergau.

1992

28 May	TNB part-privatised.

1993

22 October	National Audit Office publishes report on Pergau.

1994

17 January	Tim Lankester appears before the Public Accounts Committee.
25 January	Written statement by Douglas Hurd to the House of Commons on the Defence Protocol.
21 March	PAC report on Pergau published.
February/March	Douglas Hurd, other ministers, and representatives of consortium and of NGOs, give evidence to Foreign Affairs Committee.
20 February	*Sunday Times* publishes first article alleging high-level corruption in Malaysia.

25 February	Malaysia announces boycott of British companies for new public sector contracts.
24 June	World Development Movement seeks leave to present case for judicial review.
13 July	FAC report on Pergau published.
7 September	Malaysia's boycott of British companies for public sector contracts ends.
10 November	WDM's application for judicial review heard. Court rules that aid for Pergau unlawful.
13 December	Douglas Hurd announces new funding arrangements for Pergau that involve no further funding role for ODA.

1997

| 22 August | Inauguration ceremony for Pergau power station. |

Appendix II
The economics of Pergau: technical note

There is a standard methodology used by power system planners worldwide for deciding on the optimal expansion and mix of electricity-generating capacity for a period of years ahead. It involves projecting electricity demand, distinguishing between total demand (in kWh) and peak load (in kW), and determining through computer modelling the least cost combination of power stations, including different types (i.e. thermal, hydro, etc.) and their phasing, as well as transmission lines, to meet that total and peak load demand for a given level of security (i.e. reserve margin).

The key assumptions that have to be made concern the following variables:

- peak load and electricity demand over the planning period and its location;
- capital costs of new candidate generating plants over the planning period, their sizes and locations;
- operating costs, especially fuel costs, of both existing and new candidate plants, over the planning period;
- costs of reinforcing and expanding the transmission system.

In order to express the various and time-varying costs on a comparable basis, the planner discounts them back to a value today by applying a discount rate to a future stream of costs. Applying the chosen discount rate to a future stream of costs, both capital and operating, enables the planner to compare the costs – on a present value (i.e. discounted) basis – of alternative plans and choose the cheapest combination of power stations and their optimal phasing. The combination of power stations, which for a given forecast of peak load and electricity demand has the lowest present discounted cost, represents the optimal plan in economic terms. If the optimal plan is overridden for strategic or any other reason by the "forcing" of a plant that is not in the plan at all, or phased differently from the plan, there is a cost penalty that can be estimated through sensitivity analyses.

In applying this methodology, TNB used a standard optimisation software package used by many developing countries, the Wien Automatic System Planning (WASP) model. The WASP model was well known to ODA and World Bank economists, and accepted by them as providing an appropriate tool for examining different power station combinations and arriving at an optimal phasing and mix. In evaluating Malaysia's power plans, both institutions were happy to rely on TNB planners' running of the model. Their focus therefore was on the key assumptions that were fed into it. In the context of evaluating the case for Pergau, they were interested only in the optimal power generation plan for peninsular Malaysia since the power system in East Malaysia, 600 miles away across the South China Sea, was (and continues to be) unconnected to it.

According to the ODA/DTI mission's report of September 1990,[1] the optimal plan based on WASP runs using TNB's 1989 load forecast indicated that all new generating plants for completion prior to 1998 should be either open-cycle gas turbines (OCGTs) or combined-cycle gas turbines (CCGTs). However, for strategic reasons – i.e. for added security and flexibility – the official TNB development plan as it existed in September 1990 included one triple fired station (gas, coal or oil) for completion in 1995. The WASP model identified the cost penalty for imposing this plant on the ideal plan as RM 50 million (approximately £10 million), which was within the margin of error of the cost estimates used and considered by the TNB planners as acceptable.

At the time the ODA/DTI team visited, Pergau was not in the official TNB plan at all, even though there had been ongoing negotiations with the British contractors regarding its early construction for roughly 18 months. The mission was told that Pergau had been subject to sensitivity analysis in the WASP model. At an assumed capital cost of RM 1,250 million (£284 million) at 1990 prices, it could not be justified for commissioning before 2005; and the penalty for advancing it to 1997 was of the order of RM 400 million (£91 million).[2]

TNB were in the process of revising their development plan on the basis of a revised forecast of demand and updated assumptions on input costs. It was expected that the new plan would be submitted to the TNB board the following month (i.e. October 1990) and approved by the government sometime thereafter.

The results of the WASP model run using updated demand and cost assumptions were not available before the mission left Malaysia. However, the TNB planning staff showed the mission their updated forecast for peak load, though it had yet to be endorsed by TNB's senior management and by the government. If adopted, it was likely to be the key determinant of any variations in a revised development plan.

Table 1 shows TNB's 1989 peak load forecast for peninsular Malaysia which formed the basis of the RM 400 million (£91 million) cost penalty noted above, and the "unofficial" forecast of September 1990 – along with the actual outcomes:

Table 1 Peak load (MW) – Peninsular Malaysia

	1989 forecast	*Sept. 1990 forecast*	*Outturn*
1990	3,341	3,436	3,477
2000	7,527	8,939	9,712
2005	9,999	12,973	12,493
2010	12,927	16,223	15,072

Source: Forecasts provided by TNB to ODA; outturn data from TNB annual reports.

In the 1989 forecast, the average growth rate for the years 1990–2005 was 7.6 per cent; in the September 1990 forecast it was 9.3 per cent. The difference in terms of peak load is almost 3,000 MW in 2005, the equivalent of five plants with the generating capacity of Pergau. As the figures in the third column of Table 1 above show, TNB's new forecast turned out to be more accurate than its predecessor, though somewhat on the optimistic side.

In its report, however, the mission noted several reasons for being cautious about the new forecast. The latter was premised on Malaysia maintaining its 1970–90 average growth of GNP through the 1990s, and the mission wondered if this high growth rate could be sustained. The higher forecast also appeared to the mission to be over-influenced by the exceptionally rapid growth in electricity demand in the late 1980s, which was itself the result of extremely rapid GDP growth in the most recent years; and they thought perhaps it might be biased upwards by the wish on the part of the TNB planners to avoid a repetition of their having consistently under-forecast demand in the past.

However, far from decelerating, GDP growth actually accelerated in the early 1990s up until the Asian financial crisis in 1997; and for the whole period 1990–2008 per capita annual GDP growth averaged a very respectable 3.8 per cent.[3]

Because of their reservations about the new forecast and because it had not been formally adopted, the mission did not attempt to estimate what impact it might have on the optimal timing for the commissioning of Pergau. Had they done so, with all other assumptions unchanged, they might have inferred that its optimal year for commissioning would be brought forward a few years. However, as we will see below, when the TNB planners did incorporate the new forecast, along with other changed assumptions, into their modelling a few months later, the optimal timing of Pergau was actually pushed back to 2008.

The other key assumptions in the WASP analysis that TNB shared with the September 1990 mission were:

- Offshore peninsular gas extraction to peak in 2015.
- The price of imported coal, the cheapest alternative fuel to gas, forecast to rise in real terms by 1 per cent a year.
- The economic cost of gas projected to rise by 2.4 per cent a year to 2015, 1 per cent thereafter.
- Real discount rate of 5 per cent for calculating the depletion premium.
- Real discount rate of 10 per cent for comparing costs of different candidate plants.

TNB had previously discussed these assumptions in detail with the World Bank and they seemed to be as well founded as they could be. The assumptions regarding the cost of gas and discount rates were particularly crucial and deserve some comment.

In 1990, there were no imports of gas into peninsular Malaysia and no imports of gas were expected for the foreseeable future. The assumption was that, as and when indigenous gas supplies peaked, peninsular Malaysia would turn to other fuels (mainly imported coal and hydro). Consequently, peninsular Malaysia's offshore gas could not straightforwardly be valued by reference to international prices. Instead, it was necessary to estimate the cost of extraction and delivery and add a "depletion premium" to derive an estimate of its economic cost or value.

In 1987 the World Bank had estimated that, looking purely at cost of extraction and delivery and taking into account also the value of by-products such as propane, butane and condensates, the net cost of Malaysian dry gas to gas users would be effectively zero by 2000.

But this does not mean that the gas should be valued at zero. When a depleting resource such as gas cannot be exported, its economic value at the starting period of its extraction is relatively low; its economic value then increases over time until extraction peaks or until (if earlier) growing domestic demand outstrips the maximum feasible rate of extraction – at which point its economic value equates to the cheapest alternative (i.e. replacement) fuel. TNB planners and ODA and World Bank analysts assumed that this alternative fuel would be imported coal. The economic value of gas for each intervening year was then calculated by applying a depletion premium.

The depletion premium determines how fast the economic value of the gas increases relative to the next cheapest fuel. It depends on the rate of extraction and how many years this can be sustained before gas production peaks or demand outstrips supply, and on how much weight society places on consumption now at the expense of consumption in the future – as measured by the rate of discount. The lower the rate of discount, the higher will be the depletion premium and therefore the longer will be the period before extraction peaks; a higher discount rate will result in a smaller depletion premium, a lower price of gas in the short term, and a shorter period before extraction peaks.[4]

Using a 5 per cent discount rate for calculating the depletion premium was at the suggestion of the World Bank. This was – in the words of the mission's report – to reflect the Malaysian government's "expressed preference for resource conservation and was a way of minimizing risks of irreversible decisions". Using a different discount rate (5 per cent) for calculating the depletion premium from the discount rate (10 per cent) for evaluating the electricity generation planting options arguably involved some inconsistency. It was justified presumably on the grounds that exhaustible resources are somehow special, whereas capital and operating costs of power stations have to be assessed on a *pari passu* basis with other public sector investments for which a 10 per cent discount rate was considered appropriate.

The various assumptions shown above for when gas extraction would peak, the future price of imported coal, and the discount rate, lead to the 2.4 per cent a year real increase in the economic value/cost of gas, albeit from a very low level in 1990. It is this rising cost of gas that eventually makes other fuels competitive with gas in the model. But until gas production reaches a plateau, gas-fired generation will be the cheapest option. New triple-fired (meaning essentially coal) and hydro stations are indicated for commissioning well before gas production finally peaks because it would make no sense to build a gas-fired plant, whose expected life might be 15 or 20 years, if the supply of gas was going to be constrained within that lifespan.

The RM 400 million (£91 million) cost penalty for bringing Pergau forward for commissioning in 1997 rather than in 2005 would have been calculated by comparing the net present value of total power system capital and operating costs over a long period in two model runs that met the same security standard (i.e. one model run with Pergau being commissioned in 1997 and one with Pergau in 2005).

As noted above, the discount rate used by TNB in comparing costs and arriving at a least cost development plan was 10 per cent, which was fairly typical amongst power planners in developing countries at the time. The World Bank and ODA also considered it an appropriate rate. The consortium's advisers suggested that a lower discount rate should have been applied, and if it had been, the economics could have shifted in Pergau's favour. They suggested the use of a 10 per cent discount rate involved an inherent bias against Pergau.

ODA economists dismissed the idea of a 5 per cent discount rate as special pleading: if 10 per cent was right for evaluating investments in the Malaysian power sector as TNB and the World Bank believed it was, then it was right to apply it to Pergau. The consortium's advisers did not give any reason for suggesting a 5 per cent discount rate except that anything higher involved an unfair bias against hydro. This in itself was poor reasoning. Nonetheless, ODA should not have been quite so dismissive of the idea of a lower rate.

For years, the International Energy Agency in its annual review, *Projected Costs of Generating Electricity*, has been applying two discount rates – 5 and 10 per cent – in its evaluation of competing technologies. The UK's 2006 Energy Review used a "central case" discount rate of 10 per cent, bounded by a "lower case" of 7 per cent and a "higher case" of 12 per cent.

One reason for applying a range is to establish how sensitive particular investments are to the choice of discount rate, and it can help to confirm (or otherwise) the advantage of one investment over another.

The other reason is the uncertainty over what is the appropriate discount rate. For the last half-century and more there has been ongoing debate amongst economists as to the correct methodology for estimating the discount rate for any particular society. (For an authoritative account of this debate, see Spackman 2011a.)

There have been two main rivals: social opportunity cost (SOC) and social rate of time preference (STP). SOC refers to the risk-adjusted rate of return that can be achieved on alternative investments. It is the methodology that underlay the World Bank's and ODA's approach at the time of the Pergau decision. It was also the methodology used by the British Treasury in the 1980s to justify their requirement that nationalised industries should achieve an 8 per cent rate of return on new investments. The approach was explained in the following terms by Lawrence Summers when he was chief economist at the World Bank:

> Once costs and benefits are properly measured, it cannot be in posterity's interest for us to undertake investments that yield less than the best return. At the long term horizons that figure in the environmental debate, this really matters. A dollar invested at 10% will be worth six times as much a century from now as a dollar invested at 8%.[5]

Social time preference is essentially the premium that society places on consuming resources now compared with consuming them in the future. As a methodology for evaluating choices in the public sector, it had a stronger theoretical pedigree than SOC; but policy makers had difficulty with it because of the problems of estimation and because – since STP estimates were usually well below estimates for SOC – in conditions of capital scarcity SOC seemed preferable as a means of rationing scarce capital.

Over the past two decades, STP has gained ground amongst policy makers. The Treasury's *Green Book* (HM Treasury 2011) now recommends a discount rate for the UK public sector of 3.5 per cent based on STP methodology. This is composed of 1.5 per cent for "catastrophe risk" and "pure time preference" taken together, and 2 per cent for declining marginal utility of consumption (assuming 2 per cent p.a. future per capita consumption growth and 1.0 for elasticity with respect to marginal utility of consumption). The Treasury also recommends, as do a number of experts, a declining discount rate beyond 30 years – a 0.5 per cent reduction.

ODA were not involved in this methodological debate, and were content to stick with the SOC approach favoured by the World Bank. If ODA economists *had* applied STP methodology to estimating the discount rate for Malaysia in 1990, a discount rate of 7.5 per cent might have seemed plausible. Annual per capita GDP growth was 5.5 per cent in 1970–90, and projected growth was likely to be at least 4 per cent per annum (in the event, GDP per capita grew by an average of 3.8 per cent in 1990–2008). Spackman (2011b), after a careful review of the literature and the evidence, argues for a 1.5 elasticity, rather than the Treasury's 1.0: we have opted for the former. Applied to the 4 per cent, this produces 6 per cent for the declining marginal utility of consumption. Add 1.5 per cent for "catastrophe risk" and for "pure time preference" and we reach a discount rate based on STP of 7.5 per cent.

With hindsight, ODA economists could have usefully applied a 7.5 per cent discount rate to see how much difference it made. To have provided a definitive answer they would have had to re-run TNB's WASP model with all its other assumptions as of 1990, which they didn't have access to. But they could have done a rough calculation based on a "static" comparison – i.e. comparing Pergau with gas turbines generating the same amount of electricity (520 million kWh a year).

ODA economists assumed that, if Pergau was not going to be built, TNB would invest in OCGTs (5 x 125 MW) to meet the equivalent peaking demand. It is more likely that TNB would have invested in CCGTs (2 x 300 MW); and indeed, this is what is revealed in the optimal development plan that TNB sent to ODA in early 1991 (see Table 4). The new CCGT plant would have been used to meet base-load, displacing existing, less efficient OCGTs which would have been switched to peaking. In looking at the comparative cost of the new CCGT plant compared with Pergau, one would ideally need to net off the reduced cost of base-load generation that this would make possible (i.e. the efficiency gains from using CCGTs rather than OCGTs for providing base-load energy). This latter "displacement" saving could well be significant; but it is not possible to estimate how large it would be without knowing for how many years the "displacement" would exist – something that only a rerun of the WASP model would show.

In the following analysis, we compare the NPV cost for Pergau and alternative CCGT and OCGT plants on the assumption that they each generate the same amount of electricity a year – 520 million kWh. Commissioning of new plant on all three scenarios is assumed in 1996 (by the end of 1990 TNB was looking at 1996 rather than 1997 for the possible commissioning of Pergau). The calculations assume the CCGT plant is replaced every 20 years, OCGT plant every 15 years, and mechanical and electrical (M and E) equipment at Pergau every 20 years. The cost of gas is based on TNB's projection of a 2.4 per cent annual real increase up to 2015 and 1 per cent thereafter. Capital cost for Pergau is based on the actual contract price (RM 1,420 million at 1990 prices, of which two-fifths is for M and E). The other assumptions are as follows:[6]

Table 2 Technical and cost assumptions for Pergau and gas turbines

	Heat Rate	Outage%		Construction	Capital Cost	O and M Cost	
	Btu/kWh	*Forced*	*Planned*		*RM/kW*	*Fixed RM/kW/ p.a*	*Variable RM/mWh*
300 MW CCGT	8,532	9	10	3 years	1,423	13.08	4.34
125 MW OCGT	11,762	8	7	2 years	893	30.72	5.85
Pergau	n/a	n/a	n/a	5 years	2,367	22.50	n/a

Source: ODA/DTI Mission Report

On these assumptions, comparative NPVs at 1990 are as follows:

Table 3 Comparative NPV costs

	RM million (1990 prices)	
Discount rate	0.1	0.075
1. Pergau	1,112	1,293
2. CCGT	798	1,044
3. OCGT	720	1,066
Difference (1–2)	314	249
Difference (1–3)	392	227

At a 10 per cent discount rate, the NPV cost disadvantage of Pergau over two 300 MW CCGTs is RM 314 million (£71 million); compared with five 125 MW OCGTs it is RM 392 million (£89 million) – a cost penalty similar, though arrived at by a different route, to the cost penalty for Pergau in the WASP model. At a 7.5 per cent discount rate, the cost advantage of the CCGTs reduces to RM 249 million (£57 million); but CCGTs overtake OCGTs as the preferred option owing to their more efficient use of gas and the higher NPV a lower discount rate attributes to this greater efficiency. If the discount rate is reduced, as suggested by HM Treasury, by 0.5 per cent after 30 years from 7.5 per cent to 7.0 per cent, the cost advantage of CCGTs over Pergau reduces further by a marginal RM 8 million (£2 million).

As mentioned earlier, the cost advantage of CCGTs over Pergau, as well as OCGTs, is understated because the estimates do not include anything for the saving from CCGTs displacing existing inefficient OCGTs' higher cost base-load generation. For just one year of operation, the saving would have been RM 44 million (£10 million).[7] How much the actual displacement saving would be would depend upon how much existing OCGT capacity was available for displacement and for how many years.

There is one further advantage of gas turbines over Pergau that has not been factored into these calculations. Whereas Pergau could only operate at a capacity factor of 10 per cent, gas turbines used for peaking could operate at a higher capacity factor either for a longer peaking period or to make up for unplanned outages at base-load stations.

We conclude that on the basis of this "static" analysis and a range of plausible discount rates, on the cost assumptions available to ODA in late 1990 the NPV cost of the additional electricity generated at Pergau was substantially higher than it would have been with gas turbines.

However, there is one final and important caveat. ODA economists did not include any costing for the carbon emissions from alternative gas turbines. They were aware that Pergau was likely to be better environmentally in terms of greenhouse gas emissions, but it was early days as regards the valuation of carbon emissions and, in the words of the ODA economist working on Pergau in late 1990, he did not "believe this can be reflected in cash analysis".[8] Twenty years later, of course, carbon emissions were to be routinely valued, albeit across a wide range of estimates. We will come back to this later.

So much for the ODA economists' analysis as of the end of 1990. In January 1991 TNB planning staff sent ODA (via the British High Commission in Kuala Lumpur) an updated analysis, based on a new run of their model incorporating their new demand forecast and some other changed assumptions on input costs.[9] This showed that, far from Pergau being brought forward in the optimal plan, it was now pushed back to 2008.

Table 4 is a simplified version of the least cost development sequencing of new plant that appeared in TNB's updated analysis.

The table confirms beyond doubt that, as far as the TNB planning staff were concerned, Pergau was a low priority project. It is particularly striking that Pergau comes last of five amongst potential hydro projects. The table also shows that, if Pergau were to be "forced" for commissioning in 1996, it would be commissioned instead of two 300 MW CCGTs that, in the unconstrained model run, would be commissioned in 1997.

Table 4 TNB – optimal new plant sequences

	Pergau floating				Pergau forced			
	GT	CCGT	C500	Hydro	GT	CCGT	C500	Hydro
1993	2				2			
1994	3				3			
1995	1	1			1	1		
1996			2				2	Pergau
1997		2						
1998	1	2				2		
1999		3				3		
2000		3				3		
2001		1		Jelai		3		
2002	1	3			1	3		
2003		2		Pelus		1		Jelai
2004		4				3		Pelus
2005		3		Ulu Trg		3		Ulu Trg
2006		6				6		
2007		3		Nenggiri		5		
2008		1		Pergau	2	2		Nenggiri
2009		3				3		
2010	1	4			1	4		
Objective function: RM 30,352 million					RM 30,673 million			

Note: GT = 125 MW open-cycle gas turbine; CCGT = 300 MW combined-cycle gas turbine; C500 = 500 MW coal/gas/oil plant. "Objective function" means the discounted net present value of total system costs over the optimisation period (i.e. 50 years). The difference between the objective function with Pergau "forced" in 1996 and the objective function with Pergau "floating" (i.e. to be commissioned in 2008 according to the unconstrained least cost modelling) is the estimated cost penalty of RM 321 million.
Source: TNB communication with British High Commission, Kuala Lumpur, January 1991

TNB were now assuming a capital cost of RM 1,389 million at 1990 prices.[10] The analysis showed that, if Pergau's commissioning was "forced" in 1996, the cost penalty would be RM 321 million (£73 million).

By this time, TNB had actually agreed with the consortium on a contract price of RM 1,420 million at 1990 prices, higher by RM 31 million than the assumed price in the sensitivity analysis described above. With the extra cost assumed to be spread over five years, its NPV was RM 21 million (£5 million). Consequently, TNB's fully up-to-date estimate of the cost penalty of commissioning Pergau in 1996 rather than 2008 would have been RM 342 million (£78 million), somewhat below the RM 400 million (£91 million) previously advised. These figures all assume a discount rate of 10 per cent as per the TNB model. With a discount rate of 7.5 per cent, and a 0.5 per cent reduction for the period beyond 30 years, the revised cost penalty might have been of the order of £60 million. (We arrive at this latter figure by applying to £78 million the same percentage reduction [21 per cent] as shown in Table 3 for the reduced cost disadvantage of Pergau with a 7.5 per cent discount rate, less £2 million for the 0.5 per cent lower discount rate beyond 30 years.)

Ex post evaluation

The following paragraphs now look at how the economics of Pergau appear *ex post*. It would require a large amount of information, including operating and capital costs of existing and candidate plants, and access to the TNB's WASP model to produce anything more than rough estimates. However, it is possible to evaluate what would appear to be the key potential variants. We take as our base case the final model run that ODA economists saw in late January 1991 and the results of which are summarised in the immediately preceding paragraphs. We ignore the poor operating performance of Pergau in its first few years: if this were factored in, it would make the *ex post* evaluation look that much worse for Pergau unless an alternative gas turbine plant would have had similar start-up problems – which seems unlikely given the off-the-peg nature of CCGTs and the extensive worldwide experience of building, commissioning and operating them available to Malaysia at the time. We make the various adjustments using two discount rates: 10 per cent and 7.5 per cent.

There have of course been many developments in the Malaysian power sector over the past 20 years. Three are of particular relevance for this *ex post* evaluation. First, electricity demand – after an initial spurt in the early 1990s – grew more slowly than forecast and generating capacity expanded well in excess of what was required to meet actual peak demand. (This was partly the result of the government's encouragement of Independent Power Producers competing with TNB.) The result was a relatively extravagant, and therefore costly, reserve margin of 40 per cent in 2010.

Second, partly because of non-power system demand growing faster and due to unanticipated operational problems in extracting the gas, offshore peninsular gas supplies peaked several years sooner than had been assumed. Since 2008, gas deliveries have been in decline; and in 2011, TNB suffered severe shortages of gas, obliging it to switch to more expensive fuels. By 2013, peninsular Malaysia will become a significant importer of LNG.

Third, Malaysia was a signatory to the 1992 UN Framework Convention on Climate Change. At the climate change conference in Copenhagen in 2009, Malaysia's Prime Minister, Najib Razak, announced that Malaysia was committed to reducing the intensity of its greenhouse gas emissions per unit of GDP by 40 per cent by 2020 (with 2005 as the base). The government has a strategy in place aimed at meeting this commitment, which includes a feed-in tariff for renewable energy producers. Each of these three factors needs to be taken into account in evaluating the economics of Pergau *ex post*.

Capital costs

The capital cost of the project, as agreed between TNB and the consortium, was already more or less incorporated in the 1991 model run. The actual final net cost of the contract to TNB, including liquidated damages for delays and compensation to the consortium for unexpected design and construction changes, was RM 1,879.5 million at current prices. Excluding the payment for price escalation, the final cost at constant 1990 prices was RM 1,476 million – RM 56 million (£13 million) higher than the original contract price. The NPV of this extra cost, if spread evenly over the six years of the actual construction period, is £8 million (£9 million using a 7.5 per cent discount rate).[11]

Electricity demand

Peak load in 2005 was some 500 MW lower than in the up-dated TNB projection, and 1,150 MW lower in 2010. Other things being equal, this might have pushed the optimal phasing of Pergau back by a year or so. If TNB's January 1991 estimate of the cost penalty (£78 million) from commissioning Pergau in 1996 rather than in 2008 is averaged over the 12-year period, this could imply an additional penalty of around £6 million. We have earlier suggested that, applying a 7.5 per cent discount rate, TNB's estimate of the cost penalty from advancing Pergau to 1996 would have been around £60 million. In that case, £5 million would be the additional penalty.

Economic cost of gas

The analysis undertaken by TNB and ODA in 1990 assumed that the economic cost of gas for peninsular Malaysia would be related indefinitely to the cost of coal. The economic cost of indigenous gas would start from a low base determined by the cost of production and delivery and an appropriate depletion premium, and rise to meet the projected price of coal in terms of heat equivalence at the point when gas supplies were expected to peak (2015).

Thereafter the economic cost of gas would move in step with the price of coal. This was on the implicit assumption that peninsular Malaysia would never be an importer of LNG, and that future fuel shortfalls would be met by imports of coal or by hydro.

This was a not unreasonable assumption at the time, given the relatively undeveloped international trade in LNG, the availability of indigenous gas supplies for many decades to come, and the likely long-run availability of alternative fuels. In reality, however, peninsular Malaysia started to import gas via pipeline from Indonesia in 2002. This was on a modest scale (amounting to about 5 per cent of domestic consumption) and on extremely favourable terms: Malaysia secured a 20-year contract with a fixed price of $2.70 per million Btu, which was two-thirds of the 2002 international price for LNG and one-quarter of the LNG price in 2010. As from 2013, Malaysia will be importing LNG from Qatar to make up for a perceived lack of domestic supply, and a regasification plant is under construction on the west coast to process these imports. The terms of the contract with Qatar have not been made public, but the price is likely to be based on international market prices.

Against this background, how should we value peninsular Malaysia's gas for the purpose of comparing actuals with the estimates in the 1991 TNB model run?

One approach would be to take the price paid for Indonesian gas that, deflated to 1990 prices, was actually less in 2010 than the TNB model estimate for that year. This would further improve the competitiveness of gas turbines relative to Pergau. However, the terms of the Indonesia contract were so favourable to Malaysia and so unlikely to be repeated that it is probably right to ignore it.

A second approach would be to update the TNB estimates, taking into account the actual development of coal prices and the earlier peaking of indigenous gas supplies than TNB had assumed. The rationale for this would be that until 2010 peninsular Malaysia was basically self-sufficient in gas, and has not needed, nor has had the physical capacity, to import LNG; and furthermore, until relatively recently it did not expect to import LNG. However, since substantial LNG imports are now in the offing, this approach might be combined with valuing indigenous gas at international LNG prices as from, say, 2011.

The third approach is to value peninsular gas at international LNG prices retrospectively. This in effect is what Petronas, the national producer and supplier of gas, has done in its most recent annual reports in which it has shown the revenues it has foregone through having to sell to the power generation sector at a regulated price well below international prices.[12]

In the following analysis, we give estimates of the economic value of peninsular gas based on the second ("hybrid") approach and the third ("international prices") approach.

Table 5 shows the economic value of indigenous gas and the price of coal assumed in the 1991 TNB model run, and the actual international price of coal and LNG for the relevant years (all at constant 1990 prices). Table 6 gives international prices for LNG and coal for the whole period 1990–2010.

Table 5 Gas and coal prices – TNB model and actual

	RM/million Btu at 1990 prices				
	1990	*1995*	*2000*	*2005*	*2010*
TNB model (1991)					
Gas	3.54	3.54	3.86	4.72	5.69
Coal	4.99	5.24	5.51	5.79	6.09
International price (actual)					
Coal	5.16	4.27	2.86	4.61	6.88
LNG	9.83	8.29	10.40	12.80	19.00

Note: International prices are as per Table 6, deflated to 1990 prices as in Columns 5 and 6 and converted at 1990 exchange rate RM 2.7 = US$ 1. In order to convert tonnes of coal to Btus, we assume 6,700 kcal/kg (the figure used by TNB in 1991 model run), which converts to 26.6 million Btu/tonne of coal.

Table 6 International LNG and coal prices

	Current prices			Constant 1990 prices	
	LNG	Coal	US GDP	LNG	Coal
	($/MMBtu)	*($/tonne)*	*Deflator*	*($/MMBtu)*	*($/Tonne)*
1990	3.64	50.81	81.6	3.64	50.8
1991	3.99	50.30	84.4	3.86	48.6
1992	3.62	48.45	86.4	3.42	45.8
1993	3.52	45.71	88.4	3.25	42.2
1994	3.18	43.66	90.3	2.87	39.5
1995	3.46	47.58	92.1	3.07	42.1
1996	3.66	49.54	93.9	3.18	43.0
1997	3.91	45.53	95.4	3.34	38.5
1998	3.05	40.51	96.5	2.58	34.2
1999	3.14	35.74	97.9	2.62	29.8
2000	4.72	34.58	100.0	3.85	28.2
2001	4.64	37.96	102.4	3.69	30.2
2002	4.27	36.90	104.2	3.34	28.9
2003	4.77	34.74	106.4	3.66	26.6
2004	5.18	51.34	109.5	3.86	38.3
2005	6.05	62.91	113.0	4.37	45.4
2006	7.14	63.04	116.6	5.00	44.1
2007	7.73	69.86	119.7	5.27	47.6
2008	12.55	122.81	121.1	8.46	82.1
2009	9.06	110.11	124.3	5.94	72.3
2010	10.91	105.19	126.6	7.03	67.8

Notes: LNG price is LNG cif into Japan; coal price is steam coal cif into Japan.
Source: BP Statistical Review of World Energy June 2011. US GDP deflator; IMF Data and Statistics, www.inf.org/external/data.htm (accessed 15 February 2012).

The most striking feature in these tables is the fall in the price of coal in the 1990s, which continued until 2003; and the very low valuation of gas in the TNB model by comparison with world LNG prices. After 2003, coal prices started to increase quite rapidly, and by 2010 they had reached a level slightly above the level projected by TNB. LNG prices followed a similar, though less pronounced, pattern. The substantial reduction in international coal prices in the 1990s led Malaysia to invest heavily in coal-fired generation. From virtually nothing in the early 1990s, coal accounted for nearly one-third of Malaysia's electricity generation in 2010.

Superficially, it might appear that the appropriate comparator with Pergau could now be coal-fired plant rather than gas turbines, and that with the lower price of coal, Pergau would look even less economic. However, for technical reasons, coal-fired plant is not suitable for peaking, and therefore the comparator for Pergau has to remain gas turbines. This is borne out by the optimal sequencing data in Table 4, which shows that "forcing" Pergau in 1996 displaced gas turbines: Pergau did not displace coal-fired plant.

Applying the depletion premium methodology, the fall in the price of coal does not in itself affect the economic valuation of indigenous gas. What is relevant is the price of coal when indigenous gas supplies peak. TNB had assumed that this would happen in 2015. In fact, gas supplies from offshore peninsular Malaysia appear to have peaked in 2008 – in which case the economic value of gas would equate with the price of coal in 2008. The slightly higher actual coal price in 2010 compared with the TNB projection and the premature peaking of indigenous supply suggest that the *ex post* economic value of gas might be increased by about RM 1.2/MMBtu in that year (i.e. 6.88 minus 5.69 in last column of Table 5).

If we assume that this higher valuation of gas applies for the whole period from 1996 to 2010, the extra cost of fuel for the net additional 520 kWh generated by CCGTs if Pergau had not been built comes to RM 5.3 million annually. On a 1990 NPV basis, this equates to RM 23 million (£5 million) – or RM 31 million (£7 million) with a 7.5 discount rate.

If we assume that from 2010 gas should be valued at international prices, the projected economic cost of gas is likely to be much higher than in the TNB's early 1991 model run. In 2010, the cif price of LNG into Japan was $10.91/MMBtu, the equivalent of RM19.0/MMBtu at 1990 prices compared with RM5.69/MMBtu in the TNB model. International gas prices have been very volatile over the recent past. For example, in February 2012 the cost of US natural gas fell to a decade low of $2.3/MMBtu – 85 per cent down from its all-time high set in 2005. However, most forecasters are still expecting gas prices to increase over the next few years, notwithstanding recent developments in shale gas technology. In our analysis, we use the latest published projections by the UK's Department of Energy and Climate Change (DECC), taking their "central scenario". These are based on wholesale LNG prices into the UK, which do not necessarily reflect the costs that Malaysia would pay. But the DECC price projections in Table 7 provide as a good a basis as any for this evaluation.

Table 7 Gas price projections (2011 constant prices)

	p/therm
2010	44
2011	63
2012	69
2013	74
2014	80
2015	81
2016	81
2017	76
2018	70
2019	70
2020	70
2021 onwards	70

Source: Department of Energy and Climate Change, October 2011, *Fossil Fuel Price Projections: Summary.* www.decc.gov.uk/en/content/cms/about/ec_social_res/analytic_ projs/ff_prices/ff_prices.aspx (accessed 26 February 2012).

Deflated to 1990 prices and converted to ringitts,[13] the gas prices in the DECC projection compared with gas prices assumed in the TNB model for the period from 2011 onwards produce the following increased costs for the CCGT plant generating 520 million kWh a year:

- At a discount rate of 10 per cent, increased NPV cost of RM 67 million (£15 million).
- At a discount rate of 7.5 per cent, increased NPV cost of RM 137 million (£31 million).

In sum, the "hybrid" approach results in total NPV extra fuel cost for the CCGT plant option of £20 million with a 10 per cent discount rate, and £38 million with a 7.5 per cent discount rate.

With the "international prices" approach in which we value the indigenous gas retrospectively – as well as going forward – at international prices, we simply replace the values for 1996 to 2010 indicated above by values based on actual LNG prices. The extra fuel cost for this period compared with the fuel costs assumed by TNB comes to RM 120 million (£27 million) with a 10 per cent discount rate and RM 165 million (£37 million) with a 7.5 per cent discount rate. Adding the NPV cost from 2011 onwards indicated earlier, we get total extra NPV costs of £42 million with a 10 per cent discount rate, and £68 million with a 7.5 per cent discount rate.

Carbon emissions

A downside of gas-fired electricity generation is that it produces carbon dioxide (CO_2) emissions.[14] By contrast, CO_2 emissions from hydro are negligible. Although in the original appraisal, this disadvantage was noted, no attempt was made to put a price on it.

In the years since 1990, the impact of CO_2 emissions on global warming has become much better understood. There have been numerous attempts to estimate their social cost. The social cost of carbon (SCC) for any one year is the NPV of the future flow of damages caused by an extra tonne of carbon for a "business as usual" carbon emissions trajectory, less the NPV of the future flow of damages associated with a lower carbon emissions trajectory that is considered desirable and feasible. However, the range of estimates is enormous – even amongst those experts who share similar views on the need to combat climate change. At the lower end of the range, the American economist William Nordhaus has estimated – for his optimal policy for carbon emissions reduction – the SCC at \$7.4 per tonne of CO_2 for 2005 at 2005 prices (Nordhaus 2008, p. 83). By contrast, the Stern Review estimated the SCC in 2000 at \$25 or \$30, depending on which of two carbon emissions trajectories was chosen (Stern 2006, p. 304).

Partly because of the problems involved in estimating the SCC, for the purpose of policy appraisal the UK's Department of Energy and Climate Change (DECC) has adopted a different approach. Instead of valuing carbon on the basis of the damages caused by rising emissions, DECC has produced estimates based on the cost of mitigation – specifically, the marginal abatement cost (MAC) that the UK is likely to have to incur in order to meet its emissions targets.[15] There are two sets of estimates, reflecting the separate emissions targets adopted by the EU for traded and non-traded carbon. For traded carbon, DECC's estimates are a projection of prices for EU allowances in the EU carbon market, which in a perfect market would equate to the MAC that the UK traded carbon sector faces in order to meet its EU emissions allocation. DECC's "central" estimates for the value of traded carbon are shown in Table 8. Starting at £13 t/CO_2 in 2010, it reaches £29 in 2020 and £74 in 2030. Post-2030, DECC's projections assume that a global carbon market will be in place, with a single carbon price reflecting marginal abatement costs consistent with a global target applying to all emissions.

DFID economists have decided to use DECC's carbon value estimates for appraising and evaluating DFID-funded projects. If they were evaluating Pergau, they would be applying the DECC estimates for traded carbon since electricity generation falls within the EU's traded carbon sector. This is not entirely logical since DFID's client countries are not signed up to the EU emissions targets, and for a given emissions target their MAC may be more or less than Europe's (in Malaysia's case probably less). On the other hand, DECC's carbon value estimates do more or less reflect Europe's view of the costs that need to be incurred if serious progress is to be made in limiting its and other countries' emissions. From a European perspective, therefore, valuing the carbon emissions that the construction of Pergau avoided, using DECC's estimates, seems a reasonable approach.

Table 8 Traded carbon value projections (2011 constant prices)

	£/tonne CO_2		
2010	13	2028	65
2011	13	2029	70
2012	14	2030	74
2013	16	2031	81
2014	17	2032	88
2015	19	2033	95
2016	21	2034	102
2017	22	2035	109
2018	24	2036	116
2019	26	2037	122
2020	29	2038	129
2021	33	2039	136
2022	38	2040	143
2023	42	2041	150
2024	47	2042	157
2025	51	2043	164
2026	56	2044	171
2027	61	2045	178

Source: Department of Energy and Climate Change, October 2011, *A Brief Guide to the Carbon Valuation Methodology for UK Policy Appraisal*, www.decc.gov.uk/assets/decc/11/cutting-emissions/carbon-valuation/3136-guide-carbon-valuation-methodology.pdf (accessed 20 February 2012).

An alternative and possibly more appropriate approach is to use the Malaysian government's own valuation of carbon. As mentioned earlier, Malaysia is committed to a specific – and quite ambitious – carbon emissions reduction target. In an assessment of the socio-economic impact of its feed-in tariff programme, the Ministry of Energy, Green Technology and Water has indicated a value of RM 50 per tonne of CO_2 at 2011 prices (= £10.2 at 2011 average exchange rate) up to 2020.[16] We assume that the RM 50 figure has been calculated on the basis of the MAC that Malaysia has to incur if it is to achieve its carbon reduction target. In the short term, it is well within the range of other estimates: somewhat lower than DECC's estimates for traded carbon, but well above Nordhaus' SCC estimate and within the range of official American SCC estimates. The Malaysian valuation, however, is constant over time at least up to 2020. By contrast, most carbon value estimates – based on both SCC and MAC methodologies – increase over time. This is because, in the case of the SCC, future emissions are expected to produce larger incremental damage as physical and economic systems become more stressed and because the NPV of future damages increases the less distant they are; and in the case of MACs, because over time the easier options for mitigating emissions become exhausted. It is possible, on the other hand, that the Malaysian ministry believes that Malaysia has relatively more scope for taking mitigating action before its marginal abatement costs rise. It has not published estimates of how it values carbon post-2020.

In this evaluation, we calculate the carbon costs for a gas-fired plant using both DECC's and the Malaysian estimates of carbon values. In each case, we need to extrapolate back to 1996. For DECC's estimates we extrapolate back so as to show a 3.5 per cent annual increase from 1996 to 2010. (This is a purely mechanical application of the 3.5 per cent p.a. long run increase in DECC's forward projection.) For the Malaysian estimate, we assume the RM 50 value at 2011 prices for all years from 1996 – which compensates for the absence of any increase in the ministry's estimate for later years. In the absence of any estimate for the period after 2020, we assume the constant RM 50 value for the period 2021 to 2030. From 2030 onwards, when we assume that a global carbon market is in place, we "impose" DECC's much higher estimates.

An efficient CCGT plant typically emits around 400 tonnes of CO_2 per million kWh.[17] Thus, CCGTs generating the same amount of electricity as Pergau (520 million kWh a year) would have emitted 208,000 tonnes of CO_2 a year. Applying DECC's traded carbon value estimates, extrapolated back to 1996 as explained above and deflated to 1990 prices, the NPV cost of the carbon emissions is £21 million with a discount rate of 7.5 per cent. Applying the Malaysian carbon value estimates, also extended as explained above, we arrive at an NPV cost of £17 million using a 7.5 per cent discount rate. Since the resultant figures are so close, we can take the average between the two: £19 million.[18] Because of the uncertainty in the underlying assumptions, this figure can be no more than illustrative, but it gives an indication of the possible magnitude involved.

There is a likely offset to the extent that the CCGT plant might have displaced less efficient, existing OCGTs for base-load generation, with the OCGTs being switched to peaking duty. For a single year, this could yield a net reduction in CO_2 emissions of about 1 million tonnes, which for just one year would have yielded a saving of £6 million at 1990 prices, assuming the Malaysian carbon valuation.[19] But we don't know for sure if this "displacement" would have materialised or for how long, and for the purpose of the summary below, we ignore it.

Summary

In TNB's January 1991 sensitivity analysis, the cost penalty for advancing Pergau to 1996 was implicitly £78 million in NPV terms at 1990 prices (£60 million at a 7.5 per cent discount rate). The effect of the four retrospective adjustments on the economics of Pergau that we have discussed in this section is as follows. Plus indicates that Pergau becomes relatively more costly, minus that it becomes relatively less costly. Bracketed figures are for a 7.5 per cent discount rate:

- Higher capital cost: plus £8 million (£9 million).
- Lower electricity demand: plus £6 million (£5 million).
- Higher gas cost: minus £20–42 million (£38–68 million).

- Carbon emissions: minus (£19 million).

The total net effect of these *ex post* adjustments is as follows:

- If we assume a 10 per cent discount rate for the first three items, the cost penalty for Pergau reduces from £78 million to £53 million with the lower valuation of gas, and to £31 million with the higher valuation of gas.
- If we assume a 7.5 per cent discount rate, the cost penalty for Pergau reduces from £60 million to £17 million with the lower gas valuation, and switches to a £13 million benefit with the higher gas valuation.

These estimates are necessarily approximate because of the uncertainty about some of the underlying assumptions, and they encompass a range of over £60 million. If anything, they are likely to overstate the worsening of the CCGT plant's competitiveness because we have not included anything in our analysis for the possible "displacement" savings from CCGTs releasing less efficient, existing OCGTs for peaking duty. Such displacement would moderate the NPV cost addition for CCGTs for both fuel and carbon emissions.

Nonetheless, there is one reasonably firm conclusion that we can draw from the analysis. This is that, with hindsight, the cost penalty for Pergau was significantly less than that indicated in the *ex ante* estimates in 1990/91.

It is not possible to say with absolute certainty whether in retrospect Pergau turned out to be a worse investment than gas turbines. After making the adjustments for higher gas prices and the cost of carbon emissions, if we follow ODA and TNB analysts and apply a 10 per cent discount rate, Pergau still looks in retrospect seriously uneconomic.

Applying a 7.5 per cent discount rate, with the lower of the two gas valuations, gas turbines appear to remain the preferred choice. But with the higher of the two gas valuations, Pergau becomes by a small margin the preferred option. However, to repeat, our estimates probably overstate the deterioration in gas turbines' competitiveness. Taking this into account and looking at the estimates in the round, the balance of probability is that – even with the knowledge we now have – gas turbines would still have been a more economic investment than Pergau.

Who received the ODA subsidy?

Finally, how much of the ODA subsidy went to the contractors and how much of it went to Malaysia? In principle, the subsidy to the contractors would be the difference between the actual contract price and the price that might have been achieved if the contract had gone to international tender. The Malaysians believed they could get Pergau built by the Japanese or some other non-British contractor for RM 1,250 million (£284 million) at 1990 prices. We cannot of course know whether this could have been achieved. But if it could have been, then the subsidy to the consortium was RM 170 million

(£39 million). The net present value of the aid provided by ODA was £133 million;[20] so the balance of £94 million would have accrued to Malaysia – which more than amply compensated for the *ex ante* £78 million cost penalty that TNB's planning staff believed would be incurred by advancing the commissioning of Pergau.

Alternatively, if one were to assume that Malaysia would not have implemented the Pergau project at all without at least £78 million in aid to compensate for the *ex ante* cost penalty, in that case the implicit subsidy to the British contractors would have been £78 million and the implicit aid to Malaysia would have been £55 million.

The contract was estimated to have provided 29,000 man-months, or 2,417 man-years, of work in Britain. If we take the more conservative assumption that "only" £39 million accrued to the contractors, and assuming all of the £39 million subsidised the work in Britain and not that undertaken locally (a reasonable assumption since an alternative contractor would presumably have faced similar local costs), then the subsidy cost per man-year was £16,135.

Appendix III
Dramatis personae

British politicians

Margaret Thatcher, Prime Minister (1979–November 1990).

John Major, Chief Secretary, Treasury (1986–July 1989); Foreign Secretary (July–October 1989); Chancellor of the Exchequer (October 1989–November 1990); Prime Minister (November 1990–97).

Geoffrey Howe, Foreign Secretary (1983–July 1989).

Douglas Hurd, Foreign Secretary (October 1989–95).

Peter Lilley, Secretary of State for Trade and Industry (July 1990–April 1992).

David Mellor, Chief Secretary,Treasury (November 1990–April 1992).

David Young, Secretary of State for Trade and Industry (1987–July 1989).

George Younger, Secretary of State for Defence (1986–July 1989).

Malcolm Caithness, Minister of State, FCO (1990–92).

Lynda Chalker, Minister for Overseas Development (July 1989–97).

Alan Clark, Minister for Defence Procurement, MOD (1989–92).

Ann Clwyd, Labour Spokesperson on Overseas Aid (1989–92).

Richard Needham, Minister of Trade (1992–95).

Chris Patten, Minister for Overseas Development (1986–July 1989).

Tim Sainsbury, Minister of Trade (1990–92).

David Trefgarne, Minister of Trade (1989–90).

British civil servants

John Caines, Permanent Secretary, ODA (1987–July 1989).

Colin Chandler, Head of DESO (1985–89).

Robert Graham-Harrison, Head of South East Asia Development, ODA (until 1989).

Barrie Ireton, Principal Finance Officer, ODA (1988–93).

Dick Jones, Senior Power Engineering Adviser, ODA (1984–2006).

Tim Lankester, Deputy Secretary, Treasury (1988–July 1989); Permanent Secretary, ODA (July 1989–January 1994).

Charles Powell, Private Secretary to the Prime Minister (1983–91).

Nicholas Spreckley, High Commissioner to Malaysia (1986–92).

John Vereker, Principal Finance Officer, ODA (1985–88); Permanent Secretary, ODA (1994–2002).
Alan Whitworth, Economic Adviser, ODA (1988–99).

Others in Britain

Robin Biggam, Chairman of BICC.
Ben Jackson, World Development Movement.
John Lippitt, International Director, GEC.
Andrew Neil, Editor, *Sunday Times*.
Jim Prior, Chairman, GEC.
Christopher Rose, presiding judge for Pergau judicial review.

Malaysia

Mahathir Mohamad, Prime Minister (1981–2003).
A. P. Arumugam, Director, GEC (Malaysia) and adviser on defence procurement to Dr Mahathir.
Anwar Ibrahim, Minister of Finance (1991–98).
Samy Vellu, Minister of Energy, Telecommunications and Posts (1989–95).
Daim Zainuddin, Minister of Finance (1984–91), Treasurer of UMNO (1984–2001).

Note: The information above shows positions held during 1988–94 where relevant to the Pergau story. Many of the principal characters acquired honorific titles before, during or after the period covered in this book – Baroness, Lord and/or Sir in the case of the Britons; Tun, Tan Sri and/or Dato' in the case of the Malaysians. For simplicity, I have excluded prefixes before names, with two exceptions – Mrs Thatcher and Dr Mahathir because this is how they were nearly always described during their premierships.

Glossary

British thermal units
   Unit of energy used to describe the heat value or energy content of fuels. 100,000 Btu = 1 Therm. MMBtu = million Btu.

Capacity factor
   Ratio of electricity generated in a power plant to maximum potential output (generating capacity).

Closed-cycle gas turbine
   Turbine generator equipped with heat recovery steam generator to capture heat from the gas turbine exhaust.

Depletion premium
   Opportunity cost of consuming a non-renewable resource now rather than at some time in the future.

Discount rate
   Interest rate used to discount future quantities to the present.

Heat rate
   Measure of how many Btu for any particular fuel are required for generating a unit of electricity.

High Commission(er)
   The equivalent of an embassy (ambassador) of a Commonwealth country in another Commonwealth country.

Kilowatt/megawatt hours
   Measure of electricity generated or consumed.

Kilowatts/megawatts
   Measure of electricity-generating capacity.

Marginal abatement cost
   Cost of abating an incremental tonne of carbon or CO_2.

Net present value
   The value today of a future stream of values discounted by an appropriate discount rate.

Open-cycle gas turbine
Turbine generator with no auxiliary heat recovery system.

Social Cost of Carbon
Present discounted value of future damages caused by an incremental tonne of carbon or CO_2.

Peak load
Maximum demand for electricity during 24-hour period in an electricity generation and distribution system.

Social opportunity cost of capital
Economic rate of return that is available on alternative investments.

Social rate of time preference
Premium that society places on consuming resources now compared with some period or periods in the future.

Notes

1 Introduction

1 The government department responsible for Britain's international aid programme has had various titles. Originally, in the 1960s when first established, it was known as the Ministry of Overseas Development with its own Cabinet Minister. Under the Conservative governments of the 1970s, 1980s and 1990s, it was named the Overseas Development Administration, with a Minister of State in charge outside the cabinet and reporting to the Secretary of State for Foreign and Commonwealth Affairs. In 1997 when Labour returned to power, it was renamed the Department for International Development with its own Secretary of State, independent of the Foreign and Commonwealth Office and once again with a seat in the cabinet. Following the formation of the Conservative–Liberal Democrat coalition government in 2010, the title and independent status remained as under Labour. In this book, I refer to the department as the ODA except where it would otherwise be misleading.
2 Lewis was a native of the island of St Lucia. He studied economics at LSE and then taught at Manchester University and Princeton. He won the Nobel Prize for Economics in 1979. His book *The Theory of Economic Growth* (Lewis 1955) was one of the standard texts for development economists in the 1960s and was influential amongst official aid donors. His "dual sector" model was first described in Lewis (1954).

2 British overseas aid

1 Lancaster (1999, p. 133) quotes a government White Paper (Cmnd 239) that included the following: "The special responsibility which Her Majesty's Government has for the colonial dependencies ceases when they achieve independence. The government therefore does not envisage government loans as a normal means of assisting such countries."
2 The UN Declaration only refers to rights. But the rights of individuals or groups are meaningless unless they are mirrored by duties by others to ensure their fulfillment. In theory, those duties could attach merely to individuals. However, if the rights mentioned in the UN Declaration are to be given practical effect, the duties have to include the duties of governments. For an examination of the moral case for international aid, see Lankester (2004).
3 The most famous theoretical exposition of savings and foreign exchange gaps can be found in Chenery and Stout (1966). Chenery became chief economic adviser at the World Bank during Robert McNamara's presidency.
4 For Bauer's views on economic aid and development, see Bauer (1972). When I studied development economics in the early 1960s, Bauer's views were widely disdained. They were later to a considerable degree vindicated.

5 HC Hansard, vol 979, cols. 464–72.
6 Maizels and Nissanke (1984). By contrast, the allocation of multilateral aid was almost 100 per cent according to "recipient need". The authors measured "recipient need" by a combination of physical quality of life, low economic growth and shortage of foreign exchange. They measured "donor interest" by a combination of political, security, investment and trade interests.
7 Although the minimum grant element as defined by the OECD was the same for mixed credits and soft loans, because of the way the OECD rules required the calculation to be done, the present discounted cost of the interest subsidy under a soft loan in order to achieve the minimum grant element was usually higher than the present discounted cost of the grant under a mixed credit. In the case of Pergau, the soft loan method, which eventually had to be adopted because of short-term pressure on the ATP budget, proved much more expensive than if a mixed credit had been used (see Chapter 9).
8 HC Hansard, vol. 181, col. 32 w., and FAC 1993–94, vol. ll, pp. 23–24.
9 FAC 1993–94, vol. ll, p. 340.
10 The key provision is section 1 of the Act:

Development Assistance

(1) The Secretary of State may provide any person or body with development assistance if he is satisfied that the provision of the assistance is likely to contribute to a reduction of poverty.
(2) In this Act, "development assistance" means assistance provided for the purpose of –

(a) furthering sustainable development in one or more countries outside the United Kingdom, or
(b) improving the welfare of the population of one or more such countries.

(3) For the purposes of subsection (2)(a) "sustainable development" includes any development that is, in the opinion of the Secretary of State, prudent having regard to the likelihood of its generating lasting benefits for the population of the country or countries in relation to which it is provided.

11 World Bank (2011).

3 The Pergau hydroelectric scheme

1 According to a recent study by the Asian Development Bank, Malaysia was the only country amongst 14 Asian countries to show a decrease in its Gini coefficient over the past 15 years. But this study also shows that Malaysia still had the third highest level of inequality – after Thailand and Nepal (Menon, Mitra and Arnold 2011).
2 See Jomo (2007). The contributors to this volume are mostly critical of Malaysia's industrial policy under Dr Mahathir. The sponsorship of a few industries, such as electronics, is praised; but there is sharp criticism of waste and inefficiency in some protected/subsidised industries, especially at the heavy end.
3 For an analysis of money politics and political patronage under Dr Mahathir, see Hilley (2001).
4 Quoted in Pua (2011, p. 157).
5 The company was previously called Lembaga Letrik Negara. It was renamed TNB in September 1990 in preparation for privatisation. Throughout this book, the company is referred to as TNB, both pre- and post-privatisation.

6 The Malaysian currency is the Ringitt, RM for short. Throughout this book, unless otherwise stated, RM are converted to sterling at the exchange rate prevailing in early 1990 (£1 = RM 4.4), which was the rate used as the basis for the project contract.
7 ASD 8991 164/571/006 A.
8 ASC 9294 G.

4 Politicians and bureaucrats

1 For a recent survey, see Sabatier (2007, pp. 3–17). Sabatier outlines a number of theories coming within the public choice and institutionalism families. One theory, if it can be called that, which captures many of the features of the decision making over Pergau, is the "garbage can model" described by Zahariadis (2007). In this model, "no one person controls the process of choice. … Ambiguity is rampant … Policy makers never make their objectives crystal clear. Under conditions of ambiguity when neither the problem nor the policy preferences are fully understood, choosing the right solution becomes an almost impossible task."
2 Hashim (2002) attempted systematically to test the validity of two theories within the institutionalist family – the "advocacy coalition framework" and the "policy networks/policy communities framework" – in the context of the decision making over Pergau. She concluded that they each throw light on various aspects of the decision making but that neither provides more than a partial explanation of the whole process.
3 Ironically, one of the few economists who shared her view was the Marxist economist, Andrew Glyn, who with his associate Bob Sutcliffe, was the first to identify the secular decline in Britain's profit/GNP ratio (Glyn & Sutcliffe 1972). Glyn's later book (Glyn 2006) correctly pin-pointed the risks from excessive liberalisation of the financial markets, which became all too evident in 2007 and 2008.
4 For the best account of economic policy in the Thatcher years, see Lawson (1996). Two other interesting, and contrasting, accounts of the early period can be found in Walters (1986) and Keegan (1984). All three are agreed that "broad money" (so-called M3), which in the period 1979 to early 1981 was the main focus of monetary policy, was a seriously misleading indicator of monetary tightness. After 1981, the government adopted a more eclectic approach.
5 *The Observer*, 7 April 1989.
6 By the 1970s the Anti-Locust Research Centre had been merged into what became ODA's Natural Resources Institute, which was eventually, in 1996, taken over by the University of Greenwich.
7 It was subsequently claimed by one of Malaysia's Opposition leaders, Dr Kua Kia Soong, that a quid pro quo for the ending of the "Buy Britain Last" policy was British agreement to arrest a former Malaysian employee of the bankrupt Malaysian Bank Bumiputra whom the Hong Kong authorities were seeking to extradite on fraud charges. The individual, Lorrain Osman, wanted to have various telexes to and from the FCO made available to the Hong Kong court if he were brought to trial – which he claimed would seriously implicate senior Malaysian politicians in the failure of the bank. He was held in a British prison for seven years from 1985 until 1992 while he fought an extradition warrant. When his extradition to Hong Kong was eventually agreed, the relevant documents were never made available to the Hong Kong court because two British ministers, Lord Caithness and Frances Maude, had signed public interest immunity certificates to prevent the judge from allowing the documents to appear. Douglas Hurd informed the FAC that the certificates were issued to "assert the public interest in non-disclosure on the well-established ground that the documents dealt with the relations between sovereign states" (FAC 1993–94 vol. ll, p. 14). Whether there was any truth in Dr Soong's allegation has never been substantiated.

8 FAC (1993–94) vol. ll, p. 264.
9 HC Hansard, vol. 238, col. 803. Tim Bell subsequently wrote to Steel that his company, Lowe Bell Communications, had not been involved in any commercial aspect of Pergau or of the defence package.
10 Hurd believed that our ambassadors had to live in reasonable style if they were to be effective. Thus, in Hurd (1979, p. 48), he wrote about Carcosa, the "magnificent house of the British High Commissioner" in Kuala Lumpur. He went on: "We will not escape our part in history by camouflaging ourselves in suburban villas, as if we were Swiss or Nicaraguans." A few years later, the lease on Carcosa came to an end and the new residence was just what he feared – a "suburban villa".
11 Conference organised by the All Party Parliamentary Group on Overseas Development at the House of Commons, London, 6 June 1990.
12 *The Independent*, 18 July 1995.
13 The bloc grants given to the major UK NGOs under the Joint Funding Scheme in 1991/92 amounted to £23 million in total – roughly 1 per cent of the total aid programme.
14 To give one example of DTI's general attitude to ODA, in a radio interview with LBC Radio on 3 March 1994, a former DTI Secretary of State, Lord Young, said that he was "irritated during my time in government that ODA would go along and tell people what it was they should really have". The implication was that ODA should fund whatever recipient countries wanted irrespective of the economic merits.
15 Ambassadors and High Commissioners typically had trade promotion much higher up in their job descriptions than aid. This was to some extent the result of ODA's insistence on professional grounds that it retain responsibility for aid management through its in-country aid offices and from London. By contrast, ambassadors were fully responsible for managing the trade relationship, albeit often with seconded officials from DTI reporting to them.
16 Writing to the Prime Minister's Private Secretary on 13 March 1989, John Lippitt of GEC referred to Pergau as "the first major project to be undertaken by British contractors since the two Prime Ministers agreed that the UK would support civilian contracts of this kind late last year" (FAC 1993–94, vol. ll, p. 329). The meeting he refers to was when the two Prime Ministers signed the Memorandum of Under-standing on Defence Equipment Procurement in September 1988. In evidence to the FAC, he confirmed that in 1989 GEC were negotiating on Pergau and for defence contracts (FAC 1993–94, vol. ll, q. 862).
17 Lippitt knew about the Defence Protocol since he had accompanied Tan Sri Arumugam to the FCO to make representations about it in July 1988.
18 The changing style of public management in the 1980s can usefully be viewed through the lens of "grid/group" cultural theory as originally developed by Mary Douglas and later applied to government by Christopher Hood (Hood 1998). According to Hood's typology, public management prior to Thatcher was "high group" and "high grid" – what he calls the Hierarchist Way: public management is conducted according to well-understood general rules, and it involves "coherent collectivities and is socially cohesive". Under Thatcher, public management became "low group" and "low grid" – what he calls the Individualist Way – which results in "atomised approaches to organization stressing negotiation and bargaining". Pergau would probably have been handled better if the Hierarchist Way had still been in place, though as Hood stresses, from other perspectives – such as "policy entrepreneurship" – it has its disadvantages.

5 Dr Mahathir and the politics of Malaysia

1 Malaysia's development under Dr Mahathir to some degree fits the high modern-ism described by the sociologist, James C. Scott (Scott 1998). High modernism,

according to Scott, has three main elements: the rational engineering of all aspects of social life to improve the human condition; the unrestrained power of the modern state for achieving these designs; and a weakened civil society that lacks the capacity to resist these plans. Scott names – as examples of high modernist leaders – Walter Rathenau, Lenin, Jean Monnet, Le Corbusier, Robert McNamara and Julius Nyerere. They all, like Mahathir, believed in the power of the state, aided by "correct" analysis and planning, to achieve heroic social or wider national goals.

2 Geoffrey Robertson, *The Observer*, 28 August 1988.

3 After their meeting on 8 August 1988, Mrs Thatcher wrote in a follow-up letter, presumably referring to the Lord President's dismissal: "I have as you requested kept to myself but have noted the action taken by the King" (ASD 8788 B). Mrs Thatcher appears to have accepted Dr Mahathir's version at face value.

4 In the mid-1990s Arumugam invested $75 million in a London-based investment banking venture.

5 A well-publicised example was his alleged involvement in a share scandal in connection with the privatisation in 1990 of the national telecoms company, Syarikat Telekom Malaysia Bhd. Samy Vellu was officially cleared of wrong-doing after a 17-month investigation by Malaysia's Anti-Corruption Agency; but the allegations continued to run for many years afterwards (see Aliran Monthly 2003, p. 11, http://aliran.com/archives/monthly/2003a/11j.html, accessed 12 December 2011).

6 For a critical review, see Barry Wain in *Straits Times*, 5 April 2011. Wain writes that Mahathir "sees no reason to reassess most of the major political controversies associated with him: among them, the dismissal and prosecution of his deputy, Datuk Seri Anwar Ibrahim; the sacking of Lord President Salleh Abas; and the campaign to oust his hand-picked successor, Tun Abdullah Badawi". Wain also points to numerous factual errors and inconsistencies.

6 Arms and aid entangled

1 ASD 8788 A. A redacted version of this paragraph was provided to the FAC (FAC 1993–94 vol. ll, p. 15). The latter version referred to the grant being "no less than a specific value of the defence equipment". Later, Douglas Hurd was forced to admit that the "specific value" was 20 per cent.

2 In 2008, DESO was transferred to DTI's successor department, the Department for Business, Innovation and Skills

3 US Department of Justice, 1 March 2010 (www.justice.gov/opa/pr/2010/March/10-crm-209.html, accessed 15 November 2011).

4 The UK chapter of the pressure group, Transparency International, played a pivotal role in bringing this about.

5 ASD 8788 164 A. PS/Thatcher to PS/Younger, 21 January 1988.

6 Ibid. Major to Younger, 26 January 1988.

7 Ibid. PS/Younger, internal note, 15 March 1988.

8 Ibid. Daim to Younger, 23 March 1988.

9 Ibid. BHC to FCO, 5 April 1988.

10 *The Economist*, 5 February 1994.

11 FAC 1993–94, vol. ll, p. 88, q. 284. In view of the contradictory evidence on exactly who said what to whom, I made a request under the Freedom of Information Act to see DESO's papers regarding the Defence Protocol. My request produced nothing of substance. However, it did reveal that DESO files contain not a single paper pertaining to the Protocol for the period between 15 March and 25 May 1988. The absence of any papers in their files for the period when there was a vigorous correspondence going on between departments on the Protocol issue can only add grist to the suspicion that DESO had something to hide.

12 ASD 8788 A. BHC to FCO, 24 March 1988.
13 Ibid. Caines to Graham-Harrison, 30 March 1988.
14 Ibid. Caines to Howe, 31 March 1988.
15 Ibid. Caines to Chandler, 18 April 1988.
16 Ibid. PS/Howe to PS/Younger, 8 April 1988. The meeting took place on 3 April before Howe left for Malaysia. Howe was referring here to the OECD Consensus Agreement on Export Subsidies, which forebade an aid subsidy on one contract being used as an inducement to win a quite separate commercial contract.
17 FNF 8788 A. Caines to Ireton, reporting on conversation with Chandler, 5 May 1988.
18 ASD 8788 A. PS/Younger to PS/Thatcher, 6 May 1988.
19 Ibid. PS/Thatcher to PS/Younger, 9 May 1988.
20 Ibid. PS/Thatcher to PS/Younger, 27 April 1988.
21 ASD 164 B. Younger to Thatcher, 8 June 1988.
22 Ibid. PS/Thatcher to PS/Younger, 12 June 1988.
23 HM Treasury files, AEF-GOA/K/0019/002, *Malaysia: Economic and Political Reporting 1988*, Lankester to Major, 19 May 1988.
24 ASD 8788 C. Record of meeting, 28 October 1988.
25 Ibid. FCO record of meeting, 23 June 1988.
26 ASD 164 B. FCO to BHC, 27 June 1988.
27 FAC 1993–94,vol. ll, q. 671.
28 ESB 8991 D. BHC to FCO, 11 November 1990.
29 ESB 8991 A. DTI to ODA, 24 January 1989.
30 ASD 8788 B. BHC to FCO, 12 July 1988, and FCO to BHC, 12 July 1988.
31 Ibid. FCO to BHC, 15 July 1988.
32 Ibid. PS/Thatcher to PS/ Younger, 25 July 1988.
33 Ibid. Thatcher to Mahathir, 8 August 1988.
34 Summary of MOU can be found at FAC 1993–94, vol. ll, p. 16. Full text can be found in ASD 8788 164 A.
35 HC Hansard, vol. 237, cols 729–30.
36 *The Observer*, 7 March 1989.
37 ASD 8991 I. BHC to FCO, 22 November 1990.
38 HC Hansard, vol. 153, col. 191.
39 ASD 8788 164/854/001 A.
40 FAC 1993–94, vol. I, p. xx, para 44.
41 HC Hansard, vol. 236, col. 146.
42 FAC 1993–94, vol. ll, p. 33.
43 Kahneman (2011, p. 217), writing about the illusion of validity: "We know that people can maintain an unshakeable faith in any proposition, however absurd, when they are sustained by a community of like-minded believers".
44 FAC 1993–94, vol. ll, p. 325.
45 The Arms for Iraq Affair concerned the unlawful supply of materials by the British company, Matrix Churchill, for use in Saddam Hussein's secret weapons programme before the 1991 Iraq war. The Directors of Matrix Churchill were brought to trial, but the trial collapsed when it was revealed that the Ministry of Defence had been complicit. The revelation came from the same Alan Clark, who features in this book as ODA's harshest critic over Pergau, when he admitted under oath that he had been "economical with the *actualité*" in answer to parliamentary questions over export licences to Iraq.
46 FAC 1993–94, vol. ll, p. 24.

7 Mrs Thatcher's offer

1 FNF 8991 A. DTI to BHC, 9 November 1988.
2 ASD 8788 A. BHC to FCO, 28 November 1988.

3 FNF 8991 A. DTI to BHC, 30 November 1988.
4 ESD 8991 317 A.
5 FNF 8991 A. Record of meeting, 8 March 1989.
6 FNF 8991 A. Balfour Beatty to DTI, 8 March 1989.
7 FNF 8991 A. Shortened versions can be found in FAC 1993–94, vol. ll, pp. 25 and 239.
8 FAC 1993–94, vol. ll, p. 297.
9 Ibid. Graham-Harrison to PS/Patten, 14 March 1989.
10 Ibid. Caines to PS/Patten, 14 March 1989.
11 When the Pergau story hit the headlines in early 1994, Patten was Governor of Hong Kong. When asked about it, a spokesman said that Patten was furious about the project, and its financing was "not a proper use of aid" (*The Independent on Sunday*, 6 February 1994).
12 ASD 8991 A. PS/Howe to PS/Thatcher, 14 March 1989.
13 Ibid. PS/Thatcher to PS/Howe, 15 March 1989.

8 ODA entrapped

1 ESB 8991 317 A. Whitworth memorandum, 20 March 1989.
2 ASD 8991 A. Record of meeting at ODA with consortium representatives, 31 March 1989.
3 Ibid. Caines to PS/Patten, 6 April 1989.
4 Ibid. Graham-Harrison to PS/Patten, 6 April 1989.
5 Ibid. Patten to Prior, 15 March 1989.
6 Ibid. PS/Patten to PS/Howe, 7 April 1989.
7 Ibid. Letter from DTI to ODA, 12 April 1989.
8 ASD 8991 B. Letter from Deputy High Commissioner, Kuala Lumpur to Malaysian Minister of Energy, 17 April 1989.
9 ASD 8991 D. BHC to DTI, 12 July 1989.
10 ASD 8991 B. BHC to DTI, 1 December 1989. In many of the exchanges involving the BHC and FCO/ODA, there is lack of clarity as to the price basis of the various estimates. It obviously makes a big difference to the analysis depending on what the price basis is. In some instances, I have had to infer the price basis as best I can.
11 ASD 8991 C. BHC to ODA, 1 March 1990.
12 ESB 8991 D. BHC to FCO, 29 October 1990.
13 ESB 8991 C. *Malaysia Power Sector: Report of the Review Mission 19–28 September 1990.*
14 The interdepartmental paper for the ministerial meeting on 8 February 1991 said that "Malaysia would be paying in excess of £100 million more for electricity over the life of the project than if the money were invested in some other way, e.g. gas turbine generation" (ASD 8991 I).
15 ESB 8991 D. BHC to ODA, 24 January 1991.
16 ASD 8991 I. Letter from Ann Clwyd to C and AG, 17 October 1990.
17 *The Observer*, 9 July 2000. *The Observer*'s source for the story subsequently informed Balfour Beatty that there was no basis for the naming of that company in the story.
18 *The Independent*, 29 March 1994.
19 http://bibliotheca.limkitsiang.com/1994/03/06/dap (accessed 15 November 2011).
20 *The Observer*, 7 May 1989.

9 Crunch time in Whitehall

1 ASD 8991 I. BHC to FCO, 7 February 1991.
2 ASD 8991 H. BHC to FCO, 25 January 1991.

 3 These requirements were set out in an Accounting Officer Memorandum. They continue to be a fundamental part of an Accounting Officer's duties.
 4 In terms of the delegated authority ODA had from the Treasury, we were obliged to refer the expenditure – because it was so large – to the Treasury to provide assurance that the expenditure could be met from within the medium-term provision for the aid budget. The Treasury had approved it purely on the basis that the ODA budget was capable of covering the expenditure.
 5 The case involved the Borough of Hammersmith and Fulham, which had entered into interest swaps on a massive scale on hypothetical borrowings rather than their actual borrowings. Rather than just minimising the costs of their actual borrowings, which had been the aim of the Treasury consent, Hammersmith were essentially speculating on interest rate movements. If they had just stuck to swaps on their actual borrowings, the issue would almost certainly have never come to court. As a result of the subsequent movement of interest rates, Hammersmith faced huge losses; but as a result of the judgement, they were not liable to pay up, and the losses were borne by the banks that had entered into the swaps on the other side. In an interesting parallel to the Pergau case, the court was widely criticised for taking an unduly narrow view of the relevant legislation.
 6 The non-legal culture of the British civil service and the trend to "judicial activism" are well explained in Woodhouse (1997).
 7 "Wednesbury reasonableness" refers to a standard against which a court may decide to quash the decision of a public body. The judge in the relevant Wednesbury case, Lord Diplock, wrote that a decision could be quashed if it was "so outrageous in its defiance of logic or accepted moral standards that no sensible person who had applied his mind to the question to be decided could have arrived at it".
 8 ASD 8991 I. FAC 1993–94 vol ll, pp. 271–72 contains full summaries of the two memoranda.
 9 FNF 8991 H. PS/Lilley to PS/Mellor, 8 February 1991.
10 FNF 8991 H. Chalker to Hurd, 8 February 1991.
11 After the NAO report was published in 1993, the FCO undertook a trawl of all their relevant files to check whether Hurd had been briefed on the subject. They found nothing (FNF 9294 H, Hewitt to PS/Hurd, 13 December 1993).
12 Ibid. Hurd to Major, 16 February 1991.
13 FNF 8991. PS/Hurd to McLaren, 18 February 1991. Heywood was subsequently Principal Private Secretary to Prime Ministers Tony Blair and Gordon Brown. He was appointed Cabinet Secretary in January 2012.
14 Ibid. Mellor to Major, 18 February 1991.
15 ASD 8991 I. BHC to FCO, 7 February 1991.
16 Ibid. Caithness to Hurd, 11 February 1991.
17 Ibid. Memorandum by Barrie Ireton, 21 February 1991.
18 TNB had been "corporatized" on 1 September 1990 in preparation for partial privatisation.
19 *Sunday Times*, 20 March 1994. See also FAC 1993–94, vol ll, pp. 289–300, memorandum by Professor John Toye (para. 14).
20 In the House of Commons on 3 March 1994, the FCO minister Mark Lennox-Boyd miraculously, and no doubt inadvertently, changed the figure from 29,000 man-months to 29,000 man-*years* of employment (Hansard vol. 240, no. 76, col. 433).
21 Appendix II provides the calculation.
22 TNB would pay a lump sum of £x million in order to extinguish the loan of £y million. The difference between x and y would be the present discounted value of the interest subsidy to which TNB would have been entitled if the loan had continued to maturity. In return for ODA and ECGD agreeing to the prepayment, TNB accepted a minor reduction in the subsidy.

10 Parliament steps in

1 *The Times*, 25 October 1993.
2 *The Independent*, 24 October 1993.
3 In evidence to the FAC (FAC 1993–94 vol ll, Appendix 16, p. 301), Peter McGregor, a former Director General of the Export Group for the Construction Industries, besides offering a largely tendentious critique of ODA's appraisal of Pergau, referred to "the astonishing (and previously unprecedented) intervention of a Permanent Secretary in saying publicly that a decision was taken which was contrary to his advice". I did refer to this publicly at the PAC hearing, but this was in response to questioning several months after the NAO report had referred to my objections to the project. Until the NAO report, my formal objection was not in the public domain.
4 FAC 1993–94 vol. ll, q. 767.
5 Ibid., q. 52.
6 Ibid., p. 40, q. 53.
7 Ibid., p. 67, q. 235.
8 FAC 1993–94, vol. ll, p. 32.
9 FAC 1993–94, vol. ll, pp. 247–48.
10 FAC 1993–94, vol. l, p. lvi.
11 *The Sun*, 3 March 1994.
12 FAC 1993–94, vol. ll, p. 218.
13 FAC 1993–94 vol. l, p. lv.
14 *The Times*, 20 May 1994.
15 HC Hansard, vol. 238, cols 801–47.
16 For his pains, *The Sunday Times* (13 March 1994) described Needham as "an obscure political pigmy … prepared to wear out his kneepads kowtowing before the Malaysians". This was unfair on both counts.
17 Early Day Motion (EDM) 791 and 857, tabled 9 and 15 March 1994. EDMs are rarely debated and these particular EDMs were not. They are a means by which MPs can publicise their views on particular issues.
18 HL Hansard, vol. 552, cols 1034–71.
19 HC Hansard, vol. 253, cols 274–94.
20 I am indebted to Hashim (2002, p. 314), for this analysis.

11 Legal challenge

1 WDM submitted a memorandum to the FAC that attempted to show that increased aid to several countries was related to increasing arms sales. But their evidence of a causal link was much weaker than in the case of Malaysia (FAC 1993–94, vol. ll, pp. 112–31). WDM subsequently was instrumental in persuading the House of Commons Defence Select Committee and the Trade and Industry Committee to conduct a joint inquiry in 1995 into the financing and other aspects of government policy in relation to defence equipment exports.
2 Ben Jackson as of 2012 is Chief Executive of BOND, a membership and campaigning organisation on behalf of NGOs working in international development. Harriet Lamb is chief executive of Fairtrade Foundation.
3 R. v. Secretary of State for Foreign and Commonwealth Affairs, ex parte Word Development Movement, 10 November 1994.
4 To reinforce his argument that Rose had over-ridden the will of Parliament, Sumption pointed out that Parliament subsequently "approved without demur a supplementary estimate in an Appropriation Bill. … to allow the payments to be made to Malaysia anyway". But here Sumption missed the point. The judge had not suggested that the government should stop disbursements on the project now that its implementation

was well under way. The supplementary estimate was to enable ECGD to make the subsidy payments because these could no longer lawfully be made by ODA.

5 On the Ankara Metro project, I had personally recommended approval even though the economics of the project were unsatisfactory. In theory, I might have asked for a ministerial direction as I did with Pergau some months later. I did not because the economic case against was a good deal less damning. The example goes to show that ODA was willing to be pragmatic with ATP projects, probably too pragmatic. Our opposition to Pergau was not ideological: it stemmed from the fact that its economics was exceptionally bad by any standards.

12 The British media and trouble with Malaysia

1 *The Times*, 25 February 1994.
2 *Daily Telegraph*, 31 January 1994.
3 *The Independent*, 18 February 1994.
4 *The Times*, 4 March 1994.
5 *Financial Times*, 4 March 1990.
6 BBC TV1 interview, 25 February 1994.
7 *Construction News*, 3 March 1994.
8 *The Times*, 8 February 1994.
9 *The Guardian*, 17 February 1994.
10 http://bibliotheca.limkitsiang.com/1994/01/22/ (accessed 3 May 2012).
11 BBC TV interview with David Frost, 27 February 1994.
12 FAC 1993–94 vol. ll, p. 310. It has been suggested that Anwar was not personally anything like as affronted as Dr Mahathir and that Dr Mahathir put him up to front the issue as a test of loyalty. After he was later sacked and convicted by the courts, Anwar became one of Dr Mahathir's fiercest critics and founded his own political party.
13 It was never entirely clear what had motivated *The Sunday Times*. Some suggested it was the result of antipathy between Rupert Murdoch and Mahathir. Murdoch had been critical of Mahathir's concept of "Asian values" and his wish to export them to other countries. He had also failed to get his way with various business proposals in Malaysia.
14 Interview with Alan Whicker on ITV, 3 March 1994.
15 *The Sunday Times*, 13 March 1994.
16 *Financial Times*, 17 March 1990.
17 For example, the Conservative MP Michael Spicer in a letter to *The Times* (28 February, 1994). He also criticised the "willingness of some important British industrialists to trade the freedom of our press for Malaysian ringgits".
18 BBC 4 Radio interview, 2 March 1994.
19 *The Times*, 2 March 1994.
20 *The Sun*, 28 February 1994.
21 HL Hansard, vol. 552, col. 1039.
22 *Evening Standard*, 3 March 1994.
23 *Mail on Sunday*, 27 February 1994.
24 *The Times*, 28 February 1994.
25 *The Spectator*, 26 February 1990.
26 *News of the World*, 27 February 1990.
27 *Sunday Express*, 27 February 1994.
28 *Daily Express*, 11 November 1994.
29 *The Sunday Times*, 13 November 1994.
30 *Observer*, 13 November 1990.
31 For example, *The Economist*, 4 November 1994.
32 *The Independent*, 11 November 1994.

13 ODA objections

1 For a detailed account of the economic appraisal work, see FAC 1993–94, vol. ll, pp. 273–78.
2 ODA's environment consultants on Pergau were Environmental Resources Limited (ERL). They produced two reports: "Evaluation of an Environmental and Socio-Economic Study of the Pergau Hydroelectric Project", December 1990; and "Pergau Hydroelectric project: Environmental and Socio-Economic Issues: Report of a Consultancy Visit", April 1991.
3 FAC 1993–94, vol. ll, pp. 132–51.
4 FAC 1993–94, vol. ll, q. 77 and footnote.
5 ESB 8991 C. Malaysia Power Sector: Report of Review Mission 19–28 September 1990.
6 A combined-cycle gas turbine plant consists of one or more gas turbine generators equipped with heat recovery steam generators to capture heat from the gas turbine exhaust. An open-cycle plant has no auxiliary heat recovery and use system.

14 A fairish nightmare

1 Barker and Wilson (1997, p. 228) refers to the Pergau case: "The prime objection to this aid project was that its political justification entailed a reciprocal Malaysian decision to buy British arms and military equipment. Such a condition is unlawful … Perhaps too cautiously, the Accounting Officer formally recorded his objection on the ground of ineffective rather than unlawful or improper use of loan funds". Had I believed the funding was unlawful, I would have objected on those grounds as well. It was not until the court ruling in December 1994 that it became apparent that the funding was unlawful; and this was not because of the aid/arms linkage but because the aid was not supporting "sound development".
2 Nicholas Spreckley died in late 1994 at the young age of 59.
3 FAC 1993–94 vol. ll, appendix 25.

Appendix II

1 ESB 8991 C. Report of Review Mission.
2 The exchange rates used here and throughout this book for 1990 are: £1 = RM4.4 and $1 = RM2.7. The average exchange rate between the RM and the pound for 1990 was in fact £1 = RM 4.8. However, the contract price between TNB and the consortium was calculated on the basis of £1 = RM 4.4 (presumably reflecting the fact that in the earlier part of 1990 the RM had been stronger and the pound weaker), and this was the exchange rate used by ODA in its advice to ministers in early 1991. To avoid confusion, we have used this rate rather than the average rate for 1990. Except where we say explicitly that the price basis is for a different year, or where we give costs or prices at current prices, the reader should assume we are talking about constant 1990 prices.
3 Per capita annual GDP growth at constant prices averaged 3.7 per cent in 1980–90. For the period up to the Asian financial crisis, 1990–97, the average growth rate was 7.0 per cent (Heston, Summers and Aten 2011).
4 For a full explanation of the depletion premium concept, see Nordhaus (1973).
5 Lawrence H. Summers, "Summers on Sustainable Growth", *The Economist*, 30 May 1992.
6 These assumptions can all be found in Tables E.2 and E.3 in Annex E of the Report of the September 1990 Review Mission. The capital cost estimates for gas turbines were based on international price data provided by the World Bank. For

CCGTs, the estimate was in line with TNB's most recent contract for the purchase of CCGTs. However, TNB had most recently paid a price per kW for OCGTs some 50 per cent higher than the estimate in the table. ODA economists attributed this to the purchases having been made under pressure. Within Malaysia it was alleged that prices had been padded to enable sweeteners to be paid. If the 50 per cent higher price were to be factored into the NPV calculations, the cost advantage of OCGTs over Pergau would be reduced to about RM 170 million at a 10 per cent discount rate, whilst at a discount rate of 7.5 per cent OCGTs would be about RM 50 million more costly. But as in the Table 3 calculations, this ignores the extra value from the higher load factor at which OCGTs would be able to operate as compared with Pergau.

7 Calculated as follows. Assume heat rates for 300 MW CCGTs and 125 MW OCGTs respectively of 8,532 and 11,762 Btu/kWh (as in Table 2).This means that OCGTs require 38 per cent more fuel to generate the same amount of electricity. Two 300 MW CCGTs, with assumed total outage of 19 per cent, can generate 4,257 million kWh a year. After deducting 520 million kWh for the amount of electricity that is added to the system, the amount available for displacing higher cost OCGT base-load generation is 3,737 million kWh. At TNB's projected cost of gas in 1996 (RM 3.602/MMBtu), the fuel cost for OCGTs is RM 158 million; for CCGTs, it is RM 115 million, a difference of RM 44 million. (The figure of RM 3.602/MMBtu for 1996 is an interpolation from Table 5.)

8 ESB 8991 D. Haley to McClean, 15 November 1990.

9 Ibid. BHC to ODA, 24 January 1991.

10 TNB planners arrived at this figure by an odd route. They took the agreed contract price (excluding RM 75 million extreme risk provision) of RM 1,748.5 million and deducted RM 339.9 million for the assumed grant from ODA. The former figure was at current prices and not 1990 prices and the latter figure was wrong. However, it is clear from the papers that the figure of RM 1,389 million was run through the model as if it were at 1990 prices, and therefore the cost penalty derived from it (RM 321 million plus the extra RM 21 million for higher capital costs) is the one we have adopted.

11 Strictly speaking, in order to calculate any extra cost penalty arising from the capital cost overrun, one would also need to check whether the capital costs of a competing gas-fired plant would have turned out higher than TNB had assumed. We do not have this data. However, it is a fact that in the 1990s gas turbines became increasingly standardised amongst competing suppliers and capital costs were typically subject to less cost escalation than with bespoke hydro projects.

12 Petronas Annual Report 2011 (p. 35), www.petronas.com.my/investor-relations/Pages/annual-report.aspx (accessed 8 May 2012) gives a figure for cumulative "subsidies (potential revenue foregone)" to the power sector for the period 1997 to 2011 of RM 98.2 billion.

13 We use the UK GDP deflator and convert resulting values at RM 4.4 = £1 exchange rate. (For GDP deflator, see www.hm-treasury.gov.uk/data_gdp_fig.htm, accessed 26 February 2012.)

14 There are other greenhouse gas emissions that have a much smaller impact and that we ignore in this analysis.

15 Department of Energy and Climate Change, 2009, Carbon Valuation in UK Policy Appraisal: a revised approach, www.decc.gov.uk/en/content/cms/emissions/valuation/valuation.aspx (accessed 22 March 2012).

16 Ministry of Energy, Green Technology and Water, 2011, Handbook on the Malaysian feed-in tariff for promotion of renewable energy, www.seda.gov.my/go-home.php?omaneg=000101000000010101010001000010000000000000000000&s=28 (accessed 22 March 2012).

17 World Nuclear Association, "Comparative Carbon Dioxide Emissions from Power Generation", www.world-nuclear.org/education/comparativeeco2.html (accessed 1 October 2011).

18 In line with DECC guidance, the discount rate for calculating the NPV cost of future carbon emissions based on marginal abatement cost should be the same as the discount rate for calculating the NPV for other future costs in the economy. We have used discount rates of 7.5 or 10 per cent in the rest of our analysis on Pergau. However, using a discount rate as high as 10 per cent for calculating the NPV of climate change costs when, far into the future, these are extremely high seems intuitively implausible. Hence, we have only used the 7.5 per cent discount rate in relation to carbon emissions. (When future carbon emissions are valued on the basis of SCC estimates, the normal practice has been, for the sake of internal consistency, to use the same discount rate [usually in the range of 2.5 to 5 per cent] as used to estimate the SCC. There is no discount rate involved in estimating marginal abatement costs.)

19 Calculated as follows. Assume that 600 MW CCGT plant displaces 3,737 million kWh of base-load generation previously provided by OCGTs (see Note 7). Assuming CO_2 emissions for CCGTs of 400 tonnes/million kWh, this will translate into about 1.5 million tonnes of CO_2. For an OCGT plant, assume CO_2 emissions of 670 tonnes/million kWh, which equates to 2.5 million tonnes of CO_2. There is therefore a net saving of 1 million tonnes of CO_2.

20 As explained on page 28, because of the prepayment of the soft loan, the actual amount of aid provided turned out to be slightly less than £133 million in NPV terms.

Bibliography

A. Official documents

The key published official documents are:

1. Report by the Comptroller and Auditor General 1993, *Pergau hydro-electric project*, National Audit Office, HMSO, London. (Referred to in the text as NAO report.)
2. House of Commons Committee of Public Accounts, Session 1993–94, Seventeenth Report, *Pergau hydro-electric project*, HMSO London. (Referred to as PAC report in the text.)
3. House of Commons Foreign Affairs Committee, Session 1993–94, Third Report, Volumes l (Report, together with Proceedings of the Committee) and ll (Minutes of Evidence and Appendices), *Public Expenditure: The Pergau Hydro-Electric Project, Malaysia, The Aid and Trade Provision and Related Matters*, HMSO, London. (Referred to in the text as FAC 1993–94.)
4. Hansard: the official report of debates and other proceedings in Parliament. For the House of Commons, the Hansards referred to in the text can be found on: http://hansard.millbanksystems.com/ (accessed 9 May 2012). For the House of Lords, they can be found on: http://hansard.millbanksystems.com/lords (accessed 9 May 2012).
5. England and Wales High Court (Administrative Court) Decisions, *R v Secretary of State for Foreign and Commonwealth Affairs* ex parte *The World Development Movement Ltd.*, BAILL ll Citation Number: [1994] EWNHC Admin 1. (Abbreviated in text as R. v. Secretary of State.)

In addition, I refer to a number unpublished documents that are in ODA/DFID's, so far unreleased, files. There were several departments within ODA that dealt with Pergau, and they each kept their own files on the subject. Many of the papers were copied amongst departments, so there is inevitable duplication. Each series is numbered alphabetically. In the notes, I refer to individual files with abbreviated titles, as e.g. ASD 8788 G. The relevant file series are:

1. ASD 8788 164/854/001, *Malaysian Defence Package.*
2. ASD 8788 164/571/005, *ATP Pergau Hydro Project.*
3. ASD 8991 164/571/002, *Pergau Hydro-Electric Project.*
4. ASD 8991 164/571/006, *Malaysia ATP Pergau Hydro Electric Project Environment Assessment.*

5. ESB 8991 317/164/003, *Aid and Trade Provision – Malaysia Pergau Hydro.*
6. ESB 9294 317/164/003, *Aid and Trade Provision – Malaysia Pergau Hydro.*
7. FNL 8991 546/164/006, *UK/Malaysia Pergau Hydroelectric Power Project Grant.*
8. FNF 8788 317/840/005, *Aid and Trade Provision Arrangements Malaysia.*
9. FNF 8991 317/164/010, *ATP Pergau Hydro Electric Power, Malaysia.*
10. FNF 9294 317/164/003, *Aid and Trade Provision, Malaysia, Pergau.*
11. ASC 9294 164/571/002, *Malaysia ATP Pergau Environment Aspects.*

B. Books and articles

Barker, A. and Wilson, G. (1997), "Whitehall's disobedient servants? Senior officials' potential resistance to ministers in British government departments," *British Journal of Political Science* 27, no. 2, pp. 223–46.

Bauer, P. (1972), *Dissent on development*, Cambridge: Harvard University Press.

Cassen, R. and Associates (1986), *Does aid work?* Oxford: Clarendon Press.

Chenery, H. B. and Stout, A. M. (1966), "Foreign assistance and economic development", *American Economic Review*, vol. 56, pp. 679–733.

Collier, P. (2007), *The bottom billion*, Oxford: Oxford University Press.

Department for International Development (DFID) (1997), *Eliminating world poverty: a challenge for the 21st century*, London: HMSO.

——(2010), *Spending review.* www.dfid.gov.uk/Media-Room/Press-releases/2010/Spending-Review-2010/ (accessed 8 May 2012).

——(2011), *UK aid: changing lives, delivering results*, London: HMSO.

Donaldson, D. and Currie, J. (1991), *ATP synthesis evaluation study*, London: Overseas Development Administration.

Flint, M., Cameron, C., Henderson, S., Jones, S. and Ticehurst, D. (2002), *How effective is DFID? An independent review of DFID's organizational and development effectiveness*, London: DFID Evaluation Report EV 640.

Franks, C. (1997), "Not anonymous: ministerial responsibility and the British accounting officers", *Canadian Public Administration*, vol. 40, no. 4, pp. 626–52.

Glyn, A. (2006), *Capitalism Unleashed: Finance, Globalisation, and Welfare*, Oxford: Oxford University Press.

Glyn, A. and Sutcliffe, R. (1972), *British capitalism, workers and the profit squeeze*, London: Penguin.

Gomez, E. and Jomo, K. (1999), *Malaysia's political economy – politics, patronage and profits*, Cambridge: Cambridge University Press.

Harlow, C. and Rawlins, R. (1997), *Law and administration*, London: Butterworth.

Hashim, N. (2002), *British aid to Malaysia and Pergau dam controversy (1988–94): Aid and arms policy communities and networks, accountability and control.* Unpublished PhD thesis, London School of Economics.

Heclo, H. and Wildavsky, A. (1974), *The private government of public money: community and policy inside British politics*, London: Macmillan.

Heston, A., Summers, R. and Aten, B. (2011), *Penn World Tables Version 7.0*, Philadelphia: Center for International Comparisons of Production, Income and Prices at the University of Pennsylvania, http://pwt.econ.upenn.edu/ (accessed 26 February 2012).

Hill, H. (2005), *The Malaysian Economy: Past Successes, Future Challenges*, Working Papers in Trade and Development, Working Paper no. 2005/10. Canberra: Australian National University.

Hilley, J. (2001), *Malaysia: Mahathirism, hegemony and the new opposition*, London: Zed Books.

HM Treasury (2011), *Green Book: appraisal and evaluation in central government*, London: www.hm-treasury.gov.uk/d/green_book_complete.pdf (accessed 1 February 2012).

Hood, C. (1998), *The art of the state: culture, rhetoric and public management*, Oxford: Oxford University Press.

House of Commons Foreign Affairs Committee (FAC) (1987), *Second Report Session 1986–7, Bilateral Aid: Country Programmes*, London: HMSO.

Hurd, D. (1979), *An end to promises: sketch of a government 1970–74*, London: Collins.

——(2003), *Memoirs*, London: Abacus.

——(2010), *Choose your weapons: the British foreign secretary – two hundred years of argument, success and failure*, London: Phoenix.

Irvine, D. (1996), "Judges and Decision-makers: the theory and practice of Wednesbury review", *Public Law* (Spring), pp. 59–78.

Jomo, K. (ed.) (2007), *Malaysian industrial policy*, Kuala Lumpur: NUS Press.

Kahneman, D. (2011), *Thinking, fast and slow*, London: Allen Lane.

Keegan, W. (1984), *Mrs Thatcher's economic experiment*, London: Allen Lane.

Kenny, C. (2011), *Getting better: why global development is succeeding – and how we can improve the world even more*, New York: Basic Books.

Lancaster, C. (1999), *Aid to Africa – So much to do, so little done*, Chicago: University of Chicago Press.

Lankester, T. (2004), 'International aid: performance, prospects and the moral case', *World Economics*, vol. 5, no. 1, pp. 17–39.

Lawson, N. (1996), *The View from No. 11*, Oxford: Oxford University Press.

Lewis, A. (1954) "Economic development with unlimited supplies of labor", *Manchester School of Economic and Social Studies*, vol. 22, pp. 139–91.

——(1955), *The theory of economic growth*, Abingdon: Taylor and Francis (reprinted 2003).

Mahathir, M. (2011), *A Doctor in the House*, Kuala Lumpur: MPH Group Publishing.

Maizels, A. and Nissanke, M. (1984), "Motivations for aid to developing countries", *World Development*, vol. 12, no. 9, pp. 879–900.

Menon, J., Mitra, S. and Arnold, D. (2011), "Growth and Inclusion", in Kohli, H., Sharma, A. and Sood, A. (eds.) *Asia 2050: Realizing the Asian Century*, San Francisco, CA: Sage Publishers.

Morrissey, O. (1991), "An evaluation of the economic effects of the aid and trade provision", *Journal of Development Studies*, vol. 28, no. 1, pp. 104–29.

National Audit Office (1990), *Bilateral aid to India*, London: HMSO.

Nordhaus, W. (1973), *The allocation of energy resources*, www.brookings.edu/~/media/Files/Programs/ES/BPEA/1973_3_bpea_papers/1973c_bpea_nordhaus_houthakker_solow.pdf> (accessed 1 October 2011).

——(2008), *Question of balance: weighing the options on global warming policies*, New Haven, CT: Yale University Press.

Olson, M. (1965), *The logic of collective action: public goods and the theory of groups*, New York: Schoken Books.

Overseas Development Administration (ODA) (1975), *Overseas development: the changing emphasis in British aid policies – more help for the poorest*, London: Cmnd 6270, HMSO.

PB Power (2004), *The cost of generating electricity*, London: Royal Academy of Engineering.

Pua, T. (2011), *The tiger that lost its roar: a tale of Malaysia's political economy*, Kuala Lumpur: Democratic Action Party.

Riddell, P. (1998), *Parliament under pressure*, London: Victor Gollancz.

Sabatier, P. (ed.) (2007), *Theories of the policy process*, Boulder, CO: Westview Press, pp. 3–17.

Scott, J. (1998), *Seeing like a state: how certain schemes to improve the human condition have failed*, New Haven, CT: Yale University Press.

Sedley, S. (2012), *"Judicial politics"*, London Review of Books, vol. 34, no. 4, pp. 15–16.

Spackman, M. (2011a) *Government discounting controversies: changing prices, opportunity costs and systematic risks*, London: Centre for Climate Change Economics and Policy, LSE, Working Paper No. 67.

——(2011b) *Government discounting controversies: The valuation of social time preference*, London: Grantham Research Institute on Climate Change and the Environment, LSE, Working Paper No. 68.

Stern, N. (2006), *The Economics of Climate Change: The Stern Review*, http://webarchive. nationalarchives.gov.uk/+/http:/www.hm-treasury.gov.uk/independent_reviews/stern_ review_economics_climate_change/stern_review_report.cfm (accessed 26 February 2012).

Stuart, M. (2008), *The public servant*, Edinburgh and London: Mainstream Publishing.

Sumption, J. (2011), *Judicial and political decision-making; the uncertainty boundary*, F. A. Mann Lecture. www.guardian.co.uk/law/interactive/2011/nov/09/jonathan-sumption-speech-politicisation-judges (accessed 20 February 2012).

Tan, J. (2008), *Privatisation in Malaysia: regulation, rent seeking and policy failure*, London: Routledge.

Thatcher, M. (1995), *The Downing Street Years*, London: Harper Perennial.

Toye, J. and McQuaide, D. (1986), *ATP synthesis study*, London: Overseas Development Administration.

Wain, B. (2009), *Malaysian Maverick: Mahathir Mohamad in Turbulent Times*, Palgrave Macmillan.

Walters, A. (1986), *Britain's economic renaissance*, Oxford: Oxford University Press.

Woodhouse, D. (1997), *In pursuit of good administration: ministers, civil servants and judges*, Oxford: Clarendon Press.

World Bank (2011), *Conflict and development: overcoming conflict and fragility*, Oxford University Press.

World Nuclear Association (2009), *Comparative carbon dioxide emissions from power generation*, http://world-nuclear.org/education/comparativeco2.html (accessed 30 December 2011).

Zahariadis, N. (2007), "The multiple streams framework", in Sabatier, P. (ed.) *Theories of the Policy Process*, Boulder, CO: Westview Press.

Index

Printed in Germany
by Amazon Distribution
GmbH, Leipzig